# What is Film Theory?

## An Introduction to Contemporary Debates

*Richard Rushton and Gary Bettinson*

Open University Press

Open University Press
McGraw-Hill Education
McGraw-Hill House
Shoppenhangers Road
Maidenhead
Berkshire
England
SL6 2QL

email: enquiries@openup.co.uk
world wide web: www.openup.co.uk

and Two Penn Plaza, New York, NY 10121-2289, USA

First published 2010
Reprinted 2011

A catalogue record of this book is available from the British Library

ISBN-13: 978-0-335-23423-3 (pb)    978-0-335-23422-6 (hb)
ISBN-10: 0-335-23423-2 (pb)    0-335-23422-4 (hb)

Library of Congress Cataloging-in-Publication Data
CIP data has been applied for

Fictitous names of companies, products, people, characters and/or data that may be used herein (in case studies or in examples) are not intended to represent any real individual, company, product or event.

Typeset by Aptara Inc., India
Printed in The UK by CPI Antony Rowe, Chippenham and Eastbourne

The *McGraw·Hill* Companies

# What is Film Theory?

# Contents

# Introduction

## What is film theory?

'Film theory' is best thought of as a substantive field of inquiry in which are clustered a number of discrete theories of cinema. No one system of propositions governs the entire field – in other words, there is no single, monolithic 'film theory' that film scholars unanimously endorse. For a newcomer to the field, the nonexistence of a definitive theory of cinema can be frustrating. But we should keep in mind that the fields of the traditional arts – literature, painting, theatre, music – also house a range of theoretical perspectives, and the diversity of approaches enriches each tradition. Since the 1960s, film theory has fostered a diverse set of paradigms. Yet this is not cause for frustration. The jousting of theoretical approaches, the skirmishes among theorists, the flourishing of some theories and the decline of others – such undulations have pushed film studies into enlightening and fruitful areas of discovery. The lack of a 'master theory' of cinema, then, is not to the detriment of film theory. Knowledge springs from debate. Precisely what makes the field of film theory so fascinating – apart from the concrete emphases of the paradigms themselves – is the sheer range of theories that it encompasses, and the intellectual tussles that break out among them. *What is Film Theory?* bears witness to the exhilarating heterogeneity of contemporary film theory.

The enigma posed in the title of this book begs another question – why study film theory at all? Of what use is a theory of film? For one thing, theories of cinema can help us understand the medium better. By framing general questions about cinematic phenomena, theorists try to disclose the way films work, how they convey meaning, what functions they provide, and the means by which they affect us. Exploring theoretical questions about the medium helps us to grasp the *phenomenon* of cinema, its broad systems, structures, uses, and effects – and these prototypical features can, in turn, enable us to better understand the workings of individual films.

To read film theory, moreover, is to be enlightened to cinema's importance for this and other generations. From what angles have commentators theorized film? What questions were most pressing for the theorist at different historical junctures? How have theoretical approaches to cinema changed as the medium's technologies and conditions of consumption have changed? Film theory fascinates and instructs partly because it can illuminate cinema's role within history and culture. Theorists putting cultural forces at the centre of their concerns have furnished explanations for the social *raison d'être* of cinema; they have investigated how different audiences appropriate movies for particular purposes; and they have probed the degree to which films 'reflect' society. One major asset of film theory, then, lies in its capacity to lay bare cinema's significance for our own cultural lives, as well as for other cultures and historical epochs.

Film theory also warrants attention because it dialogically responds and gives salience to key shifts in cinema's evolution. In no sense is film theory wholly divorced from the realm of practical film-making. Rather, theory closely shadows the progress of film production, and often launches general inquiries concerning coeval phenomena, e.g. thriving generic trends, technological innovations, new forms of consumption, and so forth. Reciprocally, film theory has informed film-making, at times in purposive ways. Developing alongside film production, film theory alerts us to fresh conundrums, posits explanations, and reminds us that the cinema is a complex, sometimes enigmatic medium. Film theory endures for a simple reason: movies make us *think*.

## The advent of contemporary film theory

*What is Film Theory?* surveys the field of film theory since the 1960s. Why choose this decade as a starting point? Most generally the 1960s provide the springboard for what is called 'contemporary film theory'; more concretely, this new phase in the field's evolution can be traced to a set of historically contingent causes. It behoves us then, to provide some necessary context for the chapters that follow. If film theory swerved drastically in the late 1960s, what were the major factors propelling this shift forward?

### The academicization of film studies

*Film studies is entrenched in university departments as an academic field of study.* The academicization of film studies took root in the late 1960s, as humanities scholars imported film analysis into traditional humanistic programmes. Stimulated by a more widespread renaissance of cinephilia within American culture, young professors and students took seriously the study of cinema as an intellectual pursuit. Students in literature classes attacked *The Searchers* (1956) and *Psycho* (1960) with hermeneutic fervour. Budding philosophers debated the existential worldviews of Bergman and

Antonioni. By the early 1970s, film departments had sprung up across North American universities, though not without resistance from conservative elements within the academy. Never seeing film academia as an intellectually credible enterprise, this contingent viewed the advent of film studies with condescension and derision, ensuring film studies a bumpy pathway into the university milieu. Admitting film programmes into the academy thus entailed not only pioneering the construction of fully-fledged film departments, but also legitimating 'film' as an intellectual field of study.

University film courses proliferated rapidly, but the discipline's academic entrenchment arose out of a more diffuse set of historical circumstances. First, the unparalleled wave of cinephilia that saturated American culture at the start of the 1960s saw youth audiences feverishly devour films of different modes, backgrounds, and eras. This new generation of US moviegoers – heir to post-war 'baby boom' affluence and suburbanization – fostered a fresh appreciation of studio-era movies thanks to the network television broadcast of classic Hollywood films.

Soon the 1960s cinephile was able to draw encouragement from the critical establishment. US film critic Andrew Sarris assimilated French auteurism into American culture, arguing for the artistic credentials of Hitchcock, Hawks, and Ford. Pauline Kael, Manny Farber, and other journalistic critics celebrated the achievements of old studio film-makers and championed the fledgling work of new ones. The rediscovery of Hollywood's rich legacy helped crystallize the 1960s film culture, but no less important was the flourishing art cinema tradition in Europe. Films by Bresson, Godard, and Fellini soon became favourites of American film societies and campus cine-clubs. By the late 1960s, the European sensibility had filtered into Hollywood film-making, giving rise to a series of downbeat, counter-cultural films that included *Easy Rider* (1969), *Midnight Cowboy* (1969), *Carnal Knowledge* (1971), *The King of Marvin Gardens* (1972), and *The Conversation* (1974). This so-called New Hollywood cinema – a strain of European-influenced film-making produced within, and on the margins of, the Hollywood mainstream – showcased a new generation of self-conscious auteurs, and nourished the cinephilia of a youth audience aptly labelled 'The Film Generation'.[1]

Once the US film culture was established, a market for film academia coalesced. Students who had launched campus film clubs now lobbied for an official academicization of film studies. Of course, cinephilia alone did not propel film studies into the academy. Once university administrators realized that film programmes could be profitable, they shrewdly accepted cinema studies into the academic sphere. Film studies held an economic allure for universities, but its proponents had still to establish the field's scholarly credentials. One step towards this legitimation was the auteur theory, which seemed analogous to the concept of the author in literature. Of the director-auteur, film scholars could presuppose an œuvre, a stylistic signature, and a distinctive worldview. This affinity with literature was strategically beneficial, for if film studies could be seen to employ the same conceptual frameworks as literary theory, perhaps it could win its spurs as a reputable academic discipline in its own right. Other norms of literary studies found their way into film academia. The 1960s film critics generated a canon of artists – directors from Charles Chaplin to Roman Polanski – one goal of which was to 'establish a system of priorities for the film student' (Sarris 1996: 27). Teachers and students were thus armed with a taxonomy of directors ripe for academic discussion, much as a pantheon of great litterateurs could be examined by students in English departments.

Canons of critical *practice* were assimilated from literary studies too. A classroom emphasis on close analysis – mirroring a mode of criticism practised in the British journal *Movie* – brought film studies in touch with the literary tradition of practical criticism. Film students could analyse the form, style and themes of cinematic works just as literature students could examine such phenomena in novels and poetry. And if 'readings' dominated the New Criticism, so interpretation would be made central to the study of cinema. In part, then, film studies sought legitimation by replicating routine procedures that were firmly entrenched within other areas of the academy.

What was the significance of these developments for film theory? The concrete effects will be examined in the ensuing chapters, but it can generally be argued that 1970s film theory was strongly shaped by the attempts to prove the pedigree of academic film studies. From the late 1960s, film scholars – concerned to justify film studies as an academic discipline – cast about for legitimating paradigms, importing theories from linguistics, cultural theory and psychoanalysis. These paradigms prompted genuine theoretical inquiries – academic critics appropriated interdisciplinary theories to pose general questions about the medium of film, and the goal of enfranchisement could piggyback on the critic's quest for knowledge. Thus a Marxist account of the cinematic apparatus not only kindled theoretical debate within film studies; it also related the medium to current trends of thought regarding culture and ideology, spotlighting the wider pertinence and utility of an academic study of film. Psychoanalytic theory carried legitimizing value too. Grafting psychoanalytic templates onto a film by Hitchcock, Lang, or Preminger could produce fresh, sophisticated 'readings', the cogency of which might persuade sceptics of the intellectual weight of the discipline's object of study. Moreover, film theory continued to be underpinned by authorship and interpretation – literary heuristics and routines that helped vindicate film studies in the late 1960s. In all, the particular currents that characterized 1970s film theory bore the traces – more or less transparently – of an ongoing effort to legitimate the academic study of film.

## Resurgence in theoretical writings

*University presses launch academic film publications, and non-Anglophone theories are translated.* Concurrent with the institutional assimilation of film studies was a resurgence in theoretical writings on cinema. The early 1970s saw the launch of new US film journals, the pages of which could be filled by newly anointed cinema scholars now ensconced in campus film departments. By the mid-1970s, a host of academic periodicals was flooding the market, providing a platform for critical and theoretical discourse. Academic monographs flourished too. Universities promoted and sustained their film departments by publishing works of auteur-centred criticism, venerating directors such as Renoir, Ford, and Welles. Similarly, full-scale books were devoted to film theory, typically in the shape of survey texts and anthologies. The 1970s witnessed a fresh boom in film scholarship, but this surge of activity owed much of its impetus to the need to consolidate the field, as well as to the institutional base into which film studies had been integrated.

As film publications proliferated in the US, a parallel growth market was developing in Great Britain. Essayistic magazines such as *Sight and Sound* contributed, more or less unwittingly, to the dissemination of French auteurism, while new academic journals such as *Movie* and *Screen* pushed film criticism and theory into fresh areas. As the critics at *Movie* sought a new commitment to textual analysis, those at *Screen* inclined in the direction of film theory; indeed, the latter journal would become synonymous with many of the major trends defining film theory in the 1970s – feminism, psychoanalysis, Marxism, and semiotics. *Screen* not only initiated compelling new theories; it reprinted and showcased old ones. In the early 1970s, for instance, the journal published several (selectively chosen) manifestos that had been composed by the Formalists, Constructivists, and Futurists in the early twentieth century. Such harking back to past theories, while mediated by current purposes and concerns, reflected a growing consciousness of early theorizing about art and culture. As they crystallized theories of their own, contemporary film scholars wanted to know what had come before. Reprinting seminal essays provided one means to this goal – and it ensured that 1970s film theory was defined not only by modern trends, but by the reconsideration and discovery of earlier ones as well.

Another factor helped film theorists exhume their historical antecedents. From the late 1960s, previously inaccessible writings started to become available in English translations, expanding the relatively parochial parameters of Anglophone film theory. Previously untranslated Eisenstein could be mined for contemporary relevance, and grafted onto current theoretical concerns (e.g. Constructivism, psychoanalysis, apparatus theory, semiotics). The full breadth of Bazin's arguments concerning cinematic realism could be evaluated and juxtaposed against the views of Arnheim and Kracauer, while his modifications of the auteur theory served to powerfully qualify the version of auteurism popularized by Sarris. And contemporary theorists could discover the Russian Formalists' appeal for a systematic 'poetics of cinema', which itself prepared the way for the neoformalist perspectives of Kristin Thompson and David Bordwell.

Newer theories received English-language reboots too. *Screen* published hugely influential translations of Christian Metz, whose psychoanalytic semiology of cinema held sway for several years. By disclosing the heritage and diversity of theoretical approaches to cinema, film scholars could continue to define the field of film studies and foster a canon of critical film writings. Moreover, the rich gamut of ideas that surfaced in the 1970s was apt for contemporary assimilation – varied influences would be alloyed with current, Anglophonic concerns, and disseminated through teeming new film journals and publications.

## Politicized cultural theories

*Politicized cultural theories are meshed with academic theories of film.* Film theory after 1960 compels us for another reason – political upheavals occurring in the USA and Europe cued a major transition in the way films would be theorized in the contemporary period. If the theoretical stakes of some film theory (e.g., Bazin and Arnheim) appeared too narrowly formalistic, now film theory would be animated by a renewed political engagement, aimed explicitly at informing film practice. In Britain, the new political sensitivity was exemplified by '*Screen* theory', but the journal's Leftist tenor mirrored a more widespread acceptance of Marxist cultural theory within the academic milieu. Theorists recruited the ideological and aesthetic programmes of Althusser, Brecht and Eisenstein to exhort both politically-charged criticism and politicized modes of film-making. Needless to say, politicizing contemporary film theory constituted one more tactic of legitimation; film theory would brandish its academic stripes by demonstrating that it could shoulder weighty theories bearing broad so-cial importance.

What concrete factors motivated this political awakening? In 1960s America, political engagement had intensified with the mobilizing of a string of social movements. US liberals marched for anti-militarism and anti-discrimination. Protests broke out against the war in South Vietnam. This growing political consciousness seemed wholly detached from US film culture, but many film theorists were politically active, and disaffec-tion within contemporary society was widespread. Out of this historical context came a receptiveness to cultural critique – the American intelli-gentsia was apt to embrace the Althusserian Marxism that swept into film studies in the late 1960s.

During this period, Parisian society was afflicted by political unrest too. The student protests of May 1968 spread anti-capitalist attitudes and inspired a ground-shifting radicalism. Soon the polemicism of political indignation filtered into French film institutions. *Cahiers du cinéma* cul-tivated a stringently Marxist perspective, downplaying its auteurist her-itage and pledging itself to political criticism. French film-makers were pressed to radicalize their work by mobilizing aesthetic distance. Some film-makers (e.g., Truffaut, Rohmer) cleaved to conservative styles, but Godard pursued a so-called counter-cinema, disdaining orthodox tech-niques in favour of a provocative, anti-illusionist aesthetic. One principle of Marxist film theory, that theory ought to inform practice, gradually dwindled over time – we suggest in subsequent chapters how this vision was reconfigured to elevate other concerns. In Godard, however, Marxist film theorists had found their poster child, a film-maker committed to probing the left-wing possibilities and uses of the cinematic medium.

By the early 1970s, leftist Francophone film theory had soaked into a porous British film culture, most notably through the conduit of *Screen* theory. Althusser's 'Ideology and Ideological State Apparatuses' became a central reference point for the journal's contributors. As the 1970s wore on, *Screen* continued to play host to Continental theory, embracing the proponents of French structuralism (Metz, Barthes, Lacan, Lévi-Strauss). Assorted theories were assimilated and intermeshed, producing theoreti-cal hybrids that invariably reinforced Marxist premises. In all, the influ-ence of historical materialism on contemporary film theory is not to be underestimated.

As we have noted, film theory since 1960 compels attention partly be-cause it marks a shift toward an inquiry that is explicitly – perhaps even centrally – of a political and social bias. However, although the paradigms that emerged in the 1960s and 1970s signalled a substantive shift in the history of film theory, they did not represent an absolute break with foregoing thinking about film. A brief excursion on the emphases of early and classical film theory will lay bare the deviations and continuities characterizing the field in its different historical phases.

## Film theory before 1960

A glance at the history of classical film theory can be misleading. Film studies pre-1960 seems to pinball unpredictably between different nations, institutions, and historical moments. Theories of cinema spring forth in isolated bursts. The Soviet theorists are conjoined geographically and institutionally, but there is hardly a global community of theorists in dialogue with one another. *Prima facie*, classical film theory can look like a desultory, patchy affair. The fallacy of this impression, however, is that film writings continuously and prolifically appeared throughout the early twentieth century in many regions of the world. Much ink was spilt on this upstart medium. Formative film theory looks erratic only when the era's most significant theorists – Rudolf Arnheim, Sergei Eisenstein, Hugo Münsterberg, André Bazin, and others – are plucked out of a historical context in which film literature flourished. And if the theories themselves look disparate – and they *are* strikingly different from one another in a host of ways – they nevertheless are united by shared concerns and goals. The collective work of early film theorists (writing up to 1925) and their classical descendants (1925–60) comprise a diverse and contradictory set of premises, but each theoretical inquiry converges on a common objective: to defend film as a distinctive and authentic mode of art.

How to affirm cinema's artistic credentials? One theoretical strategy was to measure the medium against traditional criteria for art. This tactic underpins, for instance, Münsterberg's attempt to claim for cinema the goal of organic unity – the perfect synthesis of form and content – which stood as an aesthetic standard for traditional arts like painting, literature and theatre. More generally, theorists sought to particularize the essential properties of cinema, the better to mark it off as a distinctive mode of expression. What are the fundamental features of cinema? How does the medium create meaning? To what specific purposes should film be put? Such questions pushed theorists to define the specificity of cinema, but their theoretical inquiry was mediated by a defensive concern as well. If silent film theorists wanted to validate film as an art, they would have to impugn one of the prevailing prejudices of the day – namely, that photographic media, such as film, were mere copying processes, incapable of artistically shaping the things they recorded. In this view, films served up a mere facsimile of the world, a mechanical reproduction devoid of creative intervention. Believing that the burden of proof lay at their door, classical film theorists set out to demonstrate that cinema could shape its materials in artistic ways.

The exemplary figure here is Rudolf Arnheim, whose study of the silent, black-and-white cinema, *Film as Art* (1957), inventoried the means by which cinema deviated from straightforward mimesis. For Arnheim, the silent cinema transcended its recording capacity by virtue of certain medium-specific properties, as well as through particular defamiliarizing uses of the medium – as Arnheim famously phrased it, 'art begins where mechanical reproduction leaves off' (1957: 57). Silent cinema possessed intrinsic formal and technical parameters that transformed whatever was represented on screen. Technicians viewed these parameters as limitations, but Arnheim recognized that such properties were central to film's distinctiveness as an art form. For one thing, the apparent limitations of the medium yielded an imperfect recording of reality – the cinematographic process flattened out a three-dimensional world; it stripped the world of sound, colour, and other sensorial phenomena; and thanks to the boundaries imposed by framing, it fragmented reality into horizontal chunks of space. Particular uses of the medium could further wedge filmic representation and reality apart. Arnheim championed the use of surrealistic *mise-en-scène* in *Das Cabinet des Dr Caligari* (Robert Wiene, 1920); the oblique figure positions and canted angles of *La Passion de Jeanne d'Arc* (Carl Dreyer, 1928); and the drastically reconfigured spatio-temporal reality of the Soviet montagists. In all such ways, early cinema transfigured and manipulated the phenomenal world – as such, some classical theorists argued, it satisfied certain artistic criteria standardly applied to the traditional arts.

Like some other formative theorists, Arnheim prized cinema's limitations, and this position led him to inveigh against recent technological innovations (most notably, synchronized sound, colour, widescreen, and 3-D). For Arnheim, such advancements were debasing attempts to compensate for the medium's limitations, and they lured cinema away from its ontological essence (which for Arnheim lay in the medium's pictorial dimension). From a contemporary standpoint, so much clinging to prototypical parameters betrays a technological conservatism, but Arnheim's respect for the medium's limitations was central to his defence of film as a distinctive artform. Colour would pull film closer to other traditions, such as painting and dance. Synchronized sound would result in 'canned theatre', transposing dialogue and sonic effects from the stage. Both technologies, moreover, would reduce the defamiliarizing capacity that was so central to Arnheim's defence of film as art.

The resistance to these innovations was not unanimous among classical film theorists – Eisenstein, for instance, was generally receptive to the prospect of film sound and colour – but other aspects of Arnheim's approach resonated among his contemporaries and predecessors. Antici-pating Arnheim, Hugo Münsterberg cautions that 'the limitations of an art are in reality its strength and to overstep its boundaries means to weaken it' (Münsterberg 1970: 89). And more generally, Arnheim's essentialism – his concern to articulate a specificity of film – typified the ontological thrust of much film theory during the first few decades of cinema's exis-tence.

The attempt to demonstrate film's propensity for art persisted after the Second World War, but post-war film theory developed lines of argument that wholly contradicted the premises set forth by Arnheim. Foremost here is André Bazin, for whom the value of cinema lies in its indexical relation to a photographed reality. Crucially, Bazin shuffled the criteria by which film had theretofore been appraised as an artform. If Arnheim sought to show that film could be artistic despite its photographic element, Bazin simply rejected the assumption that photography was incongruous with art. Indeed, for Bazin, the essence of film art was to be found precisely in the medium's photographic dimension. Cinema possessed a peculiar ability not shared by other art forms – it could transcribe reality – and thanks to Bazin, Kracauer, and other post-war theorists, cinematic realism became a new aesthetic standard.

Bazin's tenets were sharply different from the emphases found in Arn-heim. While Arnheim belittled film's photographic essence, Bazin extolled it for its ability to 'lay bare the realities' (Bazin 1967: 15). Film art stemmed from a transformation of reality or it sprang from a 'resurrection' of the world. Arnheim admired the deranged reality of German Expressionism; Bazin's tastes favoured the everyday textures of neorealism. No less than Arnheim, however, Bazin fostered an essentialist account of the medium. For Arnheim, cinema was essentially a pictorial medium, while the Soviet theorists took film's essence to consist in editing, or montage. For Bazin, by contrast, the ontology of film inhered in a capacity to inscribe a trace of the photographed reality, delivering the world in its full complexity and ambiguity. It was precisely this direct ontological link between object and image that, for Bazin, afforded cinema its highest possibility of achieving the distinction of art.

Bazin's conviction that film art stems from an essential realism led him to affirm certain uses of film style and denigrate others. He celebrated in particular those devices which preserved spatio-temporal continuity, the better to faithfully evoke real-world experience. Spatial and temporal continuity could find expression in such compositional devices as deep focus, staging in depth, mobile camerawork, and long takes – all features that Bazin admired in the work of Welles, Wyler, Renoir, Rossellini, and Murnau. Devices such as deep focus were esteemed for generating am-biguity – as they would in reality, viewers had to scan a visual array in order to discover items of significance. Pledged to continuity techniques, Bazin manifested a general aversion to montage. He was not – as is sometimes alleged – wholly *opposed* to decoupage, but nonetheless he favoured other styles. Bazin devalued devices, such as montage, that did not accord with his conception of cinematic realism. Not only did montage rupture continuity with choppy cuts and splices, it also disambiguated and thus diminished the world, by explicitly directing the spectator's gaze to salient information. As such, montage could hardly succeed as a realist device – and thus it must be deemed extraneous to cinema's expression as art.

The film theory that emerged in the 1960s – the point at which this book begins – signalled a transition in the field's projects and concerns. No longer was the theorist embarked on a campaign to legitimate the medium. The auteur theory had helped lend credibility to the cinema, while the medium itself had yielded several accepted masterworks. Cinema's acceptance as an artform equal to that of the traditional arts had been more or less consolidated. Now theorists shifted their sights to analysing cinema as a system of social and symbolic meaning. This enterprise, and the various theoretical approaches that ensued in its wake, form the object of this book. However, the theories discussed in the chapters that follow are in no sense estranged from the early and classical traditions of film theory. Contemporary film theory frequently discloses its indebtedness to the discoveries of early and classical thinkers. Bazin's ontological inquiry connects with the writings of V. F. Perkins and Stanley Cavell. Eisenstein's politically-oriented theory was ripe for uptake by Althusserian-Marxists in the 1970s. Münsterberg's early sketch of the text – spectator interface looks ahead to the late 1980s cognitive turn. Sometimes an early or classical theorist informs several distinct contemporary approaches at once. Film theory after 1960 signalled a shift, not an absolute break, from foregoing approaches to film. And moreover, many contemporary theorists adverted to the general theoretical questions that compelled earlier thinkers like Arnheim, Bazin, and Eisenstein. What is cinema? How do films construct meaning? What functions should cinema perform? We shall see throughout this book the different ways that contemporary theorists have broached these questions.

## Using this book

*What is Film Theory?* is designed to survey and explicate the major debates within film theory since 1960. Chiefly, it aims to familiarize readers with the breathtaking diversity of approaches that has characterized the field since then. Film theory houses a range of theoretical positions, but it is also an explicitly discursive field of study. Theories do not spring from nothingness. They are agitated into being by pre-existing, inferior propositions; they hark back to archaic, forgotten hypotheses; they open dialogue with cognate theories which they serve to complement, finesse, or qualify. A contemporary film theory is characteristically reactive – in the process of defining fresh premises, it revises, extends, or overthrows established ones. This book tries to convey such dynamic interplay by charting the evolution of contemporary film theory. Chapters are organized chronologically, alighting on major frameworks as they emerge at successive or simultaneous moments in history.

Each chapter provides a detailed exegesis of some major tradition within film theory. Many of the theories we foreground have spawned fertile discussion, but it would be neither fruitful nor feasible to canvass here every text pertaining to the theory at hand. Every tradition has its exemplars – we limit ourselves primarily to discussion of these important archetypes. Accordingly, each chapter identifies major works and figures; it delineates conceptual frameworks; and it summarizes and synthesizes key arguments, occasionally coming to rest on particular case examples. Exemplary works are made salient throughout, and readers are encouraged to seek out these primary texts – all of which helped crystallize film theory in the contemporary period.

The book goes beyond simple exegesis. It furnishes original film analyses as well, exemplifying key theoretical strands through an examination of particular films. Not all works of film theory concern themselves with the individual film – a theory of cinema need only advance general propositions about the medium it studies. But the strength of a theory lies in its degree of testability against concrete examples. The analyses we present aim to demonstrate how particular theoretical approaches can illuminate individual films.

By what rationale have we chosen our film examples? Sometimes we have selected what we take to be a prototypical case study within a particular strand of theory – for instance, *Brokeback Mountain* (Ang Lee, 2005) as a focal point of debate within queer theory, or *Do the Right Thing* (Spike Lee, 1989) as a touchstone of theories surrounding racial otherness. On other occasions we have opted for lesser known, more idiosyncratic examples. An abiding objective has been to address films of different genres, milieus, and epochs, the better to demonstrate the suppleness and utility of general theories of cinema. Although we have sought, as well, to encompass films from within and without the canon, we have sacrificed reference to a large number of films in favour of a few compelling examples. By analysing closely a limited range of fiction and nonfiction films, we aim to bring into sharper focus the virtues of contemporary theory's diverse methods and approaches.

Foregrounding the ongoing conversation among contemporary film theorists is a central concern of *What is Film Theory?* Given the field's dynamic interchange of ideas, it shouldn't surprise the reader to find certain theoretical concepts resurfacing throughout the book. Some concepts blaze across several distinct research programmes. Critics migrating from semiotics to psychoanalysis, for instance, carried practices, precepts, and suppositions with them. Cinema's structures of 'identification' compelled psychoanalytic theorists and cognitivists alike. Anti-traditional storytelling caught the attention of both Marxist and poetician. And as we noted, a broader set of macro-questions have guided the theorist's inquiries, cutting across different theoretical traditions. Although we trace such connections throughout this book, each chapter can function as a stand-alone overview of a particular theoretical approach. This has been made so in order to facilitate classroom study, as well as to acknowledge the particularized interests of scholars and general readers alike. Thus the reader concerned only with *Screen* theory will find a more or less autonomous account of the subject in the pertinent chapter. For readers interested in the broader canvas of contemporary film theory, the book as a whole will serve as a thoroughgoing, wide-ranging, and analytical introduction.

Finally, film theorists work with specialized terminology, and sometimes the terms they employ can be opaque. For this reason, we have supplied a glossary of terms at the end of each chapter. The glossary words are indicated in bold on their first occurrence.

# 1 Structuralism and semiotics

## The foundations of contemporary film theory

Many writers on cinema who were active from the 1910s to the 1960s might be described as film theorists. However, a major turning point in film studies occurred in the 1960s under the influence of an intellectual movement broadly known as **structuralism**. Structuralism was a method for analysing the deep structuring logic of cultural products and practices. Everything from tribal kinship structures (Lévi-Strauss 1977) to clothing fashions and advertising (Barthes 1972; 1983) could, for the structuralists, be subjected to structural analysis. Instead of trying to discover the intrinsic meanings of surface appearances, the structuralists were committed to unravelling the hidden relations beneath surface appearances which, so they argued, provided a more substantial – and more scientific – understanding of the ways in which cultural products and practices engender meaning.

As this chapter (and most of this book) focuses on specific analyses of films, there is a large portion of investigation into the semiotics of cinema which it unfortunately does not have the space to deal with in great detail. However, readers should be aware of the desire to found a semiotics of the cinema – or a language of cinema – that was inspired by structuralism in the 1960s. The most influential scholar in this regard is Christian Metz, whose 1964 essay, 'La cinéma: langue or langage?' (Metz 1974) sought to compare the ways in which cinema conveys meanings and messages with the ways that written and spoken language does (for more on Metz see Chapter 2).

Much of the influence for structuralism was provided by the theories of Ferdinand de Saussure (1857–1913), whose *Course in General Linguistics* (1966), first published in 1916, argued that words have no intrinsic surface meaning, for the meanings of such words can only be ascertained by virtue of the relation between a word's difference from all other words. Therefore, the meaning of any one word can only be determined in relation to the deeper structure – the entire language system – within which that word is placed. For film studies and film theory, building on the foundational studies of Saussure, there were four key influences (interestingly, all of these thinkers were French):

- *Claude Lévi-Strauss* (1908–2009) is an anthropologist who made famous the structural study of **myth**. He treated myths more or less in the same way Saussure treated words. Myths as surface stories have no intrinsic meaning in themselves, but can only be understood in relation to the deeper beliefs through which social organizations are structured. Significantly, he theorized that myths arise as a way of providing resolutions to otherwise irreconcilable social differences.

- *Roland Barthes* (1915–80), whose major works were devoted to literature, also argued that cultural artefacts – clothes, advertisements, lifestyle choices – presupposed systems of deep structures through which social meanings could be classified. Like Lévi-Strauss, the notion of myth was important for Barthes, for he treated cultural products as purveyors of myths. As such, those products sought to make benign on a surface level the deeper structuring presuppositions of a culture.

- *Jacques Lacan* (1901–81) took several of Sigmund Freud's fundamental psychoanalytic principles and transformed them under the influence of stucturalism. Most emphatic was his declaration that 'The unconscious is structured like a language' (see Lacan 2006a). Therefore, for Lacan, the unconscious is not composed of elements which have intrinsic meaning, but rather, any unconscious meaning can only be ascertained by means of the differences instantiated by the overall structure of the unconscious (Lacan famously divided the unconscious into the realms of the Imaginary, the Symbolic and the Real, designations which roughly correlate with Freud's ego, super-ego and id).

- *Louis Althusser* (1918–90) was a Marxist philosopher influenced by the methods of structuralism. For the purposes of the analyses that follow, Althusser's most influential concept was that of **symptomatic reading**: the analysis of a text predicated not just on what the text declares explicitly, but also in terms of what it leaves out or even what it deliberately covers over. By excavating what has been left out at the surface level, one gains insights into the deeper structuring traits of a work, what Althusser called 'structuring absences' (see Althusser 1971; Althusser and Balibar 1970).

## Raymond Bellour, 'System of a Fragment (on *The Birds*)'

(First published in *Cahiers du cinéma*, 216, 1969; translated in *The Analysis of Film* [Bellour 2000a: 28–68]. All references in the text refer to the latter translation.)

Raymond Bellour's very close **textual analysis** of a scene from Alfred Hitchcock's 1963 film, *The Birds*, is a prime example of a structural analysis of film. Bellour seeks to account for *every shot* in a scene that lasts roughly 6 minutes. By engaging in an analysis on such a scale of detail, he then tries to surmise what visual structures – for there is little dialogue during the scene – are at work. These are not structures that would or could be recognized easily for a viewer watching *The Birds* at the standard 24 frames per second. Rather, they are structures which are more or less hidden from conscious or explicit view. Bellour nevertheless contends that the intricate structures of the scene demonstrate a level of understanding beneath the conscious or explicit story contained there. What is revealed, for Bellour, is the nature of the formation of the romantic couple in accordance with the logic of the **Oedipus complex** theorized by psychoanalysis.

Bellour's insistence on accounting for each of the 82 shots of this scene is at times bamboozling for the reader, but he is inspired by a quest for thoroughness that harks back to Lévi-Strauss's methodical studies and penchant for diagrams, and forward to Roland Barthes's more or less complete dissection of a short story by Honoré de Balzac (see Barthes 1975). Amid the apparent clutter, there are groupings used by Bellour (A1-B3) which make the scene more comprehensible and by means of which its most significant divisions are indicated.

What occurs in the scene is the joining of the romantic couple, a couple which stays together for the remainder of the film. They have met only once before: in a pet shop in San Francisco where the film's hero, Mitch Brenner (Rod Taylor), was looking for some birds as a gift for his sister on her birthday. While at the shop he engages in flirtatious conversation with another customer, Melanie Daniels (Tippi Hedren). When the birds – 'lovebirds' – Mitch seeks are found to be out of stock, unbeknownst to him, Melanie arranges to deliver the birds herself to Mitch. While attempting to deliver the birds, however, she finds Mitch has gone to the small town of Bodega Bay, north of San Francisco, and she decides to follow him in order to deliver the birds. Melanie decides to travel in a small boat across Bodega Bay so she can deliver the birds to the house – his mother's house – where Mitch is staying, along with his sister whose birthday is the occasion for the bird's delivery. Bellour's analysis traces Melanie's progress across Bodega Bay, her delivery of the lovebirds and her journey back to the pier from where she had departed (Figures 1.1–1.7).

For Bellour, the key to understanding the scene at the micro-level occurs as an effect of the relation between shots. Again, in accordance with structuralist principles, each shot gains its meaning by virtue of its difference from other shots. Central to this scene, and for American cinema in general, is the system of editing known as **alternation** or **parallel montage**. Bellour argues that the scene is ordered by means of alternation

**Figure 1.1** Alternation in *The Birds*: a close shot of 'Melanie seeing' (shot 17).
*Source*: Universal Pictures.

**Figure 1.2** Alternation in *The Birds*: a distant shot of 'what Melanie sees' (shot 18).
*Source*: Universal Pictures.

**Figure 1.3** *The Birds*: the disruption of alternation (shot 33).
*Source*: Universal Pictures.

**Figure 1.4** *The Birds*: a close shot of 'Mitch seeing'; the disruption of alternation (shot 57).
*Source*: Universal Pictures.

**Figure 1.5** *The Birds*: the seagull attacks! (shot 77).
*Source*: Universal Pictures.

**Figure 1.6** *The Birds*: the seagull attacks Melanie (shot 78).
*Source*: Universal Pictures.

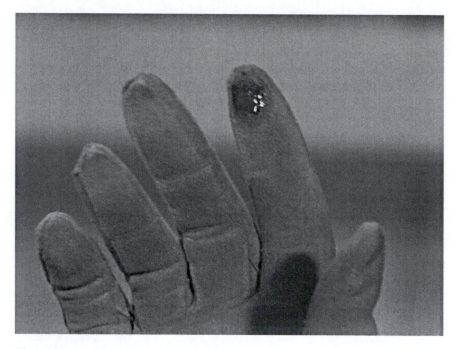

**Figure 1.7** *The Birds*: blood on Melanie's glove (shot 82).
*Source*: Universal Pictures.

between two series of shots: 'Melanie seeing' vs 'what Melanie sees'. Additionally, the scenes are ordered according to a shot-countershot form: shots of 'Melanie seeing' are *close-up* views of her, while the shots of 'what Melanie sees' are *distant shots* from her point-of-view. Therefore, the viewer's understanding of the scene unfolds principally from Melanie's point-of-view. More significant, however, are the moments where this alternation is disrupted; that is, when the rhythm of 'Melanie seeing' followed by 'what Melanie sees' is changed. These disruptions are what Bellour refers to as 'Centre A' and 'Centre B', while a third disruption occurs at the end of the scene. What does Bellour discover as a result of these disruptions?

During the period of the scene which Bellour calls 'Centre A', Melanie enters Mitch's house – without Mitch seeing this – to secretly deliver the lovebirds. The most effective shot in Centre A is shot 33 (Figure 1.3). Why is this? There are three reasons. Shot 33 is significant first of all because it disrupts the rhythm of parallel montage; it occurs where we would expect to see a shot of 'what Melanie sees', but it is *not* a shot of what Melanie sees. Rather, writes Bellour, it 'is not part of Melanie's vision, it simply underlines a detail of her action' (Bellour 2000a: 50). Second, the shot is disruptive because it is a close-up shot, so that where we would typically expect a distant shot of 'what Melanie sees' we are instead confronted with a close-up. Finally, the shot also introduces, in close-up, Melanie's gloves, a factor that will become more significant at the end of the sequence.

Bellour identifies another significant moment during what he calls 'Centre B'. As Melanie now, once again in the boat, makes her way back away from Mitch's house, the alternation of 'Melanie seeing' and 'what Melanie sees' resumes. However, this is again disrupted when Mitch notices her. The most disruptive shot is shot 57 (Figure 1.4): instead of a distant shot of 'what Melanie sees' we are instead presented with a close shot of 'Mitch seeing': he looks at her through binoculars and therefore recognizes who she is. Again, the shot is significant for being a close-up which breaks the binary scheme of 'Melanie seeing' (close shot) and 'what Melanie sees' (distant shot). It is a shot of what Melanie sees, but it also a shot of Mitch seeing.

Now that Mitch has recognized her, he is determined to get to the other side of the bay in order to catch Melanie. He jumps into a car and speeds around the edge of the bay in order to greet her as she arrives back at the pier. What follows is another series of alternating shots, 'Melanie seeing' and 'what Melanie sees' – and what Melanie sees is Mitch's car racing around the bay – as both protagonists make their ways back to the pier. At the end of the sequence Melanie is attacked by a seagull and Bellour pays very particular attention to the way in which this event disrupts the alternating pattern of editing. In shot 77 (Figure 1.5), for example, where we expect to see a shot of Mitch, instead, we are presented with a distant shot of a seagull. This does not so much disrupt the pattern of editing as it replaces Mitch with a seagull. The following shot (78; Figure 1.6), then, is not a shot of Melanie seeing, but is instead a shot of Melanie being attacked by the seagull. The inference Bellour makes is that, insofar as Mitch has been replaced by the seagull, we can presume that, within the logic of the film, the seagull represents Mitch attacking Melanie.

Finally, shot 82 (Figure 1.7), the very famous shot of blood on Melanie's glove, completes the series. Now Melanie's looking is not at someone or somewhere else, but is instead her looking at herself: she has become the object of the look – both her look and Mitch's look. Bellour notes that 'she sees herself; and if she does not see Mitch, preoccupied as she is with her wound, she knows that she is seen' (Bellour 2000a: 63). The point Bellour wants to argue from this is that Melanie is punished for her looking, and for her forwardness in approaching Mitch. 'It is her look in the very first shot [of the scene] that raises a flock of wild birds into the sky, just as it is her gift of a pair of lovebirds to a man that unleashes on Bodega Bay the irrational anger of primitive forces' (Bellour 2000a: 67).

It may seem that Bellour goes to extraordinary lengths in order to prove a small point – that the attack of the birds in *The Birds* is punishment for Melanie's sexual forwardness. At the same time, his decision to base his analysis on such an intricate picking apart of a series of shots also makes his argument remarkably convincing. Bellour's analysis remains a stark reminder of the potential complexities of meaning that can be discovered in films. One cannot doubt that he uncovers a quite stunning system of 'story pictures' in this scene. Today, however, many scholars – Bellour included (see Bellour 1985; 2000b) – are sceptical that a shot-by-shot analysis can account for the ways in which viewers typically respond to and make sense of films. Films are, after all, images that move, and draining the movement from cinema cancels out much of what is important to the experience of movie-going. However, with recent technologies such as video and DVD, the ability for film scholars to analyse films in great detail is now a widespread availability and present-day scholars could certainly gain immensely from the detailed methods used by Bellour in his classic analyses. His analysis of a small fragment of *The Birds* represents a methodical utilization of structuralist methodologies applied to a cinematic example.

## The Editors of *Cahiers du cinéma*, 'John Ford's *Young Mr. Lincoln*'

(Published in *Cahiers du cinéma*, 223 [1970]; translation printed in B. Nichols (ed.), *Movies and Methods Volume 1* [Editors of *Cahiers du cinéma* 1976]. All references to the text refer to the latter translation.)

John Ford's film, *Young Mr. Lincoln* (1939), was a relatively unsuccessful film upon its initial release, yet the editors of the highly regarded French journal, *Cahiers du cinéma*, in 1970 felt the film important enough to devote a long, intricate and very influential article to it. In the wake of the events of May 1968 (student protests and a general strike in France which nearly brought down the government), *Cahiers du cinéma* had become earnestly Marxist and believed its task was to discover the ways that films which support capitalism – implicitly or explicitly – could be distinguished from those which undermine it – again, whether such undermining was implicit or explicit (see Comolli and Narboni 1990). For these authors, *Young Mr. Lincoln* is an example of a film which appears on the surface to support capitalism and other conservative points of view, yet which, on closer inspection, reveals the limitations and problems of that system. In a first sense, then, the authors approach the film from the perspective of myth: on the surface, *Lincoln* presents a myth of the young Abraham

Lincoln, but on a deeper level, it reveals the constitutive faults which that myth attempts to cover over. But what constitutive faults does the Lincoln myth cover over? It hides, according to the *Cahiers* authors, the fact that young Lincoln founds his power and derives his success by renouncing love and pleasure. In doing so, the authors argue, *Young Mr. Lincoln* points as much to a critique of the capitalist system as it does to a condonation of it.

Like Bellour's 'System of a Fragment', the *Cahiers* article is long, detailed, exhausting and (to some extent) exhaustive. They begin with a series of hasty historical determinants: *Young Mr. Lincoln* is released in 1939, at a time when a Democrat has been President of the United States since 1933. The film therefore should, the authors infer, be committed to supporting the Republican cause against the Democratic Party, for Hollywood is big business, and the Republicans (in simple terms) by this time had become the supporters of big business in opposition to the Democratic Party's defence of big government. The *Cahiers* authors write that 'As a product of the capitalist system and of its ideology, [Hollywood cinema's] role is in turn to produce the one and thereby to help the survival of the other' (1976: 118). And furthermore, Lincoln, of course, was a Republican. The authors define another historical level: *Young Mr. Lincoln* is released at a specific historical juncture – 1939 – but it is also about a specific and very well-known historical figure: Abraham Lincoln. With this in mind, they determine that the topic of the film is 'the *reformulation* of the Lincoln myth on the level of myth and the eternal' (1976: 121). Therefore, this film should be trying to depict Lincoln as mythical, as the carrier of an eternal myth of the greatness of Republican policies.

Unlike Bellour, who analyses only a short scene in his discussion of *The Birds*, the *Cahiers* editors try to account for the whole of *Young Mr. Lincoln*. In accordance with the principles of structuralism, they try to account for the meanings of specific scenes and episodes in terms of how they relate to other scenes and episodes in the film. In doing so, they discover what they believe is the underlying structure of the film. Precisely what they discover is fleshed out in three distinct ways:

1.  A series of oppositions which Lincoln resolves.
2.  'Structuring absences'; that is, elements which are hinted at then erased from the film with the result that they function as absent principles which determine certain elements of the film's overall meaning.
3.  The renunciation of desire; in the end, the *Cahiers* editors find Lincoln himself to be lacking in power; instead he is merely the channel for a form of power greater than he.

We shall examine these points one at a time.

## A series of oppositions

At the level of myth, in accordance with the methodology central to Lévi-Strauss's investigations of myth, the *Cahiers* authors understand Lincoln's mythical status in terms of his ability to resolve conflict. Such capacities for the resolution of conflict – of knowing the correct answer – are demonstrated in the film's very first scene: the poem which opens the film. This poem, adopting the voice of Lincoln's deceased mother, asks what became of her son, Abe. Did he grow tall? Did he get to town? The poem thus directs questions towards the viewer – what will become of Abe? – to which the viewer already has answers: *we* know he will become President. Thus the film enacts, from its very outset, what the authors call a *feigned indecisiveness*: the film pretends *not to know* the answers to questions for which there *are* answers, answers that we already know. The answers to questions or problems raised by the film therefore come to be experienced as problems that have destined solutions, answers that are inscribed by destiny, almost as if by magic. The *Cahiers* authors call this the film's ideological function: the destined, automatic, natural greatness of Lincoln.

The function of finding destined, magical solutions to conflicts or problems is then repeated throughout the film:

- Blackstone's commentaries on Law are delivered to Lincoln as if by destiny. They are a solution to the farming family's inability to pay for goods (this family later becomes central to the narrative).
- He chooses his career – will he stay in the village, or leave to become a lawyer? – on the basis of the fall of a stick, a magical occurrence that 'submits the hero to predestination' (1976: 510).
- The case of the plaintiffs – a dispute over property – is resolved by Lincoln without his having to choose between the two sides in the case. Instead, the Law chooses for him. Again, a conflict or problem is magically resolved.
- In the pie judging contest, Lincoln's moment of choosing is elided in order that he never be seen to choose. Rather, it is destiny which always makes his choices for him (and which chooses him).
- In the murder case around which the film's central narrative unfolds, Lincoln steadfastly refuses to choose between the two defendants. The solution to the murder trial is magically pulled out of Lincoln's hat, like the proverbial magician's rabbit. The almanac which charts the movements of the heavens reveals the answer, as if to again prove that Lincoln finds the solutions to problems by way of predestined, eternal forces. Therefore, this is an important factor – predestination; of never having to choose – that shapes the film.

## Structuring absences

More delicate – and also more difficult to understand – is the *Cahiers* authors' use of the notion of 'structuring absences'. These are elements in the film which are hinted at – slavery, politics, sexuality – but which are then covered over. And yet, even though these concepts are made absent from the film, they nevertheless exert a force over it.

First of all, the film signals its preference for *morality* over and above *politics*, and politics becomes a structuring absence. When Lincoln, in his electoral speech near the beginning of the film, signals his preference for Republican policies – protectionism and a national bank – these policies play no further role. Rather, any politics is replaced by a commitment to the Law established in moral terms: the difference between right and wrong. And again, the basis of this morality is one in which Lincoln will not have to choose, for the moral differences between right and wrong are, for this film, eternal and predestined.

There is only one brief moment in the film when Lincoln mentions slavery, a political issue central to his presidency and the origins of the Republican Party. But as this issue is one of division, it is also made into one of the film's structuring absences so that emphasis can be put on Lincoln's powers of unity: the film refuses to exhibit Lincoln as a potentially divisive political figure in favour of his moral powers of uniting the nation behind an eternal, predestined, Republican morality.

The *Cahiers* authors then expand this reading to incorporate structuring of Law in the film. It is invariably associated with the figure of Lincoln's mother. Yet Lincoln's mother is absent (her only words are those of the poem spoken from beyond the grave). However, the absent mother is replaced by a number of figures throughout the film: Ann Rutledge (Lincoln's 'true love') and the mother of the two defendants, Mrs Clay. Significantly, it is from these characters that he receives the impetus to follow the Law: beside Ann's grave he makes the decision to go into the Law, and it is from Mrs Clay that he first receives Blackstone's commentaries. Furthermore, the *Cahiers* authors claim, an equation is made between Woman-Nature-Law (Figure 1.8), for not only does Lincoln receive the Law via women, but he also comes to understand the Law in concert with nature: he reads Blackstone's commentaries seated beneath a tree, while accompanied by Ann Rutledge on the banks of a river. Law, the film seems to be saying, is something that happens *in* nature, *by virtue of* nature, and at the origin of which is the figure of woman.

The association between Lincoln, women and his mother, becomes more important insofar as, following the death of Ann, Lincoln shies away from all sexual desire. This trait of his character is most explicitly expressed during the balcony scene in which he converses with Mary Todd (the

**Figure 1.8** 'Woman-Nature-Law': Lincoln (Henry Fonda) with Mrs Clay (Alice Brady) and her daughters in *Young Mr. Lincoln*.
*Source*: Courtesy Kobal Collection. Twentieth-Century Fox.

woman who will become his wife later in life, a period not covered by the film): he turns away from her and is instead entranced by the river. The river, of course, is associated with Ann: the absent woman–mother demonstrates her force by denying Lincoln any sexual desire.

### Renunciation of desire

Lincoln's renunciation of sexual desire opens onto one of the *Cahiers* authors' most controversial claims: that Lincoln 'does not have the phallus, he is the phallus' (1976: 517). Drawing upon theories from Lacanian psychoanalysis (see Lacan 2006b), the authors argue that Lincoln is both castrating (he *has* the **phallus**), but also castrated (*is* the phallus). In other words, the film *tries* to establish Lincoln's masculine power – on various occasions, he calls on his brute strength in order to quell disquiet: in order to keep the plaintiffs from coming to blows; he demonstrates his strength at the rail-splitting contest; and he has the power to disperse the mob when they try to attack the prison. These are all examples of Lincoln's *castrating power*. However, he is also beset by a constitutive weakness: his inability to choose, and his reliance on quasi-divine, magical forces which control his destiny. At all times, these forces are derived from women: the Law itself is passed to him by women, while his ultimate triumph in the trial is delivered to him by way of the almanac given him by Mrs Clay (the almanac also doubling as a force of nature). From this perspective, Lincoln is merely a conduit for a feminine Law, a Law which positions him as castrated, and thus, desexualized.

Lincoln's position as both castrating and castrated is the central point on which the *Cahiers* authors base their claim that *Young Mr. Lincoln* reveals the limitations of its own capitalist ideology. The figure of Lincoln can only totter between ineffectual powerlessness – as a mere channel through which an eternal, feminine, Republican Law manifests itself – or an irrational and threatening violence whose threat of force is the last resort of the Law. At the end of the film, the authors argue, '*he is an intolerable figure*' (1976: 524) (Figure 1.9).

The *Cahiers* article remains one of the most influential in the history of film theory. Extraordinary for its use of structuralist methods in delving beneath the surface text of the film, the article also courted controversy for its too heavy reliance on Lacanian psychoanalysis. Nevertheless, the article remains a landmark one for pointing out the possible underlying structures of a film that give rise to cultural and political meanings.

## Brian Henderson '*The Searchers*: An American Dilemma'

(First published in *Film Quarterly*, 34(2), Winter 1980–81; reprinted in B. Nichols (ed.), *Movies and Methods Volume II* [Henderson 1985]. All references are to the latter reprint.)

While Raymond Bellour's essay on *The Birds* was published in 1969, and the *Cahiers* essay on *Young Mr. Lincoln* was published in 1970, Brian Henderson's article on another of John Ford's films, *The Searchers* (1956), was published over 10 years later, in 1981. Henderson is also one of the foremost contributors to debates over the *Cahiers* article, to the point where he claims that, in its methodology, it presents a critique of the application of structuralism to the study of cinema (see Henderson 1973; 1973–74).

Where Bellour's analysis of *The Birds* is by and large free from a consideration of historical circumstances, and where the *Cahiers*' analysis takes into account a limited acknowledgement of historical factors, Brian Henderson's reading is very much concerned with questions of history. In many ways his article is an attempt to account for the specific historical period in which *The Searchers* was produced and released. The article title,

**Figure 1.9** Lincoln – 'an intolerable figure'?
*Source*: Courtesy Kobal Collection. Twentieth Century-Fox.

'an American dilemma', refers to Gunnar Myrdal's ([1944] 1962) book, *An American Dilemma*, which attributes to the USA a particular and on-going dilemma: the dilemma of inequality between whites and blacks. Already we might begin to see some evidence of a structuralist methodology in Henderson's article: where on the surface *The Searchers* is a film about conflict between white Americans and North American Indians, at a deeper level – at the level of structure – the film's significance lies in its being a tale of conflict between white and black Americans. One might call black Americans a 'structuring absence' in *The Searchers*.

At one level, Henderson openly notes the similarity between the content of *The Searchers* and the kinds of topics studied by anthropologists like Lévi-Strauss: kinship, race, marriage and tribal relations. And Henderson's reading is heavily influenced by Lévi-Straussian methodologies, especially insofar as he treats the film as a myth which tries to reconcile a social conflict. At the heart of the social conflict in *The Searchers* – the opposition between whites and Indians – Henderson finds one overarching opposition: that between Debbie Edwards (Natalie Wood) and Martin Pawley (Jeffrey Hunter). Debbie is a white woman who has been 'adopted' by an Indian tribe, while Martin is a part-Indian, who has been adopted by a white family. Thus, the film might be seen as one in which there is an exchange between races: what happens when a white person becomes integrated into an Indian tribe, and what happens when an Indian is assimilated into white society? Henderson further complicates these questions by recasting the opposition between Indian and white at another level: the most fundamental opposition is that between being a *relative by blood* and being a *relative by adoption*. Neither Martin nor Debbie has the 'pure' blood of the societies in which they now live, so how do societies cope with members who are not of pure blood?

While the film itself deals with these questions, there is one character through whom these questions are profoundly and ambiguously articulated: Ethan Edwards (John Wayne). Ethan is deeply suspicious of Martin's presumed assimilation into the Edwards family. These suspicions are made evident by Ethan's reluctance to accept Martin at the family dinner table early in the film, and he pokes fun at Martin throughout the film, at times referring to him as a 'blankethead' or 'half breed'. And yet, at one and the same time, he is not opposed to the idea of Martin's marriage to Laurie Jorgenson, the white daughter of a neighbouring family. With regard to Debbie, throughout the film Ethan is intent on murdering her, for her blood has been sullied by association with an Indian tribe. 'She's been living with a buck!' he declares at one point. Yet again, at the end of the film, he spares Debbie and returns her to white society. In the character of Ethan is crystallized the dilemma of relations between Indians and whites in *The Searchers*.

Henderson argues, however, that *The Searchers* is a film about relations between Indians and whites *only on its surface*. The surface story serves to cover over the genuine dilemma that is at the film's core: relations between blacks and whites in US society. Why does Henderson think this? He reads the film in this way because, at the time when the film was being produced, one of the central political problems confronting American society was that concerning relations between blacks and whites. More specifically, these issues were at the forefront of the national consciousness on account of the Supreme Court ruling, on May 17 1954, of the case of *Brown vs The Board of Education of Topeka*. This decision had decreed that the segregation of black and white students in schools was unconstitutional, thus paving the way in general for the desegregation of US society. Because the government feared that full and immediate implementation of the Supreme Court's ruling could lead to severe civil unrest, adoption of the ruling was delayed for a year in order to facilitate public debate. Therefore, during 1954–55 – precisely the period in which *The Searchers* is being planned and produced – the issue of desegregation and of relations between blacks and whites was a heated public issue in the United States.

Henderson notes the important changes made to the script during this period (1954–55), for there are very significant differences between the novel of *The Searchers*, written by Alan LeMay and published in 1954, and the finished film version of the story. The most significant differences are:

- In the novel Martin is 100 per cent white, while in the film he is one-eighth Cherokee.
- In the film Martin sneaks into the Indians' camp, kills their leader, Scar, and sets Debbie free. In the novel, however, he merely rides with the rest of the rangers and finds Debbie has already gone.
- In the film, Ethan finds and rescues Debbie. In the novel, on the other hand, Ethan is killed in the final battle. Debbie, meanwhile, in not described in the novel as one of Scar's wives, while she is in the film. Finally, in the novel Martin tracks down Debbie and embraces her, as if to make love to her, in the novel's closing episode. Laurie Jorgenson, in the novel, has married another man (Charlie McCorry) quite some time before. The film's ending is thus remarkably different from that of the novel.

The film of *The Searchers* thus emphasizes the opposition between *relations by blood* and *relations by adoption* in ways that the novel does not. Ethan, for the most part, is intent on upholding relations by blood, which is the ground for his desire to kill Debbie and for his continued ridiculing of Martin. Ethan finds it tremendously difficult to acknowledge relations by adoption. Therefore, argues Henderson, 'Ethan's insistence on literal blood lines in determining kinship, its privileges and obligations, is historically the position of the segregationist and white supremacist' (1985: 446). Ethan's position thus accords with those sections of the American population opposed to the *Brown* decision and therefore opposed to recognizing the equality of blacks and whites. Henderson concludes:

> Racism was always immoral and undemocratic but *Brown* made some of its fundamental institutions illegal . . . After *Brown*, opposing the possibility of kinship by adoption, affirming kinship by blood only, places one outside the law. Thus Ethan's exclusion from the community at the end of the film is overdetermined by its unconscious structure.
>
> (1985: 447)

What Henderson calls the film's 'unconscious structure' – the structuring absence of the opposition between blacks and whites in US society – is an outcome of his structuralist methodology. At the same time, however, for Henderson, not everything in the film can be neatly explained and contained within a unified whole. Rather, even if Ethan is revealed to be racist, or at the very least to be representative of southern American racist attitudes, he is nonetheless treated very sympathetically by the film. He is, without question, the film's hero; he is not a hated figure, but is instead a figure of great affection, even if one acknowledges the difficult and even contradictory nature of his motives and beliefs. The sympathy we have for Ethan is one of the film's finest attributes, Henderson claims, and Ethan encapsulates the complexities and tensions of the debate around the *Brown* decision during the years of the mid-1950s in the United States.

Finally, *The Searchers* is ultimately still founded on an imbalance. The film effectively declares that it is acceptable for non-whites to be assimilated into white society – as occurs with Martin – but under no circumstances should the prospect of the white person's assimilation into non-white society be countenanced; i.e., the only options entertained for Debbie are either her return to white society or her annihilation, and the apparent madness that has befallen other whites captured by Scar's tribe indicates that the only outcomes for whites in a non-white society are entirely negative. Furthermore, for Martin to be accepted into white society he has to prove that he has renounced any ties he might have had with non-white society – he must prove himself 'as fully white'.

Like Bellour's article on *The Birds* and the *Cahiers* article on *Young Mr. Lincoln*, Henderson manages to unearth a wealth of delicate material from *The Searchers*. As with each of the articles examined in this chapter, the conclusions made by Henderson are not ones that rely on overt or necessarily 'conscious' understandings of the films or sequences in question. Rather, structuralism aims to uncover a deeper level of understanding, a level which might be at odds with our overt, conscious understandings of cinematic material. Such findings are in accordance with the structuralist belief that the true, scientific nature of sign systems and systems of meaning are ones which lie beneath the surface of things, for it is only by delving beneath the surface that one can find the definitive ways in which things come to be structured.

The structuralist approach to film set the trend for the next 20 years or more in film theory. The quest to discover meanings in films which lay beneath the surface, the search for the structuring logic of a film which might be hidden inside it, obscured by the surface display, and the urge to uncover symbolic meanings which might be historically significant enough to constitute the covert structuring axioms of a film – these are the great contributions structuralism made to film theory.

# Glossary

**Alternation/parallel montage**: The system of shot/reverse-shot edit-ing that came to prominence in the early years of cinema in which the actions from two separate spaces or times could be juxtaposed by switching from the action of one scene to the action of the other.

**Myth**: The structuralist anthropologist Claude Lévi-Strauss developed a sophisticated theory of myths, declaring that myths are ways in which primitive societies find solutions to social divisions or prob-lems which would otherwise be irresolvable. Roland Barthes extended Lévi-Strauss's findings to contemporary societies, arguing that myths are ideological insofar as they render social contradictions neutral (see Barthes 1972).

**Oedipus complex**: Initially formulated by Sigmund Freud, one of the major complexes theorized by psychoanalysis. Typically, from the male child's perspective, it describes the unconscious conflict played out by the child's love and desire for his mother and his hatred for his father, insofar as the father blocks the boy's desire for the mother. The complex is 'dissolved' when the boy comes to realize that he must bow to his father's authority and allow his father priority over the mother's love.

**Phallus**: For Freud, and most importantly for Lacan, the phallus is a signifier, not an organ (i.e., penis). In a stage prior to the Oedipus complex, the child can 'be' the phallus in a quest to make up for the mother's lack of a penis; that is, the child can 'be' the phallus for the mother. Following the phallic phase and the dissolution of the Oedipus complex, the phallus assumes the role of a signifier which positions the subject in relation to circuits of desire.

**Structuralism**: An intellectual movement which tried to uncover the deep structures of social formations. A central tenet of the movement was that societies were not founded on specific, intrinsic truths, but instead were constructed out of systems of differences. The movement built on the foundations of the linguist, Ferdinand de Saussure, who argued that languages were constructed by the system of differences between individual words.

**Symptomatic reading**: A term used by the Marxist philosopher, Louis Althusser, which combines Freudian and Marxian theories to claim that social structures are often determined by deeper, hidden levels of influence which are absent from that structure's superficial appear-ances (they are 'structuring absences'). Therefore, societies can be understood by paying attention to the hidden symptoms which are absent from official discourses, but which affect those discourses in much the same way as, according to psychoanalytic theory, unconscious wishes affect our conscious thoughts and actions.

**Textual analysis**: A method of analysing written texts as well as other media such as paintings, advertisements and films in which very close attention is paid to the material evidence of the works (words, lines, editing patterns) while other factors, such as historical context or intertextual references, are downplayed. 'Textual analysis' also directly declares its allegiance to 'psycho-analysis'.

# 2 Apparatus theory
## Jean-Louis Baudry and Christian Metz

One of the motivating causes of the structuralist revolution in film studies was the desire to found a politics of cinema. The influence of the Marxist philosopher, Louis Althusser, cannot be underestimated in this regard, for his recasting of Marxist debates during the 1960s acted as a template from which theories of cinema expanded, especially in France and the United Kingdom. Althusser gave a particular emphasis to the term *theory*. In his writings he considers that the proper work of Marxist intellectuals is one in which a theoretical approach to society and politics is a necessary constituent of political action. In other words, for Althusser, theory does not follow upon the heels of practical politics, but practical politics can only be effective if guided by theory in the first place. Film theorists also took up this challenge: a theory of film was not merely one that commented on films and film-making *after* the fact but was instead geared towards guiding and informing new forms of cinema and new approaches to film-making.

If many film theorists agreed about the nature of the struggle to be achieved – that is, the struggle to define a political cinema – then they vehemently disagreed about the precise nature of what a political cinema should entail. Fierce debates on the politics of cinema raged in the French journals, *Cinéthique*, *Cahiers du cinéma* and *Positif*. Perhaps the most famous (or *in*famous) essay from *Cinéthique* during this period is Jean-Louis Baudry's 'Ideological Effects of the Basic Cinematographic Apparatus', published in 1970. What is immediately most notable in that article is its condemnation of the transparent style of Hollywood cinema. For Baudry, only cinematic forms explicitly opposed to the Hollywood style could bypass bourgeois ideology and bring about social or political change. We discuss Baudry's article in great detail in this chapter, before turning to one of the most influential essays of contemporary film theory: Christian Metz's 'The Imaginary Signifier' (Metz 1982). Finally, in this chapter we examine a cinematic case study: *Singin' in the Rain* (Donen and Kelly, 1957). Both Baudry's and Metz's essays are somewhat notorious for avoiding any lengthy discussion of actual films, so the introduction of a case study to this chapter is an attempt to see how their writings might be applied to cinematic examples.

# Jean-Louis Baudry, 'Ideological Effects of the Basic Cinematographic Apparatus'

(First published in *Cinéthique*, 7–8, 1970; translated in B. Nichols (ed.) *Movies and Methods*, Volume II [Baudry 1985]. All references are to the latter translation.)

The explicit aim of Baudry's article on the 'basic cinematographic apparatus' is to mobilize a critique of the accepted Hollywood styles of cinema. The techniques associated with the Hollywood style, based on continuity and **transparency**, are ones he attributes to a 'basic cinematographic apparatus'. Baudry then refers to the Hollywood style as one that is *ideological*. What does he mean by referring to this style as ideological? Baudry's essay was published in the same year as Althusser's very influential essay on 'Ideology and Ideological State Apparatuses' (Althusser 1971) and Baudry can be understood to be using the term ideology in the sense intended by Althusser.

Four important points can be taken from Althusser's theses on ideology, points that are not merely essential to understanding Baudry's approach to the cinematographic apparatus, but central to defining much of film theory's enthrallment with Althusser during the 1970s. The points are:

1. *Ideological State apparatuses* differ from *repressive State apparatuses*. Repressive State apparatuses are the kinds of easily identifiable governmental institutions and practices which enforce law and order and which ensure the smooth and civil running of public services – for example, the police, legal institutions, prisons, governments themselves (national and local). *Ideological* State apparatuses differ from repressive ones in the sense that they are not explicitly sanctioned under the banner of ensuring law and order, but are nevertheless institutions which reinforce the functioning of those laws and that order. Schools are one of Althusser's favoured examples: even though schools are generally considered to be places of learning, enlightenment and free thought, one significant function they perform is to produce 'good citizens', that is, they produce children who know how to behave themselves, and who learn the nature of what is deemed important, and who have inculcated in them the difference between right and wrong. At all times, according to Althusser, those values delivered to school students are the dominant, bourgeois values which ensure the continued empowerment of the dominant class. Thus, central to Baudry's thesis on the 'cinematographic apparatus' is that the cinema itself – at least in its Hollywood form – is an ideological state apparatus, an apparatus that upholds the power and privileges of the ruling, bourgeois classes.

2. *Ideology represents the imaginary relationship of individuals to their real conditions of existence*. This formulation is a complex one, because Althusser does not claim that, because of ideology, an individual's real conditions of existence become imaginary. Instead, he argues that it is an individual's *relation* to real conditions that are *represented* in an imaginary way by ideology. In other words, the real conditions might very well be right there in front of one's eyes, but the way that ideology *represents* those conditions to individuals is imaginary. We might then see this as a matter of interpretation: ideology interprets reality in such a way that individuals see that reality as if through an imaginary filter.

What, however, does Althusser mean by *imaginary*? The inspiration for this term comes from the psychoanalytic theories of Jacques Lacan, especially from his notion of the 'mirror stage', a concept which Baudry also relies on extensively for his essay (see Lacan 2006c). Lacan, in his theory of the mirror stage, argues that human beings between the ages of 6 and 18 months develop a sense of themselves as individuals who are separated from other people and objects in the world. This realization occurs as a split between the feeling or sense a child has of his/her own body and the way that the child imagines this body looks, for example, the way that this body is represented to the self as an image in the mirror. This split, therefore, can be understood as one which happens, on the one hand, between the 'real body' inside which the child lives and, on the other, the body which the child imagines it has, the body the child represents to itself. The latter representation is an imaginary one which is split, we might say, from that body's 'real conditions of existence'.

Althusser takes Lacan's theory of the mirror stage and weaves ideology into it: ideology sets in place an imaginary relation to the real conditions of existence. Baudry then takes this notion a step further by applying it to the cinema. The cinematographic apparatus – the camera, projector and screen – are the methods by which the real conditions of existence are represented in the cinema. Therefore, according to Baudry's argument, the cinematographic apparatus sets in place an imaginary relation to the real conditions of existence. On this count, the cinematographic apparatus is fundamentally ideological.

3. *Ideology interpellates individuals as subjects*. Intuitively, Althusser's assertion here is even more difficult to grasp. If individuals are not *subjects*, then what are they? And what does ideology have to do with making individuals into subjects, for can't we all be considered subjects anyway, with or without ideology? The seemingly obvious answers to these questions form part of Althusser's point: it seems entirely natural for us to conceive of ourselves as subjects because that is the reigning ideology of our day. For human beings to conceive of themselves as *subjects* is a happening

of fairly recent origin (say, of the past two or three hundred years), and Althusser contends that for humans to understand themselves as subjects is something possible only under the conditions of bourgeois, capitalist ideology. The category of the subject is one that upholds the beliefs and interests of the bourgeois classes, for it is a particular way of conceiving of what human beings are: free, isolated individuals who are solely responsible and answerable for the outcomes of their actions, rather than individuals who are determined by larger social forces.

What does Althusser mean by declaring that ideology *interpellates* individuals as subjects? Interpellation, for Althusser, is a form of recognition, so that, in ideology, individuals may be said to recognize themselves as subjects. Again, Althusser's reasoning may seem odd, for surely only if individuals are *already* subjects will they necessarily recognize themselves as subjects. Not so, however, according to Althusser. Rather, it is the very process of being recognized by ideology that makes individuals into subjects. In other words, individuals only recognize themselves as subjects if the ideology at first recognizes them as subjects.

Althusser's overarching point is therefore that *individuals are not subjects automatically* but are only made so by ideology. We shall see that this category of the subject – which both Baudry and Metz refer to as a 'transcendental subject' – has been very important for conceptualizing the positions of spectators of the cinema.

4. *Ideology can be countered by science.* If ideology is conceived by Althusser as an imaginary relation to real conditions, is there a way of breaking down this imaginary relation so that the real conditions of existence can manifest themselves? In simple terms, if ideology emanates from those elements of society which uphold the power of the bourgeois classes, then to break with ideology is to break this power. To expose the 'real conditions of existence', therefore, is to reveal the manner in which the working classes are exploited by the bourgeoisie. Althusser refers to the manner of this exploitation as the 'real relations of production'. The task of ideology, on the other hand, is to cover up the real relations of production.

Althusser refers to the domain which can expose ideology – the domain which is 'outside' ideology – as *science*. By calling it science, he does not necessarily mean the disciplines of biology, chemistry, physics, and so on, for he means those human sciences such as Marxism, psychoanalysis and philosophy – and structuralism, especially – whose very task is, according to Althusser, to theorize the real relations of production. Once again the role of *theory* is paramount here, for it is by way of the theoretical analysis of society and its structures that 'scientific knowledge' of the real relations of production can be surmised. Again, we shall see that Baudry utilizes the distinction between ideology and science in his essay.

As was noted above, Baudry conceives of Hollywood cinema as resolutely ideological. This means that, to follow in Althusser's footsteps, the Hollywood cinema must represent the real conditions of existence in an imaginary way and, in doing so, interpellate individuals as subjects. For Baudry, therefore, how does Hollywood and its cinematographic apparatus manage to do this? Baudry argues that there is one overriding reason to conceive of the cinematographic apparatus as ideological and that is that the cinematographic apparatus is geared towards denying difference in favour of unity. The apparatus achieves this unity in three ways:

1. *The 'screen-mirror'.* Just as the mirror unifies the fragmentary body of the child according to Lacan's theory of the mirror stage, so too does the cinema screen offer the spectator who gazes upon it a unity which is not typically found in reality. The cinema screen, for Baudry (and indeed also for Metz, as we shall see) thus functions in a way that is similar to the mirror of the mirror stage. Baudry notes some similarities between the way in which spectators are situated in front of a cinema screen and the way the child is positioned in front of the mirror during the mirror stage. First of all, the spectator, like the child, is immobile – the mirror stage typically takes hold before a child can crawl or walk, while cinema spectators are likewise immobilized in their seats. Second, the spectator's relation to the screen is primarily *visual* in much the same way as the child gets its bearings as a self from its visual capacities: the child's production of an imaginary relation to the self is established visually, by way of its reflection in the mirror. Key to understanding Baudry's point is that the cinema screen provides spectators with *images* instead of reality and therefore it offers *representations* of reality rather than reality itself. By doing this, the cinema represents the real conditions of existence in an imaginary way – a precise, Althusserian definition of ideology.

2. *Movement, continuity and unity.* Baudry argues that the cinema offers a *transformation* of 'objective reality'. The camera records photographic images of 'objective reality', then these images are edited and projected in a cinema theatre. At each stage of this process, a transformation occurs. The camera is a site of inscription, while the end result is a projection, with the result, Baudry claims, that

> between the inscription and projection are situated certain operations, a *work* which has as its result a finished product. To the extent that it is cut off from the raw material ('objective reality') this product does not allow us to see the transformation which has taken place.
>
> (1985: 533)

The cinematographic apparatus is an apparatus of transformation, but the processes of this transformation are typically hidden: the end product (the projection of a film) is irrevocably severed from the *real process of its **production***; that is, the end product we see in Hollywood films offers an out and out denial of the **work** involved in producing that end.

This denial of the transformational processes of cinema is the case because the traditional patterns of Hollywood cinema have provided that outcome. Even if the many frames, shots and scenes that make up a film are captured at different places and times, the traditions of Hollywood cinema have always aimed to maintain the unity of the filmic fabric, to form its disparate images and scenarios into an *organic unity*. Baudry attributes this organic unity to Hollywood's insistence on restoring continuity to discontinuous elements – what is known as continuity editing – but also to the **persistence of vision** which restores the illusion of movement to the separate, individual frames of a film. 'The meaning effect produced', argues Baudry, 'does not depend only on the content of the images but also on the material procedures by which an **illusion of continuity**, dependent on persistence of vision, is restored from the discontinuous elements' (1985: 536). Once again, therefore, the cinema is based on giving rise to an imaginary relation to reality: the 'real conditions of existence' are covered over by the processes of a transformation of reality which occurs by way of the cinematographic apparatus (camera + editing + projector). The cinematographic apparatus is, on the basis of Baudry's points here, inherently ideological.

3. *Perspective and monocular vision*: The typical way that a cinema camera – or photographic camera – captures images of reality is in accordance with the theory of linear **perspective**, or *perspetiva artificialis*, which was mathematically formulated during the fifteenth century. The system of perspective has been used widely by artists and architects ever since as a way of representing three dimensions on a two-dimensional plane. Indeed, most computer graphics which attempt to describe three-dimensional spaces also rely on linear perspective. The system of perspective is based on the notion that three dimensions can be represented on a two-dimensional plane if that representation is made to cohere with a single point. This single point is both the '**vanishing point**' of the image and the ideal position of the spectator's eye (see Edgerton 1975; White 1972). Perspective is therefore a system in which a spectator is reduced to a single point. With the system of perspective, the viewing subject is fixed in reference to a specific position: the vanishing point. The viewing subject is thus monocular, reduced to the vantage point of a single eye. In this way the system of perspective, and the optical instruments which conform to this system, not the least of which is the cinematographic

camera, generate a vision intended for the point of view of an isolated, idealized subject. As Baudry argues, 'It lays out the space of an ideal vision and in this way', he adds, 'asserts the necessity of a transcendence' (1985: 534).

The transcendence inherent in the idealized vision of the cinematographic apparatus is attributable to none other than what Baudry calls a *transcendental subject*. This transcendental subject exists beyond experience and without a body, and is, above all, an idealized subject who is the centre of a world of vision. In short, the cinema, as provided by continuity editing and the system of perspective and the idealistically transparent 'mirror-screen', gives rise to an idealized view of the world. For Baudry, this idealization of what the viewer sees is inherently ideological. In short, what Baudry means to imply is that all otherness, difference and multiplicity are reduced and denied at the cinema. Rather, what is presented there is a world which is centred and unified *on* me and *for* me. Again, Baudry's argument is one in which the cinema apparatus is produced by denying difference in favour of unity.

> And if the eye is no longer fettered by a body, by the laws of matter and time, if there are no longer any assignable limits to its displacement – conditions fulfilled by the possibilities of shooting and of film – the world will not only be constituted by this eye but for it.
>
> (1985: 537)

The cinematographic apparatus interpellates individuals as transcendental subjects: the cinema makes individuals into self-centred, self-seeking, self-affirming identities who feel as though they are the centre of the world.

Baudry does, however, consider that there might be ways of countering what he sees as being the extremely negative cinematic apparatus produced by Hollywood films. Films which expose the ideological functioning of the cinema apparatus – films which explicitly display the work involved in the transformation from 'objective reality' to screen – will be able to counteract the ideology of the dominant, Hollywood cinema apparatus. Baudry poses the question thusly: 'The question becomes: is the work made evident, does consumption of the product bring about a "knowledge effect", or is the work concealed? If the latter, consumption of the product will obviously be accompanied by ideological surplus value' (1985: 533). For him, if films are effective in displaying the work of the apparatus, then they will be able to produce a 'knowledge effect': they will be *science* rather than *ideology*. We shall pose this question to *Singin' in the Rain* at the end of this chapter.

# Christian Metz, 'The Imaginary Signifier'

(First published in *Communications*, 23 (1975): 3–55. Translated in Metz, *The Imaginary Signifier* [Metz 1982].)

Metz's extraordinary essay on 'The Imaginary Signifier', published in 1975 in an issue of *Communications* devoted to the topic of psychoanalysis and cinema, and in which Baudry also published an essay on 'The Apparatus [*dispositif*]' (Baudry 1976), takes up and builds upon Baudry's uses of the mirror stage, the system of perspective and the transcendental subject, but with an important difference: in Metz's essay there is no Althusser. The questions Metz is trying to answer in this essay are therefore substantially different from those which Baudry tried to answer in his essay on the 'cinematographic apparatus'. Baudry's analysis was guided by the distinctions between ideology and science and by a determination to configure Althusser's conception of ideology in cinematic terms. Metz completely drops or ignores these aspects of Baudry's analysis and instead sets his sights fairly and squarely on Freudian theory and on what that theory might be able to contribute to the study of the cinematic **signifier**.

The first question to ask of Metz, then, is what is a cinematic *signifier*? As we saw in the previous chapter, Metz was one of the first to apply categories derived from semiology and linguistics to the study of cinema and, in doing so, he was trying to draw comparisons between the abilities of written or spoken language to make meaning and those meaning-making abilities which pertain to cinema. The general question asked by Metz was that if language is composed of specific signifiers and traits of signification – letters, words, sentences, phonemes, and so on – then what particular traits of signification might be at work in the cinema? Metz's approaches to cinematic semiotics unfolded along these lines. His essay on 'The Imaginary Signifier' continues these researches to a degree, but is framed by one overarching question: *what does 'cinema' signify*? That is, what do we mean when we say 'cinema'? In our everyday lives and activities, what is it that we are referring to when we refer to 'cinema'?

Framing these questions also is the theory of psychoanalysis, rather than, as in Metz's earlier work, elements derived from structuralism and linguistics. Thus, Metz's explicit question in 'The Imaginary Signifier' is: 'What contribution can Freudian psychoanalysis make to the study of the cinematic signifier?' (Metz 1982: 17) There are two central concepts from psychoanalysis which Metz applies to the cinema: **fetishism**, a concept taken directly from Freud, and the *mirror stage*, which, as we have already seen, is a concept put forward by Jacques Lacan. Metz, however, positions these concepts in a very specific way. He begins by asking what it is we have become accustomed to expecting when we 'go to the cinema'. For example, how do the kinds of experiences we have (or expect to have) at the cinema differ from other cultural pursuits? Only after asking this more general question does Metz then call upon psychoanalytic theory to refine his investigation.

First of all, therefore, the question we need to ask here is: what do we expect to experience when we go to the cinema? Metz tries to answer this question by comparing the experience of cinema with the typical experience of going to the theatre. The typical experience of the theatre is, according to Metz, one in which we expect to see and hear *real actors and props situated in a real space before us*. If a chair is to be part of a play we see at the theatre then, typically, a real chair will need to be placed on the stage, a real chair which, if we so desired, we could get up out of our own seats in the theatre, walk up onto the stage and touch. By contrast, if a chair is part of a film we go to see at the cinema, then there will be no real chair placed before us. Rather, the cinema projects before us images which are no longer *real* in the same way as they are at the theatre. The cinema instead presents us with *images, projections, rays of light* and reproductions of sound. If we try to touch a chair that is part of a film, all we will manage to touch are rays of light and a screen; we will not touch a 'real' chair. This is Metz's first point: our experience of cinema is phenomenologically different from most other forms of cultural experience, for at the cinema there is quite literally no object we can touch. Instead, the images and sounds of cinema emanate from an indeterminate elsewhere.

Metz's argument expands from this first point. If we see a real chair on stage during a dramatic production at the theatre, what is the typical function of such a chair? Its function is not to make us think 'there is a chair on stage'. Rather, its function is usually to make us think it is chair which is part of a fictional scenario – within the fiction of the play we are watching, for example, it might be a chair in someone's dining room. Therefore, the chair will be a real object in front of our eyes which nevertheless refers to a fictional object situated in another time and place. In short, the chair is a *real object referring to a fictional one*. The situation in the cinema is somewhat different. Certainly, the action and the story will very likely be, as in theatre, 'more or less fictional', writes Metz. But in addition to this, he adds, 'the unfolding itself is fictional: the décor, the words one hears are all absent' (1982: 44). In the cinema therefore, there is a *fictional object* (the cinema itself) *referring to a fictional object* (the story of the film). Such, at any rate, is the way Metz tries to account for the specificity of the cinematic experience. For him, 'Every film is a fiction film' (1982: 44), not because any film's content might be fictional, but because the mode of presentation in the cinema, unlike that of the theatre, *is itself fictional*.

For Metz, therefore, the cinema does not just present a fictional *signified* (the contents of its stories) but also a fictional *signifier* (the mode or means by which those stories are cinematically formed). Metz equates the inherent fictitiousness of the cinema signifier with the imaginary: the cinema does not merely provide us with imaginary stories and scenes, but the way in which it presents those imaginary stories to us *is itself imaginary*: 'What is characteristic of the cinema is not the imaginary it may happen to represent, but the imaginary that it *is* from the start, the imaginary that constitutes it as a signifier' (1982: 44).

Why does Metz introduce the 'imaginary' as a term? Why wouldn't he simply call the cinematic signifier the 'fictional' signifier? Metz frames his entire discussion of the cinema signifier around the play of *presence* and *absence*. In its simplest terms, the imaginary is the ability to invoke absence, in other words, it is the capacity to imagine a thing is *there* when it ostensibly is *not there*. All fictions certainly engage in a process of invoking the imaginary, but the important point which Metz tries to stress is that the cinema engages the capacities of the imaginary in a very particular way. We have seen, first of all, how presence and absence are invoked in different ways in the cinema and in the theatre. The theatre is a *presence* (actors and props on stage in front of us) which refers to an *absence* (the actions and scenes of the play being performed). By contrast, the cinema is an *absence* (mere rays of light projected on a screen) that also, *doubly*, invokes an *absence* (the actions and scenes of the film being projected). The imaginariness, the doubled absence of the cinema is thus, for Metz, doubly imaginary; not merely the imaginary a film may happen to represent, but the imaginary that the cinema signifier *is* from the start.

Cinema's imaginary invocation of a doubled absence leads Metz, building on the analysis of Baudry, to ponder the relation between the cinema screen and the mirror stage. Metz does not fully endorse the mirror analogy in the way Baudry does, and Metz even declared at one point, 'I am not a Lacanian' (Metz 1979: 8). Metz's argument is that the cinema screen is *like* the mirror, but it should not be confused with the mirror of the mirror stage. If the mirror stage is an initiating phase in the child's insertion into the social world, then the screen which one watches during a cinema screening can only be likened to a mirror placed within an already constituted social world. 'A strange mirror, then', writes Metz, 'very like that of childhood, and very different' (1982: 49). Indeed, Metz goes on to refer to the cinematic situation as a 'series of mirror-effects organised in a chain' (1982: 51).

How, then, might we work out this relationship between the screen and the mirror as Metz conceives it? We can call upon the distinction between presence and absence to clarify his position:

- For the drama of the mirror stage, the child's body is present, while the child's image in the mirror is absent, even though the child experiences this image – imaginarily – as present. Therefore, the imaginary effect of the mirror stage is one in which the *absent image* is (mis)taken for a *presence*.
- At the theatre, as we have already seen, the actors and sets are present, while the action or story of the play is absent. Therefore, the imaginary effect of the theatre is, like that of the mirror stage, one in which an *absence* is (mis)taken for a *presence*. This effect has been traditionally called the 'suspension of disbelief'.
- At the cinema, the images and sounds on the screen are absent and the action or story of the film is also absent. The absent images are still (mis)taken for a presence, but all of this unfolds *on the basis of a fundamental absence*, an absence which constitutes the cinema signifier as imaginary. Metz thus calls this effect, rather than a 'suspension of disbelief', a 'doubling up of belief' (we shall come to this notion shortly). Therefore the mirror stage and the theatre invoke *absence on the basis of a presence*, whereas the images of the cinema are an *absence that itself invokes an absence*. It is in this way that Metz asserts that the cinema is both like the mirror of childhood, but also very different. The cinema is, rather, a 'series of mirror-effects'.

The greater part of 'The Imaginary Signifier' is given over to an investigation of the analogy between the psychoanalytic concept of fetishism and the cinema. According to Freud's 1927 essay 'On Fetishism' (Freud 1977b), the existence of a fetish requires *the simultaneous existence of contrary beliefs*. A fetish object has a specific function: it is an object which covers over the evident fact that the mother does not have a penis. In utilizing a fetish object – for example, a shoe or an article of clothing – the fetishist can maintain the belief that the mother is endowed with a penis (the belief that the mother *does* have a penis is an unconscious, 'primal' belief, Freud argues). And yet, the fetish has power in the realm of belief even though the fetishist knows, because it is an evident fact of the senses, that the mother does *not* have a penis. A fetish therefore has a double role: it points to the fact that the mother does not have a penis (for if the mother did have a penis, according to Freud's theory, then there would be no need for the fetish object), *while at the same time* it allows the fetishist to install a substitute for the mother's penis. The fetish therefore signifies both that the mother *does* and *does not* have a penis. Metz, following Freud, refers to this fetishistic situation as a *doubling up of belief*: the fetishist believes *both* that the mother does not have a penis *and* that she does have a penis, and it is the function of the fetish to enable the existence side-by-side of both of these beliefs.

Metz argues that a similar doubling up of belief occurs for the cinema. The spectator, while watching a film, believes both that the action on screen is not real, that it is imaginary, but at the same time, this spectator believes – unconsciously, primordially – that the scenes unfolding on the screen are real. At the very least, for Metz, the spectator takes in those scenes as believable in a convincing way, and that they are believable is a central constituent of the cinematic experience. Metz ultimately relies on a famous formulation made by the French psychoanalyst and student of Lacan, Octave Mannoni. To encapsulate the function of the fetish, Mannoni came up with the formula 'I know very well . . . but all the same . . .' (Mannoni 1969). For the fetishist proper, the formulation relates to the mother's penis: '*I know very well* the mother does not have a penis, *but all the same* the fetish object allows me to believe that she *does* have a penis.' For Metz, the formula can be applied to the cinema: '*I know very well* that what is before me are mere images projected onto a screen, *but all the same* I am going to believe in the images I see before me.' Ultimately, this might be the most important insight Metz makes into the functioning of cinema and into how, at least up until the 1970s, the term 'cinema' was understood by the majority of its audiences: we might very well know that the images we see before us are manipulated, fabricated and constructed, but for the cinema to achieve the effects we desire from it, then it necessitates that we do believe, at some level, in the veracity of its images. For Metz, this is the doubling up of belief that gives to cinema its unique effects.

## *Singin' in the Rain* (directed by Stanley Donen and Gene Kelly, 1952)

While both Baudry and Metz discuss detailed approaches to the theory of cinema and the operations performed by spectators who go to the cinema, discussions of actual cinematic examples are absent from their accounts. However, their analyses still make it possible to discuss particular films and, in the following example, we try to assess the ways in which Baudry and Metz might have thought through the experience and consequences of watching *Singin' in the Rain* (Figure 2.1).

As a product of the Hollywood system, Baudry would no doubt criticize *Singin' in the Rain* as ideological. However, at first glance many might otherwise regard the film as non-ideological, that is, as one that breaks down ideology. Certainly insofar as *Singin' in the Rain* purports to show

**Figure 2.1** Cosmo Brown (Donald O'Connor), Kathy Selden (Debbie Reynolds) and Don Lockwood (Gene Kelly) in *Singin' in the Rain*. *Source*: Courtesy British Film Institute. Metro-Goldwyn-Mayer.

what goes on behind the scenes in the making of a film, one might defend it as a film which demonstrates the *work* of a film. Is that not precisely what Baudry had called for in order to break the grip of Hollywood and its interpellations of individuals as subjects? Had he not called for films that display the work of a film, films that actually show rather than hide the transformation that takes place from the inscription (what is registered by the camera) through the editing to the projection on screen of the finished product? Inasmuch as *Singin' in the Rain* takes us, as viewers, 'behind the scenes' of the making of a film, then isn't it fulfilling the criteria of being a *non-ideological* film?

One might certainly try to make such a case, but it would be difficult to see Baudry defending such a claim. Rather, there is ample evidence to suggest that *Singin' in the Rain* is utterly ideological: it ultimately demonstrates that *bad films* are ones in which the work of the film is displayed. In *Singin' in the Rain* everything which happens behind-the-scenes – the *work* of film-making – is, in the final account, deemed fraudulent and compromised. For example, the fabrication of a romance between Don Lockwood and Lina Lamont is a behind-the-scenes insight into Hollywood stardom, but this behind-the-scenes fabrication is castigated for being just that – a sham, a publicity stunt. Also, the problems the makers of *The Duelling Cavalier* have with recording sound are again insights into the behind-the-scenes work of a film, but once again, any behind-the-scenes evidence is deemed faulty and problematic: no matter where the director places the microphone, Lina is incapable of projecting her voice in a way that will result in smooth, natural sound. Again, the foregrounding of a film's work is deemed problematic, faulty and wrong. Finally, and most emphatically, the trick necessary for producing Lina's voice (her voice is substituted with that of Kathy Selden) is also revealed as a behind-the-scenes matter of trickery and deceit. In other words, any time we are given an insight into the behind-the-scenes world of film production, such insights only serve to uphold the belief that it is only *bad* films which require shenanigans and trickery; it is only bad films which require work, effort, tricks and behind-the-scenes compromises.

Against the work that is de-valorized in the production of bad films are ones that happen *without work or effort*. Good films, the film seems to be telling us, are ones that do not require behind-the-scenes trickery. Evidence for this lack of work or effort is provided by the many musical numbers of the film. These numbers – 'Good Mornin'', 'Singin' in the Rain', 'Moses Supposes', 'Make 'em Laugh', and 'The Broadway Melody' – all occur 'spontaneously', as though they were a natural outcome of circumstances and an automatic product of the talents of Don, Kathy and Cosmo (on spontaneity in *Singin' in the Rain*, see Feuer 1986). More than anything, these song and dance routines ensure the seamless continuity of the film as a whole and assure that the finished film – *Singin' in the Rain* – provides a flawless model of the continuity system. The song and dance routines of the film are therefore exemplary of the transparency of the continuity system, while, opposed to such continuity, films which *do* demonstrate their work are failures. For further proof of this we can note the ways that audiences within the film laugh at those films which fail to live up to the standards of transparency and continuity; audiences roar with laughter when the sound is interrupted and goes out of synchronization during *The Duelling Cavalier*, as they also do at the end of the film when Lina is revealed to be a fraud as Kathy emerges from behind the curtain.

Are individual spectators thereby interpellated as subjects in front of *Singin' in the Rain*? One would have to surmise that Baudry would make such a conclusion. Spectators are encouraged to believe that fragmented subjects, such as those whose voices are separated from their bodies, are wrong, improper, and incorrect subjects who are doomed to failure, as indeed is Lina Lamont. Proper subjects, the kinds of transcendental subjects Baudry suggests are central to Hollywood spectatorship, are instead like Don, Cosmo or Kathy: self-sufficient, self-defining, and naturally successful individuals who effortlessly control their situations. Such subjects come up with quite extraordinary solutions to problems: when confronted with the impending failure of *The Duelling Cavalier*, Don, Cosmo and Kathy decide – off the tops of their heads as though it were an entirely natural occurrence – to make the film into a musical. Then, how could one solve the problem of Lina's voice? Again, our self-sufficient subjects have the answer: have her voice dubbed by Kathy. Or finally, how can Lina be exposed as a fraud after the successful premiere of *The Dancing Cavalier*? A magical solution again presents itself when Lina begins to mime on stage, so she can then be revealed as a fraud by drawing back the curtain (to the merry beat of 'Singin' in the Rain') to reveal Kathy as the real voice of the moment. These solutions are very much like those provided by Lincoln in *Young Mr. Lincoln*, solutions which appear to require no work, but instead happen naturally and obviously, by subjects who are masters of their world. Perhaps this is accentuated nowhere better than in the 'Make 'em Laugh' routine where Cosmo demonstrates the emplacement of the spectator according to the coordinates of linear perspective, as emphasized brilliantly by the *trompe l'œil* backdrop in front of which he acrobatically dances (Figure 2.2). This scene might even be taken as a perfect example of the way in which spectators of *Singin' in the Rain* are interpellated as transcendental subjects by virtue of linear perspective. All in all, a strong critique of *Singin' in the Rain* can be provided from Baudry's perspective.

What, on the other hand, might Christian Metz think of *Singin' in the Rain*? To reiterate one of Metz's guiding questions, what is it that spectators expect to experience when they go to the cinema? *Singin' in the Rain* itself provides answers to this question by virtue of the responses some of the audiences have to *Singin' in the Rain*'s films-within-a-film (*The Duelling Cavalier* and *The Dancing Cavalier*). When the cinematic machine is revealed to be faulty – for example, when the sound goes out of synchronization in *The Duelling Cavalier* – the audiences laugh and poke fun at the film. It is as though, at these moments, the film literally ceases to be a film, for it falls outside of the expectations the audience has when it goes to the cinema. In short, the cinema here ceases to function as an imaginary signifier.

But how, precisely, does this repudiation of the film occur? As Metz argues in 'The Imaginary Signifier', film – that experience which has come to be regarded as what is expected when one 'goes to the cinema' – is *an*

**Figure 2.2** Cosmo (Donald O'Connor) dances in *Singin' in the Rain*. A demonstration of perspective as ideology?
*Source*: Metro-Goldwyn-Mayer. Courtesy British Film Institute.

*absence which refers to an absence*; that is why he refers to the cinema as an 'imaginary signifier'. Therefore, for the successful projection of a film, nothing should give away the *presence* of the filmic apparatus; no faults should interfere with the doubled absence that constitutes cinema's signifier as imaginary. Therefore, the moments in *The Duelling Cavalier* when the sound goes out of synchronization are ones in which the cinematic apparatus has become present – the faults or the work of the cinema machine has interrupted the doubled absence of the cinema signifier.

As Metz emphasizes in accordance with the doubling up of belief which constitutes fetishism, the cinema signifier follows the formula of '*I know very well . . .*, *but all the same . . .*'. To reiterate the cinematic conclusion made from this: spectators double up their belief by acknowledging that they know very well this is a film made with cameras and microphones, but all the same the pleasure derived from this film depends on the magical transformation those cameras and microphones make possible. Indeed, for the majority of spectators, therein lies the glory and lure of the cinema. Quite contrary to what we would imagine to be Baudry's condemnation of the 'mirror effects' of *Singin' in the Rain*, Metz (we imagine) would rather conclude that the smoke and mirrors of *Singin' in the Rain*'s aesthetic strategies are precisely what make the film so engaging and pleasurable for many audiences. *Singin' in the Rain* can very effectively be seen as a demonstration of the ways in which the imaginary signifier functions and of the ways in which film-makers can make films which ensure the success of that signifier.

## Glossary

**Fetishism**: In Freudian psychoanalytic theory, fetishism describes a sexual perversion in which a person tries to make up for the mother's lack of a penis by inventing a substitute object. The fetish requires the simultaneous existence of contrary beliefs: at one and the same time the subject knows the mother does not have a penis (hence the need for a fetish object), but the fetish object also allows that subject to imagine that the mother does have a penis.

**Illusion of continuity/persistence of vision**: A controversial theory which seeks to account for the viewer's perception of continuous motion when presented with a succession of still images projected at 24 frames per second. The theory claims that the viewer's impression of continuous motion is the result of a limitation, or defect, of the human visual system. As the projected film image passes before the human eye, it imprints itself (or 'persists') upon the retina, yielding a fleeting afterimage that then blends into the succeeding frame. The eye/brain effectively skips over the discrepancy between the successive images and fuses them together, creating a perceptual or mental impression of continuous motion. Films are projected at a frame rate that exploits this perceptual idiosyncrasy, projecting a series of fractionally different still images that register upon the human eye an illusion of continuous movement.

**Perspective/vanishing point**: Perspective – or more accurately, the system of linear perspective – is a way of representing three-dimensional space on a two-dimensional plane. This system typically functions by means of a series of vectors which converge on a central vanishing point. The vanishing point itself was to be aligned with the location of the viewer's eye (a singular eye rather than two eyes) thus fixing the viewer's position in front of the image. The system of linear perspective was refined by Renaissance artists in fourteenth- and fifteenth-century Italy.

**Signifier/signified**: A fundamental division for Structuralist theorists. For Saussure, the division is one between the signifier as a *word*, as such, and the signified as *the concept for which a word stands*. For example, the signifier *dog* stands for the signified concept 'dog'. The idea of a dog is the signified, and the combination of signifier and signified is what constitutes a 'sign'. Furthermore, neither exists without the other: our concept of a 'dog' could not exist without the word *dog*. With respect to the cinema, Christian Metz therefore asked how does the word 'cinema' as a signifier determine what we understand of cinema as a sign?

**Transparency**: A common way of theorizing cinema has been to regard the cinema screen as akin to looking through a transparent window onto the world. Such a position regards films as works that reproduce the world automatically. Additionally, transparency describes the way in which storytelling in classical cinema is typically pursued with a desire to convey the sense that the story is telling itself automatically, without having to be created or worked upon.

**Work/production**: For Marx, history is essentially the history of modes of production. Therefore, for Marxist theorists, if films try to erase their processes of production – if they try to hide the 'work' involved in their making (see **transparency**) – then they are also denying their mode of production. To deny the mode of production, therefore, from a Marxist perspective, amounts to a blunt denial of historical forces.

# 3 *Screen* theory

## Colin MacCabe and Stephen Heath

In the previous chapter we examined some of the debates on the relation between cinema, politics and spectatorship as they were conceived
by two scholars working in France. These debates were swift in crossing
the Channel and the relationship between psychoanalysis, Marxism and
cinema reached a point of extended debate and criticism in the pages of
one particular British journal: *Screen*. For Anglo-American film studies the
impact of *Screen* was nothing less than extraordinary. Indeed, it is fair to
say that many of the central tenets laid down by that journal during its
most intensive phase of psychoanalytic Marxism are still in play in film
studies today, even if a great deal of the psychoanalytic and Marxist theory has disappeared. Primarily, what was at stake for *Screen* theory was
to find a way of theorizing a politics of freedom through cinema which
emphasized diversity over unity. If Marxist theory prior to the late 1960s
had been predicated on defining an emancipation based on a universal
consciousness, then the interruptions to this mission provided by the psychoanalytic elaboration of the unconscious proved decisive. What was at
stake was no longer the definition of a universal consciousness, but instead
was a project of articulating the diversities and multiplicities of individual
and collective experience.

*Screen* had been in existence since 1958, was run by the Society for Education in Film and Television (SEFT) and its offices were at the British Film
Institute. In 1971, however, the journal was transformed and re-launched
in a way that aimed to provide a theoretical approach to film studies with
a political edge. There followed a programme of translations of many recent articles from French scholars – the writings of Christian Metz, Roland
Barthes, Julia Kristeva and works by *Cahiers* authors, such as the essay on
*Young Mr. Lincoln*. There were also translations of some of the major figures of film theory from the 1920s and 1930s, such as Sergei Eisenstein
and Walter Benjamin. Colin MacCabe and Stephen Heath – writers of the
articles which form the basis of the present chapter – were young scholars at Cambridge University who joined the editorial board of *Screen* in
1973. The most energetic, optimistic and controversial years were those
between 1974 and 1976, when not only landmark articles were published
by MacCabe and Heath, but also by Laura Mulvey (see the next chapter).

Additionally, key essays by Raymond Bellour, Christian Metz and others were translated, not to mention significant articles by David Bordwell and Kristin Thompson as well as Edward Branigan, figures whose importance and centrality for film theory continue to this day. After 1977, however, a series of bitter and venomous debates split the editorial board – largely over the degree to which Lacanian psychoanalysis had been over-valued by the journal – and the heady days of '*Screen* theory' were in decline. At its high point, nevertheless, *Screen* was probably the most important humanities journal in English-speaking academia and it served to put film studies well and truly on the academic map.

Aside from psychoanalysis and Marxism, the most enduring influence on *Screen* theory was provided by the German writer of poems, plays and novels, Bertolt Brecht (see Brecht 1964). Brecht's major contribution to thought is generally considered to be his theory of Epic drama, a notion of theatrical drama intended to counteract the traditional notion of the 'invisible fourth wall'. The traditional notion of theatre – that of looking in on the imagined world in which a story unfolds – was thought by Brecht to encourage an uncritical, emotional response in audiences. Against an uncritical audience, Brecht desired and provided what he thought was the theoretical basis for a kind of theatre that would encourage a critical audience, that is, the kind of audience which would be encouraged to face up to and put into question 'real-world' problems. *Screen* theorists had little trouble transferring Brecht's designations for theatre to theories of cinema. If traditional films – especially those produced in Hollywood – provided escapist fodder for uncritical audiences, then what *Screen* theory enthusiastically tried to theorize were modes of cinema that could foster critical audiences. In raising these problems and trying to articulate the ways and means of a critical cinema and critical spectators, *Screen* theory expanded on many of the insights already covered in this book. In general terms, Hollywood cinema again turned out to be a negative example of cinema's possibilities while various forms of avant-garde and experimental cinema were supported for their potential to produce critical, thinking spectators. The two case studies in this chapter come from a single issue of *Screen* – an issue devoted to investigating the relations between Brecht and cinema, published in Summer, 1974.

## Colin MacCabe, 'Realism in the Cinema: Notes on Some Brechtian Theses'

(First published in *Screen*, 15(2), 1974; reprinted in MacCabe, *Theoretical Essays: Film, Linguistics, Literature* [MacCabe 1985a: 33–57]. All references in the text are to the reprint.)

MacCabe's essay is a critique of realism. The essay is also a critique, for the most part, of Hollywood cinema, so that it is fair to say that the essay, as a whole, is an attempt to criticize certain aspects of Hollywood cinema for being realist. It might be possible to declare that the overriding target of MacCabe's critique is André Bazin, the founder of the journal *Cahiers du cinéma*, whose realist approach to cinema remains the most sophisticated ever elaborated by a film critic (see Bazin 1967; 1971). The basis of the realist argument is that the most important aim for cinema is to represent reality as accurately as possible, for only by representing reality accurately will the reality of the world be laid bare for all to see.

MacCabe cannot abide by such arguments in defence of realism. To put it simply, MacCabe begins from a position which declares that cinema *cannot represent reality* in any adequate way at all. He believes that reality cannot be represented, *because reality is made of stuff that is not representable*. He goes to great lengths to stress that reality is not something you can just *see*, and therefore it is not something you can take a picture of, and nor is it something a camera or cinema camera can capture. It is not even something you can just *perceive* (hear, smell, touch, and so on). Rather, reality as such, while it is made up of things that we can see and hear and touch and so on, it is also made up of *beliefs*, *relations* and *knowledge*. Love, for example, is an important part of what we call reality, but *love* is not something you can see or touch. Capitalism is also an important part of our reality, and we can't see or touch capitalism. Rather, capitalism offers a complex structure of relations between people and things. It is for reasons such as these that MacCabe believes reality cannot be represented and, therefore, that realism is an inadequate way of articulating the true nature of the world and the social relations contained therein.

In clarifying the issues surrounding realism, MacCabe defines what are, for him, the four main types of films. These are *classic realist films*, *progressive realist films*, *subversive realist films* and *revolutionary films*.

### Classic realist films

MacCabe takes as his general model for classic realist films the devices and structures of the classic realist novel of the nineteenth century. This strategy is not as misguided as it might first sound, for MacCabe is trying to designate what in general is a guideline for what we call 'realism'. According to MacCabe, the notion of realism that commonly guides what we today understand as being 'realistic' has its origins in the nineteenth century and can be especially associated with the methods of the novels written during that period – novels by Balzac and Flaubert in France, by George Eliot, Elizabeth Gaskell and others in England. MacCabe argues that the major distinction necessary for these novels' abilities to be realistic is their characteristic division between ***subjective discourse*** and ***objective discourse***. The former are the opinions and views of specific characters – they are subjective and are typically designated in terms of a character's speech and the use of quotation marks – while the latter, which MacCabe typically refers to as the ***narrative discourse***, are intended to be the opinion or view of no-one; that is to say, the descriptive passages and third person commentaries typical in nineteenth-century novels are types of discourse which aim to establish *objectivity* beyond the subjective views and opinions of any one character. MacCabe doesn't mince his words: for the nineteenth-century novel, 'the narrative prose has direct access to a final reality' and furthermore, because of this, 'we can find the claim of the classic realist novel to present us with the truths of human nature' (1985a: 37). Or as he further claims, 'the narrative discourse simply allows reality to appear and denies its own status as articulation' (1985a: 36).

The point MacCabe is trying to make is that so-called objective discourse tries to pass itself off as entirely objective – as 'real' or 'realistic' – when clearly it must be being articulated from some point of view or another. The trick, we might say, of realism, is that it lures us into believing in the objectivity of its statements, when clearly, such statements must be the view of someone and must be expressing a point of view that comes from somewhere. In short, realism is not objective, even if it tricks us into believing it is.

What about the cinema? The popular cinema inherits the forms and structures of the nineteenth-century novel, MacCabe argues, but it also has an added advantage up its sleeve. Where novels must rely on the complications and conventions of written language in order to promote their versions of realism, the cinema can use photographed, moving images that offer a quite startling impression of reality. As MacCabe claims, 'The camera shows us what happens – it tells the truth against which we can measure the discourses' (1985a: 37). It is perhaps little wonder the cinema took over from the novel in such a convincing fashion, for it had at its disposal a mechanism which seemed to promise a satisfyingly objective view of things: moving images which could be taken directly from reality itself.

MacCabe argues that we should not be tricked into believing the reality of cinema images, for they play the same game of articulating objectivity as do nineteenth-century novels. The seemingly objective images the camera presents to us are typically juxtaposed with the subjective discourses of particular characters or points of view. If particular characters are restricted by the shortcomings of their own points of view, then it is the task of the camera itself in realist cinema to directly show us how and why they are wrong and furthermore, the camera, above and beyond the views of any particular character, can show us reality unconnected to subjectivity. The camera, therefore, against subjective discourse, pretends to directly present an objective discourse.

Examples of classic realist films should not be hard to come by insofar as, for MacCabe, they make up the vast majority of films produced, especially those produced in Hollywood. Classic realism, it should be remembered, is a *style*, so a film does not need to be *realistic* to be a classic realist film. Rather, a classic realist film organizes its discourses in such a way that an objective discourse – usually that presented by the camera – is distinct from and presents the truth of the various subjective discourses. Elements of Steven Spielberg's *Jaws* (1975) – a film that was being produced at the same time as MacCabe's essay was published – provide a good example of what is at stake for classic realism. *Jaws* begins with a series of characters who have conflicting ideas about the existence or otherwise of a killer shark. As examples of subjective discourses, on the one hand Police Chief Brody (Roy Scheider) believes there *is* a shark, while on the other hand the Mayor (Murray Hamilton) of the town of Amity (where the action of the film is set) refuses to believe in the existence of the shark. When a tiger shark is caught, there is still confusion: this shark certainly *is* a shark, but is it *the* shark, if indeed there is a shark at all? By this time, we have yet another subjective discourse: the oceanographer Matt Hooper (Richard Dreyfuss) chimes in to declare that the tiger shark is not *the* shark (Figure 3.1).

As these discussions and disagreements occur between the subjective discourses, we – the film's spectators – are given certain views of events that are beyond the views of any single character, and which none of the competing subjective discourses is privy to. The camera has already shown *us* the true state of affairs: *we* are allowed to see the attacks made by the killer shark; *we* travel underwater with the shark and see it make its first attack on the swimming girl, for example, whereas neither Brody, the Mayor, nor Hooper get to see such things. The characters are restricted to their own subjective views while *we*, by virtue of the camera, are shown the objective truth. This is what MacCabe calls classic realism: the camera shows us the objective truth of things over and above the views of any of the particular characters.

As though to reinforce the realist credo of objective observation, when the characters in the film try to discern what the truth is, they most often do so by *looking at things*. For example, the dismembered body parts of the original girl taken by the shark are examined at length in the hope that they will provide access to the truth, while Hooper and Brody also rely on looking at the insides of the tiger shark in order to see the truth of what is there. What this means is that the opinions and hunches of each of the characters can only be confirmed by an objective standard beyond the

**Figure 3.1** Matt Hooper (Richard Dreyfuss) and Police Chief Brody (Roy Scheider) examine a shark that has been caught in *Jaws*.
*Source:* Courtesy British Film Institute. Universal Pictures.

subjective restrictions of the characters. This objective standard is achieved by *looking at things*. That, for MacCabe, is what realism boils down to: the activity of looking at things, and by looking at them, seeing what the truth is. As MacCabe himself writes:

> The unquestioned nature of the narrative discourse entails that the only problem that reality poses is to go and look and see what *Things* there are. The relationship between the reading subject and the real is placed as one of pure specularity. The real is not articulated – it is.
>
> (1985a: 39)

To emphasize and expand on his point, MacCabe also engages in a lengthy discussion of an essay by Sergei Eisenstein and of Alan Pakula's 1971 film *Klute*, neither of which we have the space to discuss here. MacCabe does, however, pursue several alternatives to classic realism.

## Progressive realist films

What MacCabe calls progressive realism is, we would argue, what many filmgoers would recognize as being 'political' cinema, that is, films that are more or less like typical Hollywood films, but which are politically progressive. Some examples of this type of film have recently been quite successful, even when produced in Hollywood. *Syriana* (Stephen Gaghan, 2005) and *Good Night and Good Luck* (George Clooney, 2005) were impressive Hollywood attempts to propose politically left-leaning narratives from within the forms and structures associated with classic realism, while there is a range of potentially progressive films distributed throughout the history of film, from D. W. Griffith's *Intolerance* (1916), to Costa-Gavras' *Z* (1969) or Matteo Garrone's *Gomorrah* (2008). Probably the most influential film-maker who can be described as a progressive realist is Ken Loach, whose early television documentary, *Cathy Come Home* (1966), is mentioned by MacCabe. What is most characteristic of Loach's films – for example, *Hidden Agenda* (1991), *Land and Freedom* (1995), *The Navigators* (2001), and others – is a Bazinian commitment to the abilities of the film camera to record reality in an unmediated way. Thus, Loach's films – and others that can be described as progressive realist films – fall prey to the same problematic MacCabe identifies in the typical, classic realist film; that is, they still offer the true version of reality as one that exists from a single, unified perspective: 'What is . . . still impossible for the classic realist text', MacCabe writes, 'is to offer any perspectives for struggle due to its inability to investigate contradiction' (1985a: 44). Progressive realist films can only present us with society's injustices in the hope that merely exposing these injustices will be enough to make them go away. MacCabe remains highly sceptical that any such exposure of the real can provide a genuine level of political emancipation. With those limitations in mind, he moves onto another filmic category – those films which open up the possibility of subversion.

## Subversive realism

A film which features moments or strategies of subversion is one which, even though again it is predominantly realist in style, nevertheless offers an elaboration of what MacCabe refers to as 'various settings' (1985a: 48). A subversive film is one which offers at least the potential of breaking away from a single, unified discourse on truth. MacCabe doffs his cap to the *Cahiers* editors by declaring that they had identified in *Young Mr. Lincoln* an example of a film which, even though it is predominantly classic realist in style, nonetheless offers moments of subversion (see Chapter 1). Other films – such as Roberto Rossellini's *Germany Year Zero* (1948), a film championed by André Bazin and felt to be one of the classics of realist cinema (see Bazin 1997) – could push beyond *moments* of subversion and offer *strategies* of subversion. 'Instead of a dominant discourse which is transgressed at various crucial moments [in the manner of *Young Mr.*

*Lincoln*] we can find a systematic refusal of any such dominant discourse' (1985a: 48). A recent example of such a film is Gus Van Sant's *Elephant* (2003), which we approach at the end of this chapter.

MacCabe nevertheless identifies a certain 'block', as he calls it, to such films. Even though they gesture towards breaking free from the realist heritage of cinema, they nevertheless fail to do so. For MacCabe, even if such films do demonstrate 'various settings', they shy away from presenting the clash that is at the origin of these settings; that is, they do not demonstrate the contradictions which have caused the disruptions at their core. MacCabe puts it this way, vis-à-vis Rossellini's films:

> If the reading subject is not offered any certain mode of entry into what is presented on the screen, he is offered a certain mode of entry to the screen itself. For the facts presented by the camera, if they are not ordered in fixed and final fashion amongst themselves, *are* ordered in themselves. The camera, in Rossellini's films is not articulated as part of the productive process of the film.
>
> (1985a: 49)

In this way, MacCabe comes very close to critics like Jean-Louis Baudry (discussed in the previous chapter) with the claim that in order for a film to truly undermine the system of classic realism, it must expose the production conditions of the film's 'work'; that is, it must foreground its processes of production.

## Revolutionary films

Beyond strategies of subversion and progressive realism, MacCabe argues for the possibility of something quite bold: revolutionary films. He presents his case thus:

> The question I want to raise here, and it must be emphasised that it can only be raised, is the possibility of *another* activity which rather than the simple subversion of the subject or the representation of different (and *correct*) identities, would consist of the displacement of the subject within ideology – a different constitution of the subject.
>
> (1985a: 51)

MacCabe wants something quite ambitious – 'a different constitution of the subject' – and this is an ambition that has arisen again and again in conceptions of film theory. MacCabe's explicit reference is to Althusser, and his theorization of the revolutionary text can be placed alongside Baudry's critique of the cinematographic apparatus. Where Baudry emphasized the necessity for showing the *work* of cinematic production in order that the spectator, too, would have to work, MacCabe, taking his cues from Brecht, places emphasis on the notion of *production*. If, during a typical trip to the cinema, the spectator is placed outside production in a leisure space and time entirely devoted to non-production (a manner very often associated with film in terms of 'escape' and 'forgetting one's cares'), then, from MacCabe's perspective, that is the very *problem* that faces cinema. Only by placing the spectator *within the realm of production*, instead of concealing those processes, can a revolutionary cinema emerge. As examples of revolutionary films, MacCabe focuses on *Kuhle Wampe* (directed by Slatan Dudow, 1932) – a film in which Brecht participated – and *Tout va bien* (1972), a film directed by Jean-Luc Godard and Jean-Pierre Gorin. It is the latter we shall interrogate at the end of this chapter. Before we can do that, however, we first want to examine another key example of *Screen* theory.

## Stephen Heath, 'Lessons from Brecht'

(First published in *Screen*, 15(2), 1974. Reprinted in F. Mulhern (ed.) *Contemporary Marxist Literary Criticism* [Heath, 1992]. All references in the text are to the reprinted version.)

As wide-ranging and ambitious as MacCabe's essay in the same issue of *Screen*, Heath's 'Lessons from Brecht' reads like a manifesto, a plea for a better, more political cinema. Heath was a major figure – for Anglo-American audiences, he might be perhaps *the* major film scholar of the period. His *Questions of Cinema* (Heath 1981) offer a summation of many of the debates of the period, and includes essays on the topics of cinema and gender, the cinema apparatus (on which Heath also co-edited a collection of essays; De Lauretis and Heath 1980), on 'suture' (a concept which the present book has not the space to consider) and structures of narrative. 'Lessons from Brecht' is not, however, included in *Questions of Cinema*. (For an extraordinary, contemporary review of *Questions of Cinema*, see Carroll 1982. The essential elements of Carroll's review would later develop into 'post-theory'; see Bordwell and Carroll 1995.)

  'Lessons from Brecht' elaborates an argument that is still prevalent in film studies. The major distinction Heath theorizes is between **separation** and **distanciation**. For Heath, the traditional structures of film encourage the spectator to adopt a position of separation from the cinema screen, whereas a revolutionary cinema, inspired by Brecht, is one that would encourage a position of distanciation in the spectator. What, therefore, is the basis of this distinction?

## Separation

In order to account for the notion of separation, Heath relies on Freud's notion of fetishism. We have already seen how Christian Metz understood the 'imaginary signifier' of cinema from the perspective of fetishism, but while Metz's analysis was avowedly neutral, for Heath, the fetish structure of cinematic representation is something which must be criticized and opposed. Where Metz emphasizes the doubling up of belief that arises from the structure of fetishism, Heath, on the contrary, stresses the way in which the fetish delivers to the spectator a belief in his or her *plenitude*, *stability* and *unity*. Heath states:

> [T]he fetish assures the subject's position, his identity. All this is to say that fetishism is a structure . . . and that this structure focuses a centre, the subject it represents, which derives its unity, its un-troubled centrality, from the split it operates between knowledge and belief, between knowledge which disperses the stability of the subject, opens a production of desire in which the subject has ev-erything to lose, and belief in which the subject positions himself in his structural plenitude.
>
> (1992: 234–5)

There are a number of crucial argumentative terms in use here which hold the key to Heath's argument. **Knowledge** is that which reveals the true nature of existence for the subject, whereas the **belief** which is imparted by the fetish is something which definitively elides knowledge. If we think about how this functions specifically in terms of the fetish object (see Chapter 2), then, for Heath, the fetish object is an object of belief which reassures the subject, which makes him or her 'happy' (as Freud states; Freud 1977a: 354), but which is entirely at odds with the true nature of things: the mother quite simply does not have a penis (that is, *knowledge*) whereas the fetish object dupes the subject into believing that she does have a penis (this, for the subject, entails a false *belief* in the fetish).

That is a first issue: in the structure of the fetish, knowledge is covered over by belief. But Heath also claims that knowledge *disperses* the stability of the subject, while the fetish, on the other hand, delivers to the subject an illusion of coherence and plenitude. The subject's coherence and plen-itude are a result of what Heath calls *separation*: the subject is maintained in his or her unified coherence in a way that places the subject outside the true nature of the object; the fetish separates the subject from a true knowledge of its object; the fetish object acts like a barrier of belief which separates the fetishist from the truth of knowledge.

Heath links the structure of the fetish both to the photograph and to the cinema. His essay, like MacCabe's, is in many ways a response to Roland

Barthes' essay, 'Diderot, Brecht, Eisenstein' (Barthes 1977a), a translation of which was published earlier in *Screen* and which was later collected in a book edited by Heath (Barthes 1977b). Heath's point is this: under the conditions of fetishistic separation, the spectator can take pleasure in the photographic or filmic image because he or she remains 'outside this existence' (1992: 235). The identity of the spectator is therefore assured because the spectator is *separated* from that which is represented. In turn, Heath links this separation with Marx and Freud and 'the essential denial of work, production, the refusal to grasp the positions of subject and object within that process' (1992: 235). Once again, therefore, in a way that pertains to the arguments we have already seen put forward by MacCabe, Baudry and the *Cahiers* editors, Heath is critical of forms of cinema in which there is a denial of work and an elision of production. That fault is what separation makes possible.

## Distanciation

Heath draws from Brecht a succinct notion of distanciation as that which overcomes separation. If traditionally at the theatre the audience is separated from the actors by means of footlights or an orchestra pit, or simply by means of the spatial separation between the stage and the audience, then the only way of overcoming this separation is to break down that distance. This entails nothing less than doing away with the 'fourth wall, that fictitious wall that separates stage and audience' (Brecht, quoted by Heath 1992: 237). Perhaps the strange outcome of distanciation is that the notion of distance is one that actually brings the audience closer to the action; indeed, it is designed to bring them *into the action* entirely, to the point where any separation from the play or film is negated. As Heath describes, 'The aim is no longer to fix the spectator apart as receiver of a representation, but to pull the audience into an activity of reading' (1992: 239). Here, then, the members of the audience are no longer separated from what is represented and they are no longer separated from the processes of producing what is represented. Rather, by way of distanciation, the audience is *pulled into the work*. Heath quotes at length from Brecht:

> It is also as spectator that the individual loses his epicentral role and disappears: he is no longer a private person 'present' at a spectacle organised by theatre people, appreciating a work which he has shown to him; he is no longer a simple consumer, he must also produce. Without active participation on his part, the work would be incomplete . . . Included in the theatrical event, the spectator is 'theatralised': thus less goes on 'within him' and more 'with him'.
> (Brecht, quoted by Heath 1992: 240)

For Brecht, ultimately what this means is 'the production of **contradictions**'; not the promulgation of fetishistic beliefs of coherence and plenitude, but on the contrary,

> a dialectical procedure by which the spectator is placed in that *critical* position on which Brecht lays so much emphasis and which means not simply that the spectator criticises but also that his own position is given as critical, contradictory, that he is pulled out of his fixity.
>
> (1992: 240)

For Heath, this is how a critical spectator can be advocated – not only in the theatre, but more pertinently in the cinema.

It is in this way that Heath manages to forge a distinction between films that function in a way to fix the subject into a position of unity and coherence – something achieved by way of the fetishistic structure of representation which serves to *separate* the viewer from a film's processes of production – and films which operate in such a way as to maintain the subject in a state of contradiction and dispersal, something achieved, according to the Brechtian tenets of distanciation. Some of the specific filmic methods of distanciation are investigated below.

## *Elephant* **and** *Tout va bien*

In 'Lessons from Brecht', Heath's discussions of particular films are somewhat piecemeal, and while MacCabe is more generous in his discussions of actual films, his analyses can hardly be said to be conclusive. Therefore, in the final section of this chapter, we approach two films to discuss them in the light of *Screen* theory.

*Elephant* is a film directed by the American film-maker, Gus Van Sant, in 2002. It is an innovative film that uses very long takes and an extremely mobile, 'steadicam' camera which seems to float through scenes. The use of long takes is one of the strategies usually favoured by a realist cinema, and Van Sant also adheres to other overtly realist modes: he uses non-actors (the film features 'real' school students), and all filming was done on location. The film charts the events that occur on what seems to be an average school day at an average American high school. The major narrative event of the film was inspired by the tragic shootings that occurred at a high school in the town of Columbine in 1999, so the film's climax provides us with images of the deaths and terror that are the result of such an event.

The film pursues a very specific organizational structure. It is structured according to a series of interlinked episodes but, perhaps most markedly,

**Figure 3.2** Subversive realism in *Elephant*.
*Source*: Courtesy British Film Institute. Fine Line Features.

the film does not unfold according to a linear, chronological time. Instead, the film jumps from one period in time to another, so that events which have occurred earlier in terms of the story sometimes times occur later in terms of the film's plot. Furthermore, the film is divided into eight specific segments, each of which is separated by an intertitle heading, a very Brechtian technique of distanciation. Each segment tends to focus on one particular character or group of characters. In doing this, *Elephant* provides an exemplary case of a film which provides what MacCabe calls 'various settings'. All points of view are given more or less equal weight so that no *one* character's role is privileged over any of the other characters (Figure 3.2). There is, as MacCabe might say, a 'systematic refusal of any dominant discourse' (1985a: 48).

Nevertheless, even if the film does manage to present these various points of view, it fails to provide an adequate social or political context within which the events of the film take place. The film cannot provide an underlying logic which would allow us to understand what is at stake politically in the shootings that are the film's central event. Instead, in accordance with an inherently realist logic, we are merely shown what things there are, as if all we have to do to understand the world is to see those things. Such a strategy would be entirely ineffective for a scholar like MacCabe. For him, we can assume, *Elephant* is incapable of delving

**Figure 3.3** The factory set in *Tout va bien* Anouchka Films.
*Source*: Courtesy British Film Institute.

into the wider structural issues which could further inform us as to why these shootings have occurred.

*Tout va bien* (directed by Jean-Pierre Gorin and Jean-Luc Godard in 1972) is singled out for praise by MacCabe, and he has been a long-time champion of the films of Jean-Luc Godard, culminating in a biography published in 2003 (MacCabe 2003). There are elements in *Tout va bien* which instantly qualify it as a Brechtian film. One of the characters, Jacques (Yves Montand) even makes explicit reference to Brecht. He does this while directly addressing the camera – a Brechtian feature which recurs throughout the film. One of the more famous Brechtian moments of the film occurs right at the beginning when we see cheques being signed for the various arts, crafts and businesses that went into the making of the film. Hence, right from the outset, we are privy to the fact that what we are seeing is a *production*, and even more than that we are shown certain aspects of that production process.

Another Brechtian element in *Tout va bien* is the set in which the action of the factory strike takes place (Figure 3.3). We see into this set as though it were a doll's house, so that we are made fully aware of the artifice involved in constructing the filmic world. The film is also narrated to us at various points by two interlocutors whom we never see, but only hear. At the beginning of the film these interlocutors discuss how to make a film, that films usually feature love stories, and that a budget for the making of a film can be found if it features big stars. And verily, *Tout va bien* does feature two world famous film stars: Jane Fonda and Yves Montand. Our interlocutors interrupt their description of a typical film by demanding something different: we shall not be presented with a love story; rather, we shall have a story of today, with workers, farmers, petit bourgeois and middle classes, and we'll place the main characters of the film among them. This is indeed what occurs in *Tout va bien*.

The strategy of making a *different* film is one that is directly opposed to a typical, mainstream, Hollywood film. This is the strategy the film is determined to pursue and it is certainly one of the reasons MacCabe thinks the film might qualify as a revolutionary one. As we declared earlier, it is, for MacCabe, as much as for Heath, only if the spectator is placed within the realm of *production* that a film can be truly revolutionary. Placing the spectator within the realm of production is what *Tout va bien* tries to achieve. It achieves this first of all by its adoption of Brechtian strategies – that is, of demonstrating the processes of a film's production – and also by having the film's main protagonists themselves placed within the realms of the production. As the film unfolds, we discover our protagonists caught up in a strike at a food production factory. In an even more explicit fashion, during a sequence in which various workers at the factory describe the unpleasant nature of their day-to-day work, their descriptions are intercut with inserts of our protagonists themselves on the production line, dismembering carcasses and stuffing sausage meat into their casings. The film's main protagonists are therefore inserted into the realm of production.

*Tout va bien* also tries to link its personal love story, the romance between Jacques and Susan (Jane Fonda), to wider historical processes. There is little doubt that the film draws an analogy between the trouble and strife of the factory (especially insofar as it emerges as a consequence of the struggles of May '68) and the difficulties that occur in Jacques and Susan's relationship. The argument these two characters have half-way through the film hinges on their work practices – on the fact that Jacques has 'sold himself out' since May '68 by making television commercials instead of focusing on feature films, and the fact that Susan feels it impossible to write in a politically effective manner any more (she is an American broadcast journalist) (Figure 3.4). Thus, the film's 'love story' is inextricably caught up in the process of production itself.

Finally, the film, after having made links between the personal and political, now proceeds to make a further link between the real of production and that of consumption. The famous tracking shot at the supermarket

**Figure 3.4** The personal and the political: Jacques (Yves Montand) and Susan (Jane Fonda) in *Tout va bien* Anouchka Films.
*Source*: Courtesy British Film Institute.

near the end of the film is overlaid by Susan's declarations that going to the supermarket is essentially no different from going to work. Everyone merely goes about their business without paying heed to anyone else; shoppers are too busy and too single-minded while shopping to notice any of the activities of the wider world, in precisely the same way that workers in a factory become buried in their work on an assembly line in ways that prevent them from engaging with the wider world. While we can certainly claim that *Tout va bien* is somewhat heavy-handed at times, there is also little doubt about the scale of its aims. This film goes a long way towards being a *revolutionary* film in MacCabe's terms.

However, in a subsequent article, MacCabe ultimately ends up being somewhat reticent about the revolutionary potential of *Tout va bien* (see MacCabe 1975). He criticizes the film for its lack of a punctuating text – many earlier films of Godard's had featured much more complex inter-relations between onscreen titles, sounds and images (MacCabe 1975: 55). For MacCabe, this diminishes the film's Brechtian strategies, and the film ends up replacing politics with morality (readers will remember that the *Cahiers* editors issued a similar criticism of *Young Mr. Lincoln* – see Chapter 1 above). Moreover, the film defines an objective discourse, for the truth is associated with the claims of the working class, and therefore the film falls into moments of classic realism. Finally, with its focus on the romantic narrative, *Tout va bien* ends up not being a political film about changing the world but rather a moral film 'put in terms of changing one's subjective state' (MacCabe 1975: 56). It is less a film about how to change the world than it is about trying to amend one's own subjective practices. This therefore disqualifies the film from being properly revolutionary. (MacCabe later reiterates this view; MacCabe 2003: 233.)

MacCabe's ultimate dissatisfaction with *Tout va bien* demonstrates the ultimate failure of *Screen* theory itself: its politics tended to override anything to do with cinema. One gets a sense that there was never going to be a film or set of films that would entirely satisfy the criteria of a revolutionary film, and there is a sense that no film was ever going to provide enough distanciation to bring about radical social change. The stakes and aims of *Screen* theory were therefore impossible to attain. The only satisfactory outcome of *Screen* theory is an enduring dissatisfaction with cinema as such, a feeling that no film can ever be quite good enough to inspire a revolution.

## Glossary

**Belief/knowledge**: *Screen* theorists, in the wake of Marx, Brecht, and Althusser, made a distinction between belief and knowledge. Belief refers to modes of understanding which are essentially ideological insofar as they are typically based on false assumptions (such as religious beliefs). For Stephen Heath, the kinds of beliefs central to dominant cinema are 'fetishistic beliefs'. Knowledge, on the other hand, arises from an understanding of the contradictions central to the historical modes of production. As such, knowledge transcends fetishistic beliefs and ideological falsehood.

**Contradiction**: Derived from Marx, contradiction refers to opposed social forces; for example, the opposition between proletariat and the bourgeoisie. *Screen* theory therefore favoured the kinds of films which would make social contradiction obvious; that is, films which would clearly demonstrate the unequal relations between proletarian workers and bourgeois owners of production.

**Distanciation**: Derived from Bertolt Brecht's theories of epic drama – what Brecht termed the *Verfremdungseffekt* – distanciation in the cinema implies a breaking down of the processes of separation. When distanciation occurs, therefore, the spectator is no longer separated from the drama but instead becomes part of the drama. According to the theory, distanciation enhances a spectator's critical faculties, so that being part of the drama involves the engagement of one's critical processes of judgement. Such critical faculties are thought necessary for the advancement of a political (i.e., Marxist) cinema.

**Narrative (objective) discourse/subjective discourse**: Colin MacCabe's distinction between narrative discourse and subjective discourse is a variation of the long-held distinction between the use of third-person and first-person narrative. MacCabe, however, applies the distinction to cinema, so that the camera is effectively the centre of objective, third-person narrative discourse over and above any of the specific, subjective, first-person points of views of any of the characters. This prioritizing of the objective narrative discourse is central to what MacCabe calls 'classic realism'.

**Separation**: A term derived from Lacan, who relies on the Latin '*se parare*' to claim that separation entails a process of 'engendering oneself'. For *Screen* theorists, therefore, in the cinema, the way in which the typical spectator of the classical cinema is separated from the screen is likewise a process in which the spectator is 'self-engendered' as a fixed and unified subject.

# 4   Feminism and film

## Visual pleasure and
## identificatory practices

The intersection between feminist theory and film has occasioned some of the finest work in the history of film theory. Indeed, it is fair to say that the models of film theory which we have examined so far are ones that were slowly and surely replaced during the 1980s by a questioning of the problem of individual identities. Much of this move from a universal politics to a politics of emancipatory identification occurred under the influence of feminist film theory. The quest for feminist film theorists was one of refining the models of Marxist emancipation, for such models typically began and ended with men. Feminist film theory therefore set itself the task of affirming the distinctiveness and particularity of women's identities in the face of the universal narratives of men. The significance of this move should not be underestimated, for the feminist models of film and their concentration on identifying and defending women's identities are one of the models that during the 1980s and 1990s replaced the Marxist theories of the 1970s. This form of 'identity politics' plays a significant role for feminism and film, but it is also one of the models of theorizing that informs the next chapter of this book. The intervention of feminism in film theory is therefore of lasting importance, for it helped film theory move away from the dogmatic, universalizing trends of the 1970s to more nuanced and complicated visions of film and cinema.

What, then, are the questions feminist film theory asks? A starting point and assumption is that men and women are unequal, that women are designated – for one reason or another – as inferior to men, and that the prevailing structures of society are those which place women under the domination of men. To begin with, therefore, the status of women can be mapped, to a certain extent, onto the struggle for the status of the proletariat in Marxist theory. That is, women, like the members of the working classes, are held in positions of subservience by the wider structures of social and political existence. When feminism began to be theorized in film studies in the early 1970s, it took its reference points from the combination of psychoanalysis and Marxism that had already proved so influential for film studies. Like *Screen* theory, feminist film theory gained a foothold in the academy by looking at the ways in which psychoanalysis could explain, at a psychical level, why societies (especially in the industrialized West) came to be structured in ways that rendered certain members of the population – workers and women in these instances – subservient to those who exploited them – bourgeois, capitalist males. We might therefore posit a first phase of feminist film theory as one which tried to explain the ways in which the traditional modes of cinema assisted in the process of rendering women subservient. By proving the subservience of women, these early scholars could begin to imagine strategies and modes of film-making that could then lead to the emancipation of women. In this chapter we focus on four contributions to feminist film theory, the first from 1975 and the last published in 2006. We feel that the range of discussions across these four essays define, in a condensed way, the development of feminist film theory since the mid-1970s.

Today, however, there might be some pressing questions to be asked. If feminist film theory was central to film studies between the 1970s and 1990s, then today its position is increasingly under pressure. If the voices expressed in a special issue of *Signs* published in 2004 are anything to go by, then one is almost tempted to say that the project of a feminist film theory has ground to a halt. There is a sense in which, as one contributor puts it, 'many of the battles have been won' (Kuhn 2004: 1221). What has become important for women and film studies today, it seems, is for women to find the voices with which to express themselves and to defend the importance of expressing that which can be expressed as a woman. There are many examples of such a will-to-expression (for example, the foremost journal of feminism and film, *Camera Obscura*, has been building an 'archive for the future' since its thirtieth anniversary issue in 2006), the voicing of attitudes, pleasures and beliefs which, prior to the engagement between feminism and film, had not been articulated.

## Laura Mulvey, 'Visual Pleasure and Narrative Cinema'

(First published in *Screen*, 16(3) Autumn 1975: 6–18; reprinted in L. Mulvey, *Visual and Other Pleasures* [Mulvey 1989a]. All references are to the reprint.)

Mulvey's essay remains a remarkable one, for it condenses into a few short pages a vast range of ideas relating to the cinema, many of which have been slowly worked through and teased out in the years since. Though film theory and feminism have moved on considerably since the publication of Mulvey's article, the insights and formulations at its centre continue to inspire and intrigue scholars and students. Probably the most provocative statement of the essay, and one which by and large sums up Mulvey's position, is stated in the following way:

> In a world ordered by sexual imbalance, pleasure in looking has been split between active/male and passive/female. The determining male gaze projects its fantasy onto the female figure, which is styled accordingly.
>
> (1989a: 19)

The first point to note is that, for Mulvey, the world is ordered by sexual imbalance: men and women are unequal, and this inequality is the originating point of a feminist critique. Second, the feelings of pleasure and the activities of looking are structured and formed in such a way as to cater for the specific needs of men. The structures of pleasure, looking and pleasure-in-looking are ones that are definitively male: males take pleasure in looking, while women are there *to-be-looked-at*. The result of such a structure is that males assume an *active* role in processes of looking and pleasure, while women assume a passive role: women are the *objects* of pleasure whose role in the structure is that of being looked at. Finally, the male gaze – the activities of the male's looking – is determining for women; it is as though women exist in order to satisfy the desires and pleasures of men. As such, women are, Mulvey claims, 'styled accordingly'.

This sexual – or gender – imbalance is something Mulvey believes exists in the wider world (for that is the position from which she begins), but it is something which is reinforced, aided and abetted by the dominant, Hollywood cinema. Mulvey makes an equation between what the dominant cinema presents and the wider social world, which is to say that the dominant cinema reflects the sexual imbalance which exists in the wider world. She writes: 'However self-conscious and ironic Hollywood managed to be, it always restricted itself to a formal *mise en scène* reflecting the dominant ideological concept of cinema' (1989a: 15). There are two specific results of this Hollywood ideology. On the one hand, Mulvey advocates an *alternative* cinema which can challenge the Hollywood ideology, while on the other hand, she calculates the ways in which the Hollywood cinema reinforces – and indeed exacerbates – the gender inequalities of the social world. We shall begin with the latter claim.

Hollywood films consolidate gender inequalities by relying on two specific formal strategies. First, they encourage **scopophilia**, and second, they encourage **identification** with certain characters. To explain how these processes function, Mulvey relies upon psychoanalytic theory. Scopophilia is 'pleasure in looking', and Mulvey delivers a fine explanation of the way in which this typically functions in Hollywood cinema:

> Although the film is really being shown, is there to be seen, conditions of screening and narrative conventions give the spectator an illusion of looking in on a private world. Among other things, the position of the spectators in the cinema is blatantly one of repression of their exhibitionism and projection of the repressed desire onto the performer.
>
> (1989a: 17)

The conditions which produce this effect are, for Mulvey, psychically complex. If, in the 'real world', any person engaged in processes of spying, of 'looking in on a private world', would feel rather uncomfortable in doing so, then there is no such discomfort while at the cinema. Indeed, whereas such a process in the 'real world' would not be socially supported or advocated, at the cinema it is a positive necessity. What this means more generally, according to Mulvey, is that what is normally problematic in the real world can, on the contrary, in the cinema deliver an experience of pleasurable satisfaction. Indeed, any sense of exhibitionism that may accompany the subject in everyday life – the fact that one is seen and looked at – can be safely and securely ignored while at the cinema; all senses of exhibitionism can be projected onto the screen performers, for they are the ones who are there to be looked at. The pleasure in looking that is central to the mainstream cinema is therefore a matter of scopophilia, and taking her cues from Freud (1977a), Mulvey argues that the activity of looking in the cinema produces pleasure of a specifically sexual nature; that is, scopophilia is the pleasure produced by looking at another, at an object – or character – that is separated from the self.

The second specific process essential to Hollywood's formal qualities is that of *identification* with characters. Taking her inspiration this time from Jacques Lacan's account of the 'mirror stage' (Lacan 2006c), Mulvey argues that identification is not a matter of looking at another person or object that is separated from the self, but is on the contrary a matter of recognizing a character who is *like oneself* (or what *one would like to be*). This identification is typically made with the hero of a film; the hero of a film is never the object of the spectator's look as an erotic object – the spectator's relation to the hero is not one of scopophilia. Rather, it is one of seeing a hero who is potentially like oneself.

Hence, putting the pieces of this argument together: the spectator at the cinema identifies with the male hero of a film while the females in a film are the objects of a scopophilic pleasure-in-looking. This, for Mulvey, constitutes a basic structuring device of the Hollywood cinema. In addition to this, males are associated with narrative – for it is the male hero of the film who drives the narrative. Women, on the other hand, are associated with spectacle, for it is as spectacle that they are looked at, while at the same time the (male) spectator's activity of looking will not interfere with the flow of the narrative. To put it succinctly, the woman is there for display purposes only. (Mulvey obtains many of her ideas here from Freud's essay, 'On Narcissism' [Freud 1984].)

These are the basics of what Mulvey conceives as being the gender division functioning in mainstream, Hollywood cinema. However, there are further complications in her argument. She considers, for example, that the woman is the signifier of *lack* according to psychoanalytic theory; woman is the sign of castration, and therefore she arouses not just pleasure for the man, but also anxiety, what Freud called **castration anxiety** (the anxiety caused by the 'lack' of the penis which signifies sexual difference [on these points see Freud 1977c; 1977d, Lacan 2006b]). Therefore, films have developed specific methods for dealing with this castration anxiety which the female figure produces. On the one hand, pursuing a strategy of what Mulvey calls **voyeurism**, the female figure can be tamed, unveiled, demystified and, in extreme cases, punished – punished for little other than her being a woman. Such strategies are common in *films noirs*, but Mulvey specifically concentrates on three films directed by Alfred Hitchcock (*Vertigo* [1958], *Rear Window* [1954] and *Marnie* [1964]). In each of these films, the woman emerges as a potential threat to the male and is therefore accordingly tamed or punished. (It should also be noted that Raymond Bellour's article on *The Birds* which we discussed in Chapter 1 draws conclusions not dissimilar to Mulvey's thesis here.) The other strategy by means of which Hollywood films deal with women as potential sources of castration anxiety is by way of idealization – what Mulvey refers to as a strategy of **fetishistic scopophilia**. Here, the film makes the woman into an idealized figure of incomparable beauty and virtue so that, in her perfection, she cannot possibly cause a threat to the male. Mulvey equates such beauty with the fetish; feminine beauty serves to cover over any lack that might be perceived in the woman. This strategy is one Mulvey ascribes to the films of Joseph Von Sternberg, especially those films in which Marlene Dietrich plays the heroine (e.g., *Morocco* [1930]).

Mulvey thus paints a rather bleak picture of the ways in which Hollywood films muster their forces behind the upholding of males as the prime movers of life while women are effectively bound and gagged by devious strategies of nullification. Her theses should in no way be reduced to simplicity, for we believe that many present-day films perpetuate the conditions of which Mulvey was so critical.

Mulvey was, at the same time, keen to express an alternative. If Hollywood films exacerbated the gender inequalities that exist in the wider world, then not all films had to do so. Indeed, forms of cinema could be conceived which would directly counter Hollywood's gender imbalance. Mulvey is direct: her article is motivated by a desire to destroy the pleasure of Hollywood cinema, of 'daring to break with normal pleasurable expectations in order to conceive a new language of desire' (1989a: 16). Her anti-Hollywood motivations in this article can therefore be placed alongside those of *Screen* theory, as her arguments are motivated by a desire to counter the Hollywood cinema with a politically progressive alternative. 'The alternative cinema', she claims, 'provides a space for the birth of a cinema which is radical in both a political and an aesthetic sense and challenges the basic assumptions of the mainstream film' (1989a: 15). Mulvey was herself a film-maker, and her films of the mid-1970s were sombre challenges to the Hollywood status quo. But perhaps no other film-maker of the 1970s had such a profound effect on debates on feminism and film than did Chantal Akerman, whose extraordinary films of that period, *Je Tu Il Elle* (1974), *News from Home* (1977), *Rendezvous d'Anna* (1978), and the most exceptional of all, *Jeanne Dielman* (1974), are landmarks in the desire to invent a new cinema which challenges the hegemony of male pleasure and voyeurism. (On Mulvey's approach to works such as these, see Mulvey 1989b.)

Discussions of Mulvey's essay abound, and it continues to attract and provoke (for example, see Merck 2007). Undoubtedly the greatest criticism, from a feminist direction, was that Mulvey's argument contained no possible place for women. *All* spectatorship seemed to be reserved for men (for her thoughts in this regard, see Mulvey 1989c). Probably the most significant response for feminism thus became the desire to theorize female spectatorship and this was a project that occupied much of feminist film theory during the 1980s and beyond (see, for example, Studlar 1988; Doane 1988, 1991; Penley 1989; Williams 1989; Clover 1992; Creed 1993). The essay we examine below can also be seen as part of the quest to theorize female spectatorship and it is to that essay we now turn.

## Elizabeth Cowie, 'Fantasia'

(First published in *m/f* 9, 1984; revised in Cowie, *Representing the Woman* [Cowie 1997]. All references to the revised version.)

Originally published in 1984, Cowie's essay first of all engages in a long and intricate interpretation of the Freudian – and post-Freudian – notion of **fantasy**. Amid all of this exegesis and explanation it becomes difficult to discern precisely what it is that Cowie is trying to say. But we can find a reasonably clear statement of her position right at the end of the article.

She argues that a film like *Now, Voyager* (directed by Irving Rapper, 1942), one of the films she discusses in her article, avoids an ending in which the male is produced as hero. Therefore, even though this is a Hollywood film, it is quite unlike the kinds of films that were the focus of Mulvey's 'Visual Pleasure' article. Furthermore, the terms of fantasy turn out to be crucial:

> Fantasy fails therefore to produce the fixed and polarised posi-
> tions – and identities – of men and women required for a feminist
> politics basing itself on a theory of patriarchy. Indeed, while
> the issue of feminine desire is introduced...the position now
> arises as to the nature of this 'femininity' and in what sense it
> is an attribute of women, and if it is, how far it is always and only
> an attribute of women.
>
> (1997: 164)

Cowie's position thus represents a significant turnaround when compared with Mulvey's. What is at stake is no longer identifying in films or in Hollywood cinema a 'world ordered by sexual imbalance' (Mulvey), for fantasy, according to Cowie's analysis, fails to result in such polarizing oppositions, and nor does it give rise to a system of patriarchy in which women are subordinated in a world determined by and for men. If this is the case, where is *feminism*? Is not the quest of feminism, as so clearly spelled out by Mulvey, one of identifying and striving to overcome what is a manifestly unequal relation between the sexes? If Cowie is not trying to draw attention to this inequality, then what precisely *is* the nature of her endeavour? Her answer is an uncomplicated one, but it is one that is embedded in an entirely new research programme for feminism and film. During this phase, feminist film theory becomes devoted to the study of *feminine desire*, to the nature of 'femininity' and to the question of whether femininity may or may not be a set of attributes reducible solely to the domain of women. Cowie's challenge – and it is not hers alone; it is one that has occupied many feminist film scholars (Studlar 1988; Williams 1989) – seems worlds away from the clear-cut, energized and vociferous distinctions that formed the basis of Mulvey's contribution to feminist film theory. Broadly speaking, however, the kinds of questions raised by Cowie were to become central for feminist film theory during and after the 1980s.

How, then, does Cowie reach her conclusion? Her crucial intervention concerns the nature of identification in the cinema. For Mulvey, identification was something that occurred between spectators and characters. In her account, as we have pointed out, there are only positions of identification for male spectators, for these spectators identify with the male heroes of films. Cowie, on the contrary, stresses that we do not so much identify

with the *characters* of a film as with *the positions or situations in which characters find themselves*. Cowie's position therefore represents a substantial change from the arguments associated with Mulvey. For Mulvey – and for many other psychoanalytic film theorists – identification is based fundamentally on *misrecognition*; that is, on identifying with something or someone who is manifestly not oneself. Because of this misrecognition, identification in the cinema is a process of distortion. For Cowie, processes of identification as articulated through fantasy are not distortions, but are, on the contrary, expressions of deep wishes. Therefore, a film like *Now, Voyager* presents a series of *situations which elaborate deep wishes*, and the expressions of these wishes can result in modes of identification for the film's viewers.

As we have already stated, there is a great deal of complex psychoanalytical theorizing in Cowie's essay. We feel, however, that there are two important factors which form the basis of Cowie's arguments. The first is an explanation of *fantasy*, adapted from a very influential essay published in the 1960s by two students of Jacques Lacan, Jean Laplanche and Jean-Bertrand Pontalis (Laplanche and Pontalis 1986). Cowie takes one major point from their essay, and this point has had a lasting influence on film studies:

> Fantasy involves, is characterised by, not the achievement of desired objects, but the arranging of, the setting out of, desire; a veritable mise en scène of desire...The fantasy depends not on particular objects, but on their setting out; and the pleasure of fantasy lies in the setting out, not in the having of the objects.
>
> (1997: 133)

To have a fantasy, therefore, is not to have a fantasy about obtaining an object, whether that object is a partner in love, a new car, a fine house, or whatever. Rather, it is a matter of imagining oneself to be in a situation – a 'scene' – which maps out the possibility of pleasure. What such fantasies typically entail is a change in one's social circumstances; that is to say, what is typically at stake in fantasizing is a change in one's relations to other people. If one fantasizes about obtaining a new job, for example, then such a fantasy is not simply about having a better job. It will also usually mean imagining one has more money, and that one will be better able to provide for oneself or one's family – thus, raising one's profile in the eyes of family members – or that one will be more respected by virtue of having a better job, and so on. In short, such a fantasy entails a change in one's relations to other people, to one's family, colleagues, and social circle; a change in one's position in the world. (Cowie refers to Freud's essay 'A Child is Being Beaten' [Freud 1955] to chart the different positions one can take within a fantasy scenario.)

Cowie's second significant point taken from psychoanalytic theory relates to Freud's considerations on 'Creative Writers and Day-dreaming' (Freud 1985). Following Freud, Cowie claims that what is most important for day-dreams and other fictional pursuits (such as are depicted in novels and films) is not an *escape from reality*, but rather is a matter of finding the ways in which fantasies can *intersect with reality*. Fantasies, Cowie argues, are very much wishes for a change in the circumstances of social reality, and what creative writers, film-makers and other purveyors of fiction achieve is a public expression of the ways in which social reality might be different. What is central for the writer of creative fiction – or for a film-maker – is to compose a fantasy in such a way that readers or viewers will *enter into the fantasy*. This entering into the fantasy is therefore, for Cowie, perhaps the most important aspect of fiction films:

> We enter the fantasy structure and identify *as if* it were our own. This is not a cognitive mistake, we are not deceived or deluded by the fiction, we have not misrecognised or disavowed the otherness of the film's fiction ... We do not take the character's desire as our own, but identify with the character's position of desire in relation to other characters.
>
> (1997: 140)

Cowie's most important breakthrough is this: when *identifying* in the cinema, we do not identify with a particular character and in doing so thereby 'lose' our sense of self. Rather, we identify with a character's *position* or *situation* in relation to other characters. Cowie, at the end of her chapter, engages in a discussion of two films: *Now, Voyager* and *The Reckless Moment* (directed by Max Ophüls, 1949). In each of these films she notes the different situations characters find themselves in and the ways in which these positionings create specific 'settings for desire'. For the purposes of our discussion here, we have chosen to focus on *Now, Voyager*.

Cowie argues that *Now, Voyager* is, above all else, the presentation of a series of wishes. The wishes are those of the film's main character, Charlotte Vale (Bette Davis), as the film is essentially her story. Three main wishes are elaborated:

1. Charlotte's wish to be recognized as someone.
2. Her wish for a 'secret love'.
3. Her wish to be a good mother.

The presentation and evolution of these wishes throughout the film occur as an unfolding of various 'settings of desire'. First of all, for example, Charlotte is presented as drab, lacking in confidence, and definitively under the thumb of her mother, and her role in the family is seen as being one of accompanying her mother in old age. Early in the film, however,

**Figure 4.1** Jerry Durrance (Paul Henreid) and Charlotte Vale (Bette Davis) in *Now, Voyager*.
*Source*: Courtesy British Film Institute. Warner Bros.

Dr Jaquith (Claude Rains) begins to recognize and understand Charlotte with interest and care, especially when he notes her interest in romantic novels and smoking, both of which Charlotte's mother disapproves of. The recognition and condoning of her 'secret' wishes enable Charlotte to begin to find ways of expressing herself. She subsequently blossoms while on the cruise ship where she is definitively recognized as a captivating woman by many of those on board, and especially by Jerry Durrance (Paul Henreid), with whom she has an affair (Figure 4.1). Her wish to be recognized as someone is fulfilled on the cruise.

This wish soon becomes somewhat complicated, especially given the fact that Jerry is already married. Charlotte's subsequent attachment to an eligible and eminently desirable bachelor, Elliot Livingston (John Loder) – further evidence of her ability to be recognized as someone – ends when

Charlotte calls off their engagement. We might see this as her 'trying out' of a wish which she decides she does not wish for at all. What her renunciation of Elliot is evidence of, Cowie argues, is Charlotte's wish for a 'secret love' with Jerry, and this secret love finally takes the form of caring for Jerry's neglected daughter, Tina (Janice Wilson). This resolution allows Charlotte to occupy a number of positions:

- She becomes a mother to Tina and thus plays a role that her own mother did not (a *good* mother rather than a *bad* one).
- At the same time she becomes a daughter again, for it is through Tina that she can resolve the tensions she had with her own mother.
- Looking after Tina allows her to maintain her 'secret love' for Jerry, for it is through Tina that she maintains contact with him.

All of this is a way of saying that, for Cowie, *Now, Voyager* presents the setting forth of a number of scenarios of desire, a number of different fantasies which allow Charlotte to shift and change her relationships with other people. Cowie concludes in turn that it is Charlotte's trying out of a number of subject positions which allows the spectators of the film to also try out their own positions. By entering into the film's fantasies, by identifying with the 'settings of desire' in which Charlotte partakes, the spectators of the film also imagine themselves in those roles as occupying those positions. Cowie's argument therefore changes radically the stakes of feminism and film when compared with Mulvey's position in her 'Visual Pleasure' article. Where Mulvey finds no place for women to occupy during the screening of popular, Hollywood films, Cowie finds instead a very complex set of relations between spectators and the fantasy scenarios represented in popular films. These fantasy scenarios, argues Cowie, offer women various positions to identify with, positions by means of which the status and value of the feminine can be negotiated.

## Jackie Stacey, 'Feminine Fascinations: A Question of Identification?'

(Published as Chapter 5 in *Star Gazing: Hollywood Cinema and Female Spectatorship* [Stacey 1994: 126–75].)

Stacey's book, *Star Gazing*, very much sets itself the task of moving beyond the narrow uses of psychoanalysis in feminist film theory. While she does use some concepts drawn from psychoanalysis (in particular, from the writings of Jessica Benjamin [Benjamin 1990]), she endeavours to reformulate notions of identification in the cinema above and beyond the ways in which identification has typically been used by psychoanalytic film theorists. In this way, her approach can, on the one hand, be placed along-side that pursued by Elizabeth Cowie. Like Cowie's, Stacey's approach reprimands psychoanalytic film theorists (such as Mulvey, Baudry and Metz) for reducing processes of identification in the cinema to the production of *fixed* and *singular identities*. Like Cowie, who advocates processes of multiple and shifting processes of identification, Stacey too is adamant that identification in the cinema is a process whereby spectators have the ability to assume shifting, varied and multiple positions. On the other hand, however, Stacey's arguments are very different from those of Cowie. Instead of relying on theories of psychical structure derived from psychoanalysis, Stacey instead relies on the testimony of actual spectators, that is, the statements and views of people who go to the cinema (or, as Stacey's investigation is historical, people who *did go* to the cinema). Given her perspective, one which relies on a field of investigation that has become known as 'audience research' (for more on audience research, see Chapter 9), her conclusions are somewhat different from those of Cowie.

In what ways does Stacey's work contribute to feminist film theory? Her work gathered comments and views from women who were regular cinemagoers in Britain during the 1940s. Therefore, it was an attempt to gather information about the pleasures and expectations women had when going to the movies during a period when movie-going was at its height. Her research might therefore be seen as a direct test of the theories expressed in Mulvey's 'Visual Pleasure' article. Where Mulvey found no satisfactory processes of identification for women in the cinema – identification was solely the reserve of males who identified with the male heroes of popular films – Stacey wanted to determine empirically whether this was the case. By doing so, she was giving a voice to women and allowing them the possibility to express their own tastes and pleasures. Needless to say, contra Mulvey, Stacey discovered a range of identificatory practices in which women engaged when going to the cinema.

For the women who were the subjects of her study, Stacey concluded that there were two fundamental types of cinematic identification: 'Cinematic identification fantasies' and 'Extra-cinematic identification practices'. There are a range of sub-types of these two main categories, but for our purposes we will focus on three types:

1. Transcendence
2. Aspiration and inspiration
3. Extra-cinematic identification practices

Stacey draws a fundamental distinction between types of identification which engage in *fantasy* and those which engage in actual *practices*. Fantasy identifications are ones which occur only in the imagination of the spectator and which are 'make believe' (1994: 137), whereas practices are activities which lead to material changes in the spectator, such as the acquisition of new shoes or clothes, or the adoption of a new hairstyle based on the hairstyle of a character seen in a movie. Category (1) relates to identifications based in fantasy, while category (3) involves identificatory practices; category (2) lies part-way between fantasy and practice.

## Transcendence

A typical statement of a spectator engaging in activities of what Stacey calls transcendence is provided by one of the respondents, Elizabeth Rogers:

> I preferred stars who were unlike everyday women because I went to the cinema to escape into a world of fantasy, wealth, and above all, glamour. I preferred those unlike me because I could put myself in their place for a short while and become everything I wasn't – beautiful, desirable and popular with the opposite sex.
>
> (1994: 150–1)

For situations like this, Stacey argues that there is a temporary identification between the spectator and the onscreen star-character, but that this identification is only temporary, so that a separation between the self of the spectator and that of the character is maintained. '[T]here is a temporary fantasy self which takes over, and yet the star's identity is still primary here', writes Stacey. '[T]his temporary, one-way movement', she continues, 'leaves the spectator's own identity apparently unchanged by the process' (1994: 151). The identifications at play here are therefore temporary ones so that the fundamental identities of viewer and film star or film character remain unchanged.

## Aspiration and inspiration

The second kind of identification Stacey discovered were ones in which the star-character would provide something of a 'role model' for the spectator, something to aspire to, even if the spectator knew that they would never be quite like the star. Therefore, such identifications involved a partial change in the spectator's own identity, because they provide a sense of something to aspire to, something to aim for. A characteristic example of this kind of response comes from Norah Turner:

> Hollywood stars in the roles they depicted were all the things we'd have liked to have been, wearing glamorous clothes and jewels we had no chance of acquiring, and doing so many wonderful things we knew we would never have the nerve to do.
>
> (1994: 152)

**Figure 4.2** Bette Davis as Judith Traherne and George Brent as Dr Frederick Steele in *Dark Victory*.
Source: Courtesy British Film Institute. Warner Bros.

Marie Burgess, another example, stated that movie stars made her 'feel like the unattainable could be reached' (1994: 159), while Joan Clifford admitted 'I liked seeing strong, capable and independent types of female characters mostly because I wished to be like them' (1994: 154). This category of identification is therefore one in which the boundary between spectator and star-character becomes blurred to a certain degree.

### Extra-cinematic identification practices

With this type of identification, changes to the spectator are definitive insofar as they involve material changes to the spectator's practices. These are transformations which occur outside the cinema; hence Stacey calls them 'extra-cinematic'. And they are not momentary or short-lived transformations, but are ones which involve substantial investment and dedication on the part of the spectator (Figure 4.2). Vera Carter sums up the kinds of identification involved here:

> I was a very keen fan of Bette Davis and can remember seeing her in *Dark Victory* . . . That film had such an impact on me. I can

remember coming home and looking in the mirror fanatically
trying to comb my hair so that I could look like her.

(1994: 167)

Stacey concludes that such processes are ones in which the identity of the
spectator attempts to merge with the star-character in some material way,
and that such processes involve 'the production of oneself simultaneously
as subject and object in accordance with cultural ideals of femininity'
(1994: 168). Here, therefore, the boundaries between spectator and star-
character are definitively blurred.

There is no question that Stacey's work opened up substantially the
field of female identifications in the cinema. From the position of Mulvey
in which there were no possible feminine identifications at all, through
Cowie's explication of the shifting and multiple nature of fantasy identifications in the cinema, Stacey's work approaches something like the
full complexity of operations that function in 'going to the cinema' for a
range of women. Perhaps most marked in Stacey's book is the notion that
women go to the cinema as a way of modelling their own subjectivities,
not in ways that provide negative fantasies about female inequality or
subservience, but in ways that provide women with something to aspire
to and which can lead to active, material changes in women's lives. As
Stacey states, 'Identification involves not simply the passive reproduction
of existing femininities, but rather an active engagement and production
of changing identities' (1994: 172). Going to the cinema was a chance
for women to take on new identities, to potentially change their ways of
being, and to adopt new modes of existence.

## Barbara Klinger, 'The Art Film, Affect and the Female Viewer: *The Piano* Revisited'

(*Screen*, 47(1); 2006 [Klinger 2006].)

A recent essay written by Barbara Klinger opens up new ways of thinking about the relationship between female spectators and cinema. Before
we examine Klinger's arguments in detail, however, we might first of all
begin to understand how feminist film theory redirected debates in film
theory on a more general level. Feminist film theory redirected the kinds
of debates associated with Marxism and Apparatus theory – which were
based on meta-narratives of universal emancipation – towards debates involving the expression and articulation of *individual identities*. Stacey, for
example, does not rely on drawing conclusions which might be pertinent
to *all* spectators, and she does not even rely on stamping out models of

spectatorship for *all women* to potentially adhere to. Instead, she relies on a careful explanation of the myriad ways in which individual women might engage with the cinema. Therefore, her arguments do not make claims for a universal emancipation of women, but work to advance our understanding of the different modes of spectatorship which function for women in the cinema. Her arguments thus take film theory away from positions associated with universal emancipation to ones in which the articulation of *difference* is paramount.

Klinger's argument can be seen as a tentative advancement of Stacey's innovations. Taking as a starting point the pertinence of individual responses to films, Klinger works towards deepening her understanding of her own, acutely personal response to a particular scene from a particular film. In closely examining her own responses to this scene, she works towards uncovering the many complex relations and influences that function in watching a film. By delving as deeply as possible into the personalized evocations emitted by the scene, Klinger works towards enhancing her understanding of her own particular, individual identity. As she puts it, her essay tries to unravel 'a certain combination of aural and visual elements within the context of a particular structuring of female experience that focuses on momentous shifts in identity and self-recognition' (2006: 40).

Again we might ask: what contribution does Klinger's essay make to feminist film theory? Her accentuation of the highly personal and subjective, we would argue, is an extension of the kinds of political arguments put forward by Colin MacCabe, Stephen Heath and others during the 1970s and 1980s. If we again think of MacCabe's arguments on 'Realism in the Cinema', he was attempting to highlight the shortcomings of what passed itself off as 'objective discourse' in favour of the articulation of specific subjective responses (see Chapter 3 above). What this necessitated was, in MacCabe's words, the theorization of a 'subject in process', a term borrowed from the writings of Julia Kristeva (see Kristeva 1998), and 'a new political model of subjectivity' (MacCabe 1985b: 9). Furthermore, MacCabe strove to produce a 'theory of identity' which could 'allow for a genuine heterogeneity and contradiction in our diverse identifications' (1985b: 10). It seems to us that feminist film theory has gone a long way in discovering ways of theorizing the 'subject in process' and the nature of 'diverse identifications', discoveries which are evident in the work of Cowie, Stacey, and many other feminist film theorists. Klinger expands on the discoveries made by a generation or more of feminist film theorists and takes them to a new level of personalized sophistication, of uncovering a 'subject in process', an amalgam of 'diverse identifications' which is unprecedented in film studies. Her expression of a specifically feminine viewpoint adds further to our understanding of feminine identities.

Klinger focuses most closely on Jane Campion's 1993 film, *The Piano*, already the focus of much feminist criticism. *The Piano* is an especially evocative film, set in an isolated settlement in New Zealand during the late nineteenth century, about a woman who is trapped in a cruel and loveless marriage. The film's heroine, Ada (Holly Hunter), though unhappy in her marriage, finds solace in playing her piano. At the same time, she develops a romantic attachment to a swarthy, tattooed local man George Baines (Harvey Keitel). She eventually breaks with her husband and leaves New Zealand with Baines and her piano. On the voyage away from the coast of New Zealand, she decides to throw her piano overboard, perhaps because it has become a symbol of her old life, a solemn reminder of her loveless marriage. Now, the film seems to be saying, she can begin life anew, she no longer needs her piano. As the piano sinks to the bottom of the sea, Ada's ankle becomes entwined in a rope that is attached to it and she is swept overboard. She manages to climb free, and is brought back to the boat safe and sound.

At the end of the film, she is living happily with Baines. And yet, the film concludes with a scene in which Ada again imagines being attached to her piano as it plunges to the sea floor. This is the scene which captivates Klinger in her article.

> Ada has not left the past entirely behind after all; she still enter-
> tains the thought of her own death, visualized as a combination
> of a dream, a wish and a haunting. Through her internal voice,
> Ada discusses how at night she thinks about the fate she almost
> encountered. She imagines her piano in its ocean grave and sees
> herself tethered to it, as she once was, by an ankle caught in a
> rope.
>
> (2006: 22)

Klinger refers to this scene and the emotional, affective response she has to it as an example of an 'arresting image'. The scene is one that, for *her* – and not for everyone; Klinger does not try to universalize her own responses, but rather tries to investigate them as *subjective* – has an exceptional emotional fullness, comparable to what Roland Barthes once called, with reference to photography, a photograph's *punctum* (Barthes 1981). The arresting image is the direct counterpoint to what MacCabe calls *objective discourse*, for this is an extremely personalized, subjective, ambiguous, contradictory and uncertain form of discursive enunciation.

Klinger tries to mine her own experiences in order to determine why this particular scene from *The Piano* has such an affective charge for her. She finds corresponding images and evocations in other films she has seen (Hitchcock's *Rebecca* [1940], Godard's *Two or Three Things I Know About Her* [1966] and Cooper and Schoedsack's *King Kong* [1933]), but ultimately the resonance of the 'arresting image' from *The Piano* forces Klinger to the limits of personal confession. The fullness of the scene's affective power is a response to an element from Klinger's own past and of the ways in which her past intersects with that evinced by *The Piano*. The final scene of *The Piano*, a scene so affecting for Klinger, reminds her of a childhood dream:

> In the nightmare, I awoke with my heart pounding from a bad dream, only to see a large figure standing in the doorway. The figure turned out to be a big, hairy ape who then commenced to chase me all over the countryside. In a final attempt to escape, I leapt straight up into the air in a 'dream shot' framed much like a photograph or a movie image. Within this frame, I could see my ankle and foot at the top and my pursuer's paw and arm reaching up from below ... [T]hen, the ape grabbed my ankle and I realized that I was doomed. Shortly thereafter, I really woke up and realized, as one does, that it was just a dream.
>
> (2006: 36–7)

Klinger eschews a Freudian interpretation of this dream and instead focuses on the way in which the affective sensations evinced by the dream were reignited while watching the final scene from *The Piano*. It is this affective resonance that is important for Klinger's argument. Pointing out the ways in which films have the ability to work at this level – that is, as a combination of past and present; in terms of the dynamics of regression and memory which intersect with what is seen, heard and felt in the present – is the aim of Klinger's analysis. She concludes in the following way:

> Hence, while particulars between spectators surely vary, *The Piano* invites personalization ... through its graphic reenactment of a drama of female identity that has the potential to intersect in heterogeneous ways with viewers' experiences.
>
> (2006: 40)

Klinger's argument is a culmination of the significant shift that occurs in film theory with feminism. The personalized, female response which is validated and investigated for its significance is a long way away from the reduction to masculinity to which women seemed to be consigned by Mulvey's article 'Visual Pleasure' (and possibly by other theorists, such as Baudry and Metz). As we declared at the beginning of this chapter, the contribution made to film theory by feminism cannot be underestimated, for it is under the influence of feminism that the entire terrain of film theory shifts radically, from the dogmatic Marxism of the 1970s in which the pleasures of cinema-going were held to be highly suspect, if not outright damaging, to the acceptance and interrogation of concrete cinematic pleasures, with a hope of understanding them more clearly and with a good deal more sympathy.

## Glossary

**Castration anxiety**: In psychoanalytic theory, castration anxiety refers to the unconscious fear that one will be castrated. For males, therefore, this anxiety is closely linked with the Oedipus complex and the boy's fear that, as a consequence of his desire to be with his mother, he will be punished by the father. The boy specifically fears that this punishment will take the form of castration insofar as he is aware that some humans (girls) do not have penises. The fear of castration is thus closely linked with the dissolution of the Oedipus complex.

**Fantasy**: Like identification, fantasy is a contested term in film studies. Elizabeth Cowie takes her definition from the work of the psychoanalysts, Laplanche and Pontalis, in order to argue that fantasy refers to the *setting of desire*. As a result, fantasy designates the way in which humans learn to desire. For Jackie Stacey, by contrast, fantasy identifications in the cinema are ones which are make believe and which occur only in a viewer's imagination. For this reason, Stacey opposes fantasy to practice, with the latter involving 'real' instances instead of make believe ones.

**Fetishistic scopophilia**: As an outcome of psychoanalytic theory, fetishistic scopophilia is specifically linked to sexual gratification derived from the pleasure in looking at a sexual object. For Laura Mulvey, fetishistic scopophilia is more specifically a way in which films nullify the potential castration anxiety caused by female characters. By making female characters attractive and desirable, some Hollywood films encourage male spectators to engage in fetishistic scopophilia and thus repress the threat of castration.

**Identification**: A much contested term in film studies. For Christian Metz, identification is split between primary and secondary processes of identification. The former entails, broadly speaking, the spectator's identification with the camera, while the latter designates a spectator's identifications with characters. For Laura Mulvey, identification is a process of spectators' imagining they are the character in the film, so that one identifies with a character whom one wishes to be like. For Jackie Stacey, on the contrary, there are several types of identification which spectators can assume, while for Elizabeth Cowie, spectators identify less directly with characters and more with the range of roles or positions certain characters occupy in a narrative.

**Scopophilia**: Literally meaning 'pleasure in looking', from the psychoanalytic perspective theorized by Laura Mulvey, scopophilia refers to
the ways in which Hollywood films encourage the visual pleasure of
looking in (male) spectators.

**Voyeurism**: Voyeurism is generally considered synonymous with
scopophilia. Laura Mulvey, however, theorizes voyeurism as a way in
which Hollywood films tame the threat to male spectators posed by
female characters. Under conditions of voyeurism, some Hollywood
films subdue or punish their female characters in order to bring them
under male control.

# 5 Cinemas of the other

## Postcolonialism, race and queer theory

What we here call 'cinemas of the other' is an attempt to chart three movements in film theory which have been, broadly speaking, indebted to *Screen* theory and feminist film theory. These are ***postcolonial*** *film theory*; *theories of* ***race*** *and cinema*; and ***queer*** *film theory*. These movements are united by their attention to *minority groups*, that is, to groups of people who have been underrepresented or misrepresented in cinema. By bringing attention to such minority groups, these groups can be encouraged to speak for and represent themselves. One of the aims of these theories, then, is to take the burden of representation away from the dominant centres – Hollywood, especially – in order to make it possible for minority groups to represent themselves in ways that are not determined by mainstream, dominant modes. One might immediately begin to see where such positions fit in with feminist film theory, for feminist film theory was based on trying to give women a voice, a position from which to speak for themselves in the cinema. If women's place in the cinema was determined by men, then the task of feminist film theory was to put women's place in the cinema back into the hands of women. Much the same problem faces the domains of 'otherness' approached in this chapter: if colonial nations, minority races, gays, lesbians and other queer identities had all been determined by a dominant mode of representation – typically that of white, European males – then the task of defining cinemas of the other was to take that determination away from the centre in order to give it back to those people whose own identities and destinies were at stake.

The relationship between 'cinemas of the other' and feminist film theory might initially seem clear enough, but what is its relationship to *Screen* theory or Apparatus theory? First of all, there is little doubt that both Apparatus theory and *Screen* theory were focused on European traditions of film-making and emerged out of European traditions of thought (structuralism, semiotics and Freudian psychoanalysis). At the same time, however, Jean-Louis Baudry's critique of the apparatus was precisely a critique of the *fixity* and *universality* with which the dominant cinema produced spectators as Subjects (with a capital 'S'). His critique of the dominant mode of cinema's apparatus was also a call for a *different kind of cinema*, one that would dismantle both the fixity and universality of Hollywood's ideological apparatus. For *Screen* theory too, while its call for a new kind of cinema was based on an anti-realist, modernist impulse, we nevertheless see such calls repeated in defence of 'cinemas of the other' so that, to a large extent, the theorization of cinemas of the other is an extension of the positions articulated by *Screen* theory. Some writers argue, for example, that a cinema of the other cannot rely on classic realism (in the sense given to this term by Colin MacCabe), while others argue that Brechtian strategies of foregrounding and distanciation are precisely what are needed to produce a cinema of the other. We shall see how these arguments unfold throughout the chapter.

## Getting beyond representation

Theorizing 'other' cinemas does have a long history in film studies. However, most scholars agree that until the 1980s the majority of such studies were theoretically naïve. Prior to the 1980s, therefore, the thrust of such arguments was that Hollywood cinema (and other arms of the dominant, European cinema in France, Italy, the United Kingdom, and so on) privileged the representation of white, heterosexual males of European origin so that all other forms of humanity were subordinated to this dominant. Therefore, the white, male cowboy was the measure by which the backwardness of American Indians could be measured; the Arab or Asian terrorist was the 'baddy' whose obliteration served as the marker of the white hero's virility and success; the black mammy or butler (or worse, the evil savage represented by a character such as Gus (Walter Long) in D. W. Griffith's notorious *Birth of a Nation* [1915]) were the subordinated 'others' by which the upstanding communities of whites could be judged; while the representation of deviant sexuality was almost entirely hidden by the demand for strict heterosexuality in the cinema. Scholars interested in exploring the cinemas of the other therefore began by denouncing the negative stereotypes by which minority subject positions were represented in dominant cinema. Pointing out the ways in which 'other' subjects were subordinated to the dominant (white, male) 'Subject' was thus a means of criticizing dominant cinema for the limitations of its representative strategies.

Alongside this process of unearthing negative stereotypes emerged strategies of counter-representation; that is, ways of film-making which provided *positive* images of previously misrepresented 'other' subjects. One branch of the underground cinema in the United States – typified by the work of Andy Warhol, Kenneth Anger and Jack Smith in the 1960s – provided a blueprint for self-representation of gays and lesbians in the cinema; the rise of Blaxploitation films in the United States in the early 1970s provided an outlet for the self-representation of blacks (though films made for blacks have a long history in the USA); while film-makers of 'other' nations – in Africa and South America, for example – thrived in the 1960s and beyond under the urge to provide positive representations of the otherwise neglected subjects of colonial nations.

It is undeniably true to assert that film *theory*, in these cases, lagged a decade or so behind film *practice*, dominated as theory was by an emphasis on theorizing Hollywood and the 'art' cinemas of Europe. One trope running through interventions in the 1980s, when cinemas of the other began to be approached with some theoretical complexity, was the feeling that, in order to theorize these cinemas, it was necessary to go beyond the dichotomy of positive and negative images. For film theory, it was not enough merely to vilify the negative images of the other and to affirm positive images, for such arguments were, by necessity, ones that treated cinematic images as realistic. Robert Stam and Louise Spence make this claim in their important introduction to a special issue of *Screen* from 1982 on 'Racism, Colonialism and the Cinema' (Stam and Spence 1985). They write that

> While posing legitimate questions concerning narrative plausibility and mimetic accuracy, negative stereotypes and positive images, the emphasis on realism has often betrayed an exaggerated faith in the possibilities of verisimilitude in art in general and the cinema in particular, avoiding the fact that films are inevitably constructs, fabrications, representations.
>
> (Stam and Spence 1985: 634)

What Stam and Spence therefore call for is a particular attention to the *cinematic* possibilities of otherness, one that goes beyond a mere pointing out whether images of otherness are positive or negative. The battle between positive and negative images of otherness nevertheless remains a heavily debated terrain on which these theories are played out. We shall see throughout this chapter how distinguishing between positive and negative images remains an important, if still overemphasized area of debate, even while theoretical approaches have become more subtle.

Some ways of navigating one's way through these debates is discussed by Stuart Hall in one of the major interjections on these issues. Hall is a prominent scholar associated with the field of Cultural Studies in Britain whose writings on television and film have had a major impact on the field. He is also a scholar of Caribbean origin, born in Jamaica, who has spent his adult life in Britain. When invited to give a talk at the opening of the inaugural Caribbean film festival in 1989 he reflected on what it might mean to define oneself as 'Caribbean'. He considered that defining a Caribbean identity could be positioned between the two poles of *similarity* and *difference*:

- On the one pole, identities are defined by similarity, that is, by the aspects of a culture which unite it. 'Within the terms of this definition', writes Hall, 'our cultural identities reflect the common historical experiences and shared cultural codes which provide us, as "one people", with stable, unchanging frames of reference and meaning' (Hall 2000: 705). Any cultural identity is therefore united by the similarities of a cultural heritage.
- At the other end of the spectrum, Hall emphasizes the ways in which the identity of a culture is also always permeated by *differences*. He argues that there will always be differences between the members of any culture, so that any sense of cultural unity, while identifying and producing aspects of similarity, must also try to account for the specific differences which define it. 'In this perspective', Hall states, 'cultural identity is not a fixed essence at all' (Hall 2000: 707). Rather, this sense of identity is one in which any identity is defined by way of a constant 'becoming', by the ways in which any identity will change and transform throughout history.

As such, Hall argues, calls for cultural identity cannot ever be claims to return to an origin, to a 'true' or 'pure' heritage that existed before such identities might have been contaminated by colonial settlement or cultural domination. Any idea of a true heritage has already been lost to history and cannot ever be reclaimed. What Hall prefers to emphasize, therefore, are the ways in which cultures, but minority cultures especially, must work towards constantly transforming and redefining their own identities in ways that both reflect the similarities of the past and look forward to the differences of the future. 'The **diaspora** experience', Hall concludes, 'is defined, not by essence or purity, but by the recognition of a necessary heterogeneity, diversity, by a conception of "identity" which lives with and through, not despite, difference; by **hybridity**' (Hall 2000: 713). We shall see how these positions are articulated and disputed in each of our analyses of 'cinemas of the other'.

## Postcolonial cinemas and theory

(Robert Stam and Louis Spence, 'Colonialism, Racism, and Representation', in B. Nichols (ed.), *Movies and Methods*, Volume II [Stam and Spence 1985].)

We have already had cause to mention Stam and Spence's important essay on 'Colonialism, Racism and Representation' from 1982. They emphasize the need to go beyond theories of representation in order to invent ways in which colonial and postcolonial cinemas can be conceived as definitively anti-colonial. But before explaining precisely how such methods might be effective, they put forward some definitions of colonialism, racism and the Third World. **Colonialism** refers to the domination by European powers (including the USA) over less powerful nations, especially colonies and former colonies in Africa, Asia and South America. The *Third World* refers to the historical victims of processes of colonization; that is, of countries and peoples who have suffered from the effects of colonization. Stam and Spence further claim that *racism* is, in essence, an outcome of colonial policies; that blacks, Asians, Africans, Arabs and other native people had been – and continue to be – systematically subordinated by their European conquerors.

Colonial film-makers, in specific attempts to challenge the powers of their oppressors, sought to produce films which would give positive voices to colonized people and enable them to tell their own stories. Many such films, however, were forms of *progressive realism*, the likes of which we encountered in our discussion of realism in Chapter 3. Stam and Spence agree with MacCabe's verdict that progressive realism can never be entirely satisfactory in pointing to the underlying structural causes of political problems, problems such as those of colonial oppression. As they claim, in terms that echo MacCabe's, '"Reality" is not self-evidently given and "truth" cannot be immediately captured by the camera' (1985: 639). As a result, Stam and Spence stress the need for the specifically cinematic qualities that must accompany calls for anti-colonialist film-making: such film-making must demonstrate an awareness of the power of the medium. 'Its emphasis', they argue, 'should be on narrative conventions, genre conventions, and cinematic style rather than on perfect correctness of representation or fidelity to an original "real" model or prototype' (1985: 641). Here, they emphasize two aspects of cinemas of the other on which we are keen to focus: (1) it is not enough merely to offer positive representations of oppressed peoples; and (2) there is no way to return to an 'essence' of a people in order for those people to express themselves; rather, any process of representation must focus on the hybridity of any cultural identity.

Stam and Spence choose, as a film which exemplifies their argument, Gillo Pontecorvo's groundbreaking critique of the colonial struggle in Algeria, *The Battle of Algiers* (1966). They claim that Pontecorvo's film is well aware of the mechanisms typically at play in mainstream films, so that the film aims, from the point of view of the Algerians, to question French oppression by using the same techniques that might be used in an ordinary fiction film. As a result, Algerian characters in *The Battle of Algiers*

**Figure 5.1** 'Passing' as French in *The Battle of Algiers*.
*Source*: Courtesy Kobal Collection. Igor Film.

are shown as sophisticated, daring and even as seductive objects of the cinematic gaze. Such impressions are, however, deliberately turned back against the gazes they seduce, and this is achieved in a cunningly manipulative manner. Stam and Spence argue that the standout sequence is one in which three Algerian women deliberately adopt the dress, make-up and mannerisms of French women in order to gain easy passage into the European district of Algiers (Figure 5.1). One of the women even actively courts the gaze of a French soldier whose flirtatious banter at once signals the success and attractiveness of the Alegerian's disguise while simultaneously castigating the French gaze for so easily judging the correctness of human beings by their appearance. The critique becomes even more stinging when each of the women launch successful terrorist attacks by planting bombs at various bars and cafés in the European district. Stam and

Spence are impressed by this strategy for the simple reason that it does not make the claim of essentializing Algerian identity. The sequence does not try to pretend that the Algerians are more caring or more authentic than their French oppressors. It shows, on the contrary, that the Algerians are quite willing and able to trick and double-cross their colonial oppressors using any tactic that might suit. These tactics might include indiscriminate murder on a large scale and other unapologetic acts of terrorism. And yet, for Stam and Spence, even more than this, the film's strategy is inherently cinematic:

> The film makes us want the women to complete their task, not necessarily out of political sympathy but through the mechanisms of cinematic identification: scale (close shots individualise the three women); off-screen sound (we hear the sexist comments as if from the three women's aural perspective); and especially point of view editing.
>
> (1985: 642)

Stam and Spence's point is thus that, to create an anti-colonialist cinema one must portray anti-colonialist sympathies, yes, but one must also utilize the techniques and methods of cinema in order to create those sympathies. It is not enough to merely portray 'truthful' stories that might chart the indignities of a colonial regime. What is even more necessary is the adoption of the cinema and its techniques as political weapons in which antipathy towards a regime can be actively expressed and sympathy with the oppressed produced. 'Indeed', as Stam and Spence claim, 'examining the film as a whole, we might say that Pontecorvo "hijacks" the techniques of mass-media reportage – hand-held cameras, frequent zooms, long lenses – to express a political point-of-view rarely encountered in establishment-controlled media' (1985: 643).

But is *The Battle of Algiers* a *post*colonial film? Is it not simply an *anti*-colonial film? *Postcolonial* generally refers to conditions which pertain to nations subsequent to their struggles for independence. Postcolonialism refers to the mixtures, tensions as well as the positives that have accrued from the multicultural melting pots of many formerly colonized nations, so that a postcolonial film might well be from Algeria, India or Haiti, but also from the United Kingdom (for example, *Sammy and Rosie Get Laid* [directed by Stephen Frears, 1987], *Mansfield Park* [Patricia Rozema, 1999], or *Bend it Like Beckham* [Gurinder Chadha, 2002]) or the United States (*Mississippi Masala* [Mira Nair, 1992], or the Oscar-winning *Crash* [Paul Haggis, 2005]) or Australia (*They're a Weird Mob* [Michael Powell, 1966], *La Spagnola* [Steve Jacobs 2001]). The key theorists of postcolonialism, while not necessarily focusing on film, are Edward Said (1978, 1993) and Homhi Bhabha (1994), and readers might wish to consult such works.

**Figure 5.2** Jesminder Bhamra (Parminder Nagra) with her teammates in
*Bend it Like Beckham*.
*Source*: Courtesy British Film Institute. Twentieth Century-Fox.

However, we wish to defend the field of postcolonialism as still one of
contestation, so that while so-called 'postcolonial' films might celebrate
the richness of hybridity and diversity, they are also bold enough to bring
into question the kinds of power relations which structure social fields.

A film such as *Bend it Like Beckham* opens up, for example, a number of
issues. It is directed by a quintessential postcolonial film-maker, Gurinder
Chadha, director of *Bhaji on the Beach* (1993) and *Bride and Prejudice* (2004).
*Bend it Like Beckham* tells the story of a teenage, second-generation Indian
immigrant, Jesminder Bhamra (Parminder Nagra), whose main aim and
desire in life is to play football (Figure 5.2). She is a very talented footballer, but such talents are not held in high regard by her parents. On the
contrary, her parents are determined to uphold the characteristics of their
Indian cultural traditions. Therefore, the film portrays one of the major
challenges of postcolonial, multicultural life: how does one manage to
maintain one's cultural traditions when relocating to another culture?
And furthermore, how does one make valuable links with a new culture
while at the same time keeping in touch with the traditions that are part
and parcel of one's own cultural identity? This challenge is precisely the
one defined by Stuart Hall in terms of *similarity* and *difference*.

*Bend it Like Beckham* ends triumphantly with Jesminder accomplished as a women's footballer. However, the film, while celebrating the multicultural melting pot of postcolonialism, also importantly signals the ongoing struggles of colonial mentality beneath the surface of multicultural positivity. One of the main reasons Jesminder's father finally accepts her desire to play football is that he had himself been denied the opportunity to play cricket when he settled in the United Kingdom. He was determined that the colonial racism which had prevented him from achieving sporting success should not be repeated in his daughter's case. Therefore, we would foreground the continuing anti-colonial message at the heart of *Bend it Like Beckham* as being consistent with the colonial struggles represented in *The Battle of Algiers*. Perhaps the guiding precept here is that in order for something to be postcolonial, it must first of all be anti-colonial.

## Cinema and race: three readings of *Do the Right Thing*

(Houston A. Baker, 'Spike Lee and the Culture of Commerce' [Baker 1993: 154–76]; Douglas Kellner, 'Aesthetics, Ethics, and Politics in the Films of Spike Lee' [Kellner 1997: 73–106]; Jonathan Rosenbaum, 'Say the Right Thing (*Do the Right Thing*)' [Rosenbaum 1997: 13–21].)

With a black US President now residing in the White House, and given the proliferation of African-American film stars (from Sidney Poitier through Eddie Murphy, to present-day stars like Denzel Washington, Will Smith, or Halle Berry), pop stars (from Little Richard to Snoop Dogg; from Diana Ross to Beyoncé) and sports stars (Jackie Robinson to Kareem Abdul-Jabbar to the Williams sisters), one wonders whether there is still a race 'problem' to worry about. And yet, while stars might be one thing, the lives and fortunes of those who fail to reach stardom is another thing altogether. There is no question that in the United States – and in many other nations of the world (the United Kingdom, Australia, France, Germany, and so on) – blacks and people of non-white backgrounds typically find themselves at a social and financial disadvantage. The systematic entrenchment of these disadvantages still demands examination and political action. Here, one is forced to envision areas in which the right questions are difficult to discern, let alone the right answers. If we aim for racial equality, then does this automatically mean that blacks are supposed to be *the same as* whites; i.e., that blacks be assimilated into white culture in the manner proposed by a film like *The Searchers* (see Chapter 1 above)? Or are we supposed to defend the 'multicultural' position which advocates a harmony of racial and cultural *differences*? Furthermore, blacks themselves face the problem of negotiating the similarity/difference dichotomy themselves (how does one stay 'true' to one's 'blackness'?). Should the problem of race and cinema be one of exposing the shortcomings of the many mainstream films which still feature racial stereotypes and which produce representations of blacks as deficient in one way or another (i.e., as criminals or junkies, stereotypes which today take the place of the earlier stereotypes of mammy or butler, coon or mulatto)? Or should film theory aim to articulate the ways in which black characters can be the equals of whites in order to affirm the fundamental 'humanity' of all human beings? Or, in an echo of the colonialist struggle in *The Battle of Algiers*, should film theory advocate a provocative and challenging role for blacks in cinema, one in which they counter the systemic social and political forces which oppress them, by violent means if necessary?

Film and theories of film must try to do all of these things, and working through such questions enforces film theory's re-engagement with the call of *theory* in the Althusserian sense. The questions, however, remain difficult ones with long histories. Here, we do not at all aim to chart the history of those questions and struggles as they pertain to cinema. Instead, we shall examine three interpretations of one particular, ground-breaking film: Spike Lee's *Do the Right Thing* (1989). A number of questions should be borne in mind, even if there are few ways to provide answers to such questions. How can one make a black cinema? Is there a black aesthetic? How does one provide positive representations of blacks in a positive way? By making them the same as whites, that is, by making them aspire to the same things to which white people aspire? Or by making them antithetical to everything which a white society stands for (a society, which, after all, has built much of its success as a result of the oppression of blacks)? But also, what about other 'races' – Italians, Hispanics, Koreans, and so on – races or ethnicities which are represented in *Do the Right Thing*? Should they be reviled as antithetical to black power, or are they located as part of a wider ethnic and racial struggle? Finally, is there such a thing as a black politics? And if there is, what is its relationship with cinema?

*Do the Right Thing* is an important film, but important for whom? The film courted a great deal of controversy when released, for it achieved the double act of endorsement from the black community for offering a challenging vision of the plight of young, urban, black Americans while also having to bear the wrath of conservative critics, most of whom derided the film's ending as one which could incite racial violence. Interpretations of the film remain plagued by a search for perfect solutions, so that the film is praised for what it achieves, while at the same time critics seem certain that what *Do the Right Thing* achieves is never quite enough. In short, the film tries to 'do the right thing' but, for most critics, it does not do that thing well enough.

This points to an impasse in film theory, for much of film theory has been plagued by the search for films which 'do the right thing' (see the end of Chapter 3 above for *Screen* theory's version of this impasse). As a result, film theorists have often been overly enthusiastic about finding faults in the films they analyse. Such searches appear to us to be somewhat futile, for one can always find fault with something if one is determined to find it. More than anything, *Do the Right Thing* might very well be an example of a film which undermines theory insofar as its strategies and conundrums appear to outdo and override all attempts to reduce the film to specific aesthetic and political categories. If nothing else, *Do the Right Thing* appears to us to be a film which forces film theory to face up to its own difficulties.

Houston A. Baker, in an essay published not long after the film's release, argues that *Do the Right Thing* presents a more positive view of the plight of urban blacks than had an earlier effort of Lee's, *Joe's Bed-Stuy Barber Shop: We Cut Heads* (1983), a film set in the same Brooklyn neighbourhood of Bedford-Stuyvesant as *Do the Right Thing*. Baker concentrates on the patterns of 'getting by' and 'making a living' that are a day-to-day struggle for blacks living in such communities. As he claims, 'Getting paid is what counts in *Do the Right Thing*' (1993: 173). When Mookie (Spike Lee) is paid double at the end of the film, Baker interprets this outcome as a significant affirmation of his actions. The evening before, in the film's climactic sequence, Mookie had thrown a garbage can through the window of Sal's Pizzeria, a local, Italian-American pizza restaurant for which Mookie made deliveries, thus setting off a period of looting and rioting in which Sal's was gutted by fire (Figure 5.3). Baker interprets Mookie's action as a symbol of violence – of violent political action, in the manner advocated by the black political leader of the civil rights era, Malcolm X (about whom Lee subsequently made a film and whose memory, along with that of Martin Luther King, looms large over *Do the Right Thing*). This leads Baker to defend the film's message as ultimately one of black empowerment through violence: 'If Mookie has truly done the "right thing"', he argues, 'then the movie seems to suggest that a violently aggressive Black energy of revolt can lead to Black empowerment' (1993: 173).

Such a reading certainly raises as many questions as it might answer. What is a 'black' movie? For Baker, a properly black film seems to be one that advocates black empowerment. A black film, from this perspective, is supposed to provide models of the ways in which blacks can act politically so as to improve their social and economic situation. We can see nothing wrong with such proclamations of socio-economic empowerment, but it is difficult to see precisely where a *film* fits into such an agenda. If the guiding precepts of film theory are 'what is cinema?' and 'how do films make meaning?', then the answers to such questions that we can assume

**Figure 5.3** Spike Lee as Mookie and Danny Aiello as Sal in *Do the Right Thing*.
*Source*: Courtesy British Film Institute. 40 Acres and a Mule Filmworks.

from Baker are somewhat narrow. We must assume that his answer to the question, 'what is cinema?' would be something like: cinema is a vehicle for the enhancement of specific political struggles. Furthermore, we might assume that his answer to the question of how films make meaning would be that films make meanings by providing positive (or negative) models of how to act. To put it another way, films are supposed to show us how to 'do the right thing'.

And yet, doing the right thing is not as straightforward as it might seem. Where Baker sees Mookie's actions as positive and empowering, others interpret him as a deeply flawed character who is not so much a role model as a symptom of black urban apathy and selfish individualism. Ed Guerrero, for example, writes that 'Mookie is a feckless middleman, a slacker, an urban survival capitalist bent on profitably negotiating all of the neighbourhood's varied racial factors and ambushes, while doing just enough in the way of work to get by' (Guerrero 2001: 33). These are difficult interpretive nodes that *Do the Right Thing* encourages by way of its complexity, but we are also uncertain that such attempts at interpretation can yield definitive results. Instead, we see such debates as reducing films to expressions of positive and negative images and it is a major problem that pervades the study of race and cinema. If Mookie is interpreted as unreservedly positive, then his action of throwing the garbage can through the window will be seen as a positive one; if we interpret him as a negative role model, then his action will be more questionable and his grab for money at the film's end as utterly opportunistic. Perhaps a more challenging way of viewing Mookie is to see him as embodying both positive and negative characteristics, but adopting such a perspective makes him a far more complex character from whom political points are not so easy to score.

Douglas Kellner is one of the few commentators to pick up on some of the film's overt aesthetic strategies. First, he notes *Do the Right Thing*'s approach as being akin to that of Brechtian modernism and therefore with strategies which have a long history in film (see Chapter 3 above). Second, he points out that the film's *mise-en-scène* is studded with multiple references to everyday urban existence, especially in the styles of clothing worn by the film's characters. From the Brechtian point of view, then, *Do the Right Thing* is something of a 'learning play' in which various positions are articulated, and in which various 'things to do' are postulated, but where, in the final account, no 'right thing' or correct position is authorized. There are also more obvious and overt Brechtian strategies, especially the celebrated and infamous 'racial slur' sequence, a sequence which definitively breaks the flow of the narrative and severs the cinematic illusion (as consistent with the ways in which Brecht has been taken up by film theorists). From the perspective of the cultural politics of identity and style, Kellner charts the myriad ways in which characters' T-shirts, sneakers, or musical preferences play key roles in defining their identities. 'Identity', Kellner claims, 'is thus mediated by mass-produced images, and image and style are becoming ever more central to the construction of individual identities' (1997: 81).

Kellner decides that the consumerist ideology of cultural style ultimately overrides the film's Brechtian strategies. For him, Lee's politics are too diffuse and imbued with an individualist, middle-class, consumerist ethic that blocks *Do the Right Thing* from achieving any serious systemic political critique. He writes that 'Lee's politics are, for the most part, culturalist, focusing on black identity and moral decisions concerning race, gender, and personal identity' (1997: 90). Insofar as that is the case, Kellner concludes that Lee 'fails to address the reality and dynamics of class oppression' (1997: 91). Again, therefore, we are left with a critique of *Do the Right Thing* for the fact that it fails to do the right thing. For Kellner, what is at issue here in the critical judgement of a film is its ability to *reflect accurately what reality is*. From this perspective, reality is a matter of class oppression and the cultural politics of style are merely so many ways of ignoring and covering up the systemic oppression of class, a significant proportion of which is built on the oppression of blacks. Insofar as *Do the Right Thing* fails to reflect this so-called reality accurately, the film fails Kellner's reality test. Once again, from the film theory perspective, we tend to see such an approach to the evaluation of a film as one that is quite severely flawed, one that, even in its desire to assert aesthetic strategies and Brechtian modes, still reduces a film to its positive or negative images.

One of the more challenging interpretations of the film simply admits that there are no 'right things' to do and that *Do the Right Thing* is precisely about the difficulty of making decisions about what the right things are. Jonathan Rosenbaum, in an extended review of the film, tries to dissect *Do the Right Thing* in terms of the typical kinds of expectations audiences have when they go to see a film. In the manner of *Young Mr. Lincoln* (see Chapter 1), we might say, audiences typically want to be delivered a message about the difference between right and wrong; that is, audiences want to be clearly shown what are the 'wrong things' and what are the 'right things' one is supposed to do. Lee, in *Do the Right Thing*, resolutely refuses to tell us what the 'right things' are, and this is the film's most inspiring challenge. Rosenbaum speculates:

> What if [*Do the Right Thing*] postulates – as I believe it does – that given the divisions that already exist in the social situation the film depicts, it's not even possible for any character to 'do the right thing' in relation to every other character.
>
> (1997: 16)

What we in fact have here is an assertion of Colin MacCabe's rejection of an overarching objective narrational point of view on the action. Rather, *Do the Right Thing* presents a series of subjective perspectives, none of which is entirely privileged over the others, and each of which has its faults in relation to the others. In *Do the Right Thing*, it is quite simply impossible to draw specific conclusions about who *has* and who *has not* done the right thing. This is especially so, Rosenbaum contends, in relation to the film's closing scenes. He declares:

> [O]ne might intuit that some of the film's black characters associate their trashing of the pizzeria with 'fighting the power', but there is nothing in the film that suggests that they're right about this . . . Indeed, the movie takes great pains to show that the characters who tend to talk the most about 'fighting the power' in less hysterical situations – Radio Raheem, Buggin' Out, and Smiley – are relatively myopic and misguided.
>
> (1997: 17)

Of course, this is in no way to declare such characters *wrong* either. And that, for Rosenbaum, is exactly the point: their actions and views are *right* for some situations, for some settings and for some people, but they are not unequivocally right for all situations, settings and people. More than at any point in the film, that is the case for Mookie's throwing of the garbage can. At the vexed moment when Mookie is trying to decide how to respond to Raheem's killing, he simply has no idea what the right thing to do could possibly be. Furthermore, he knows that, whatever he does, it will be right for some people and wrong for others. Hence the dilemma central to the film and its portrayals and characters: how is one supposed to do the right thing? It is a question for which there are no clear answers.

We have therefore provided three views on *Do the Right Thing*. The first, by Houston A. Baker, defends the film's portrayal of black violence by asserting that it serves as a way in which blacks can achieve a level of empowerment. The second, by Douglas Kellner, criticizes the film for failing to accurately develop the underlying causes of class conflict which Kellner believes (in a manner very close to that of *Screen* theory) is necessary to a proper portrayal of social reality. A third reading, by Jonathan Rosenbaum, defends the film's ambiguity, its inability to ascertain what the right things to do are. We hope these views give some insight into the complexities and difficulties that face discussions of race in the cinema.

## Queer film theory: three readings of *Brokeback Mountain*

(D. A. Miller, 'On the Universality of *Brokeback*' [Miller 2007]; Charles Eliot Mehler, '*Brokeback Mountain* at the Oscars', [Mehler 2007]; Hiram Perez, 'Gay Cowboys Close to Home' [Perez 2007].)

Is *Brokeback Mountain* a queer film? The success of this mainstream, Hollywood film which features a homosexual couple has resulted in widespread and sometimes pointedly nasty debates in the queer community (and beyond) over the perceived qualities of the film. From such a perspective some might be tempted to reduce queer film theory to a simple scorecard of 'yes' or 'no' to the queer question. However, we would wish to stress that queer film theory is less about simply affirming queerness and criticizing stereotyped, negative representations of queer sexualities. Nor do we see queer film theory as defending queerness at all costs, so that any mention of normalized heterosexualities is automatically dismissed as backward and disempowering. Such debates merely end up reducing queer film theory to a matter of *positive* and *negative* images. Queer film theory, we would like to argue, is a matter of affirming the potential queerness of all sexualities – that is, of pointing to and articulating the gay, lesbian, bisexual, transgender and other possibilities of the cinema as such.

Queer film theory, like the other theoretical approaches to cinemas of the other approached in this chapter, is devoted to questioning cinema's modes of expressing power. Where postcolonial film theory questions relations of power in colonial and postcolonial settings, and approaches to race in the cinema ask questions of power in relation to race, queer film theory interrogates the cinematic expression of power's relation to sexuality. Its key question might be: how are some types of sexual practices and relationships depicted in comparison with other, possibly deviant or perverse sexual practices? Like its subordination of colonial and racial others, mainstream cinema has typically elevated relationships centring on heterosexuality and the nuclear family above all other types of sexual relationship. (On this score, one might merely note the long history of 'missing children' films, from *Rescued by Rover* (Cecil Hepworth, 1905) or D. W. Griffith's *The Adventures of Dollie* (1908), through Hitchcock's *The Man Who Knew Too Much* (1956), to the *Home Alone* (1990–97) franchise to note that one of the central plots of Hollywood cinema is that of restoring the nuclear family to its pristine fullness). Mainstream film has also tended to downplay or outlaw sexual relationships which might endanger the sanctity of the heterosexual family (e.g., *Fatal Attraction* [Adrian Lyne 1987], or Otto Preminger's *Advise and Consent* [1962]). While mainstream cinema has tended to remain stubbornly heterosexual, there is nevertheless a significant history of gay and lesbian films, dating more or less back to the origins of feature film-making itself (see Dyer 1990). One task for queer film theory is thus to unearth the histories of these productions and to examine and explain the ways in which they have provided a means of expression for gay, lesbian and other sexualities throughout the history of cinema. Such films are predominantly ones made for and by gays and lesbians and, as such, they have circulated outside the mainstream. For some theorists, that is precisely what queer cinema should be: something *outside the mainstream* which provides a constant and necessary challenge to the mainstream. On this model, queer cinema should be a counter-cinema, just as queer practices are counter-practices which aim to undermine and point to the deficiencies and restrictions of mainstream sexual practices. If queer films prove to be offensive to mainstream audiences, then that is precisely what they should do, for 'queer' is by definition, something *queer*; something strange and *not normal*, and all the more subversive for resisting any attempts at normalization. Perhaps the major thinker of recent times who has set the tone for queer theory is Judith Butler (see Butler 1990, 1993). Another approach taken by queer film theorists is to reclaim mainstream films for queer audiences. This kind of approach is a matter of 'reading against the grain'; that is, of examining films which on the surface are manifestly heterosexual, but if looked at more closely or examined from a specifically queer perspective, can be affirmed as queer (see Doty 2000).

Queer film studies and queer cinema turned a definitive corner at the beginning of the 1990s when a proliferation of films burst onto the market. These films were most prominent on the film festival market, but some films also crossed over to the mainstream (see, for example, *My Own Private Idaho* [Gus Van Sant, 1991]; *Poison* [Todd Haynes, 1991]; *The Living End* [Gregg Araki, 1991]) making enough of an impact to be dubbed 'new queer cinema' (see Rich 2004). There were a number of synergies at work here: the gay and lesbian community had begun to rebuild its confidence following the fear and danger of the AIDS crisis which had reached its height in the mid- to late 1980s; the very term 'queer' had begun to take over the lesbian, gay, bisexual and transgender moniker, LGBT (originally a term of derision used by homophobes to vilify other sexualities, 'queer' was reclaimed by the LGBT community during the 1980s as a positive term in much the same way as blacks appropriated the word 'nigger'); and the very queerness of these films foregrounded new practices and sexualities that weren't merely gay or lesbian, but which were more defiantly hybrid, mixing sexuality, race, class and gender as well as other practices such as illicit drug use, prostitution and, in the case of Jennie Livingston's *Paris is Burning* (1990), the New York drag ball scene, among other things. The new queer cinema signalled a new era of confidence, self-expression and defiance.

Some writers have recently claimed that the new queer cinema has run out of steam or that its moment has passed. If we compare Gus Van Sant's early queer-flavoured works (*My Own Private Idaho*[1991], *Even Cowgirls Get the Blues*[1993])[1] with his more conservative output in the late 1990s (*To Die For* [1995], *Good Will Hunting* [1997]), or Peter Jackson's turn from the queer-inflected *Heavenly Creatures* (1995) to the *Lord of the Rings* trilogy (2001-2003) and *King Kong* (2005), or the Wachowski brothers' beginnings with *Bound* (1996) to the somewhat less queer *Matrix* films (1999–2003), then certainly one might feel this to be the case. Nevertheless, there have been recent successes – Todd Haynes' *Far From Heaven* (2003) is especially notable. And then, Hollywood has gone and produced what might possibly be the most mainstream queer film ever: *Brokeback Mountain* (directed by Ang Lee, 2006). Only the question that has vexed commentators ever since its release is: is this *really* a queer film?

We do not wish to defend any right or wrong answer to this question. The question is nevertheless an important one, and questioning the film around whether its representation of homosexuality is positive or negative has divided the queer community in ways that allow us to investigate the current state of queer film theory. Much of the queer community's problems with the film stems from its publicity, the enthusiasm with which the film's director, Ang Lee and producer, James Schamus, down-played the gay aspects of the film. They wanted to affirm that, instead of being *just* a gay movie – or even a *gay cowboy* movie – it was in fact a universal love story. Queer critics immediately protested that to be queer was precisely to be antagonistic to anything that might be universal, so that downplaying its gay characteristics was to automatically default on the film's status as queer. Against that argument, however, many queer critics have defended the film as a finely nuanced and moving depiction of the difficulties of gay existence in the United States during relatively recent times (the film is set between 1962–1983).

To add one final spice into the mix, there was also a substantial eruption of homophobia from high profile American media personalities who were plainly fearful of going to see the film lest they might turn gay themselves, in itself an extraordinary display of how ignorant and bigoted large sectors of the population still are (in the United States, at least; David Letterman and Larry David provided the most public of the homophobic displays – on these points, see Rich 2007). As part of a dossier of responses to *Broke-back Mountain* published in *Film Quarterly* in 2007, mostly by well-known film historians and theorists, Robin Wood – a long-time film scholar who is openly gay – reflected that, even if there had been some media fear about the film, such fear was far from what he had experienced when he first saw the film in a large cinema in Toronto:

> Here we have a film that twenty years ago would have been treated with abhorrence, a film in which, less than a half-hour in, two handsome young men, both familiar to the youth audience, go far beyond the exchange of a carefully prepared and tasteful kiss, having violent and passionate anal sex, and it is greeted by large mixed audiences with almost universal enthusiasm.
>
> (Wood 2007: 29)

Such progress, as Wood sees it, leads him to unreservedly endorse the film; 'its influence can only be positive', he writes (2007: 28).

And yet, there's that word 'universal' again. To an extent, this is where D. A. Miller, in the same *Film Quarterly* dossier, launches his attack on the film, by far the most theoretically nuanced yet to be published. '[N]ot withstanding the scene of two men fucking', he writes, 'no one has stepped forward to attest to any *sexual* excitement in the film' (2007: 50). What Miller claims therefore is that the film *represses* the queerness of its sex-uality. As such, it is difficult to see how the film could be regarded as queer. In expanding his critique of the film, Miller decries the film as one that is restricted to a standardized, mainstream Hollywood form. It is, in other words, an example of what Colin MacCabe would call classic realism

**Figure 5.4**  Ennis Del Mar (Heath Ledger) and Jack Twist (Jake Gyllenhaal) in *Brokeback Mountain*.
*Source*: Courtesy British Film Institute. Focus Features/Paramount.

(as described in Chapter 3 above). The film clearly divides its points of view into ones which are *objective* – ostensibly the position held by the cameras and by the audience – and those which are *subjective* – the views of Ennis Del Mar (Heath Ledger) and Jack Twist (Jake Gyllenhaal) (Figure 5.4). What results is, therefore, a cinematic discourse in which the objective, guiding, overarching narrative point-of-view is *heterosexual*, while the subjective perspectives of the gay characters are deemed just that: aberrations or deviations of the objective, heterosexual norm. What makes the film a 'universal story of love' is therefore a product of its cinematic mode of storytelling, of its 'classic realism', which ensures any universal love story will always be a love story defined along heterosexual lines. This is certainly the guiding theme of Miller's essay.

There have, however, been fervent defenders of the film in the gay and queer communities. Some writers have tried to urge queers to support the film as an important and courageous expression of queer sensibilities, while some commentators have gone so far as to declare that the film deliberately repudiates and brings into question some of the theoretical excesses which characterize queer theory itself. One writer, Charles Eliot Mehler, argues that *Brokeback Mountain* offended both the right and left extremes of politics: rightists were offended by its homosexual narrative while queers, as voices of the left, were outraged that the film wasn't gay enough. What is most likely at stake here is the film's rejection of a camp aesthetic. Mehler steps up his critique by claiming that *Brokeback* might be considered an *anti-queer* film insofar as it is so openly and honestly homosexual. That is to say, rather than celebrating mixed, hybrid, extreme, interracial or whatever forms of queer sexuality, *Brokeback* concentrates on an entirely standardized and somewhat banal gay relationship. As Mehler argues, 'It would be difficult to imagine the typical queer theorist invoking a category such as "guys who look like guys who like guys who look like guys"' (2007: 147). Mehler is thus claiming that *Brokeback* rediscovers an 'ordinary' gay relationship that has none of the bells, whistles, wigs, implants or strap-ons which would make the film properly 'queer'. But he also sees this as the film's main benefit: that it moves the depiction of homosexuality away from the depiction of excess – it removes the spectre of *exoticism* from the homosexual, and thoroughly banalizes him. The thoroughgoing ordinariness of the depiction of Ennis and Jack amounts to an offense of both left and right ends of the political spectrum:

> *Brokeback*, in fact, is noteworthy for its depiction of the ordinary. But the unwritten code of the Hollywood heterosexual hegemony (and seemingly the queer-culture hegemony as well) encourages viewing the homosexual as sensationalistic, *the homosexual at a safe distance*. By failing to conform to this code, *Brokeback Mountain* posed a threat to both the Hollywood heterosexual power structure *and* queer theory.
>
> (2007: 148)

The most sophisticated defence of the film has been written by Hiram Perez who tries to understand why the queer community so easily labelled the film as 'not a gay movie'. 'Rather than opening new possibilities of identity', Perez writes, '"not a gay movie" rules out any engagement with the inherent contradictions of identity' (2007: 72). Much like Mehler, therefore, he argues that definitions of gay and queer have been too focused on urban practices of identity-mixing and hybrid sexualities so that an understated homosexual relationship located far from the bright lights and underground scenes of a metropolis is a category that doesn't fit into what has become accepted as queer. Perez is keen to point out that, according to reports and interviews, *Brokeback Mountain* did resonate with many gays located in small, country American towns, so its effect on that level should not be underestimated.

Perez's boldest interpretative move is to consider Ennis Del Mar as a very 'particular expression of queerness'. He is a *gay cowboy*, and for Perez, the cowboy legacy is crucial to defining Ennis' queerness. Traditionally, the cowboy figure resides on the fringes of civilized society and often outside the law (indeed, we have seen such a case in our discussion of *The Searchers* in Chapter 1). This automatically tips Ennis' existence towards that of queerness: against the 'civilized' and 'normalized' modes of contemporary social existence, he is an outsider who accepts an identity beyond the realms of what is to modern sensibilities considered normal or desirable. Perez emphasizes Ennis' queerness in contrast to Jack's repression: Jack is the one who wants something akin to a gay marriage with Ennis, while Ennis, Perez argues, remains wedded to wandering and working as a rancher. Ennis has left his own marriage and being unmarried is how he feels most comfortable with himself. He is satisfied with his occasional sexual encounters with Jack and doesn't want to be pushed into the restrictions of marriage, for it is Jack who passionately urges Ennis to escape with him and it is by no means clear that Ennis would ever want to do such a thing. The film is therefore not a story about *how society prevented two homosexuals from living happily ever after*, but is a story about the different ways in which two gay men attempt to deal with their relationship. Jack wants marriage; Ennis, on the other hand, prefers the fringe-outlaw status of the cowboy who, from time to time, engages in passionate sexual encounters with a man he loves. Jack wants a gay life that is *like a heterosexual romance* – a position Perez calls gay assimilation, i.e., where gays are accepted as being *just like heterosexuals*. Ennis' position, by contrast, is more radically queer: he wants a life that is well away from any of society's norms and it is his character which gives to the film its radical edge.

The question of *Brokeback Mountain's* queerness – or its lack of queerness – will no doubt continue to be debated. Here we have presented three cases: one in which D. A. Miller convincingly criticizes the film for its realist narrative discourse because, he claims, that discourse is decidedly heterosexual; another from Charles Mehler which defends the homosexuality of the film rather than its overt queerness; and a third from Hiram Perez, in which the emphatic queerness of the film is placed on the shoulders of the 'gay cowboy', Ennis Del Mar.

## Glossary

**Colonialism/postcolonialism**: Colonialism refers to the ways in which imperial, European nations subjugated the native populations of the countries they conquered (their colonies). For example, France subjugated the native populations of Algeria (among others), while Britain is held responsible for subjugating a vast range of native populations, from Australia to India to North America. Postcolonialism, on the contrary, refers to ways of describing and analysing the new-found social and cultural experiences of those populations that are no longer colonized, but which nevertheless continue to incorporate aspects of their former colonial power into their everyday attitudes and practices. From this perspective, postcolonialism refers to the ways in which previously colonized peoples have adapted, in both positive and negative ways, to the effects of their colonial heritage.

**Diaspora**: Diaspora refers to ethnic populations who have moved, for one reason or another, from their traditional homeland. The African diaspora, for example, refers to the scattered populations around the world, from the Caribbean to the United Kingdom, of people whose ethnic origin is African.

**Hybridity**: For postcolonial theory, hybridity generally refers to ethnic mixing (hybrid = mixture). In this way, hybridity sets itself in opposition to racial purity.

**Queer**: Originally a word meaning strange or peculiar, in the mid-twentieth century, queer became a negative term designating homosexuality. However, in recent times, the word has been reappropriated as a positive one to embrace a wide cross-section of non-heterosexual identities, such as gay, lesbian, bisexual or transgender identities. The term does not necessarily exclude heterosexuals, however, who may also engage in queer sexual practices.

**Racism**: Racists believe that humans can be distinguished by virtue of their specific racial or ethnic traits. In making such distinctions, racists typically highlight the differences between races in order to claim that some races are better or worse than others. Racism is therefore the belief that humans can be qualitatively differentiated on the basis of their racial characteristics.

# 6    Philosophers and film

## Gilles Deleuze and Stanley Cavell

The first six chapters of this book tell a story of how contemporary film theory developed from the quest to define a politics of cinema, inspired first
of all by theories of structuralism and semiotics and moving ultimately
to theories of diversity and otherness as foregrounded by the influence
of theories of gender, race, sexuality and postcolonialism. The final four
chapters of this book depart in fundamental ways from the line of film
theory which begins with structuralism, though each of the theories we
now encounter is ultimately bound up with the theories we have so far
outlined. This chapter deals with two theories of cinema which emerged
alongside the debates grounded in structuralism and *Screen* theory, but
they each offer ways of thinking about cinema that are significantly different from the politically inspired responses we have so far examined.

Gilles Deleuze and Stanley Cavell are philosophers. Many philosophers
have written about the cinema, but the works of Deleuze and Cavell have
had an enduring effect on film studies. Their works intersect with the
strands of film theory we have examined so far in interesting and controversial ways. There is a substantial amount of secondary literature now
written on each of these philosophers' contributions to film theory and it
is likely that their influence will be felt for many years to come (on Deleuze,
see Rodowick, 1997; Flaxman 2000; Bogue 2003; Pisters 2003; on Cavell,
see Rothman and Keane 2000; Mulhall 2008). For these reasons, we feel it
is important to account for their contribution to film theory.

## Gilles Deleuze (1925–95)

Deleuze was a French philosopher who had great affection for the cinema.
He was the writer of many philosophical works and is probably best known
in Anglo-American circles for the provocative works he co-authored with
Félix Guattari, *Anti-Oedipus* and *A Thousand Plateaus* (Deleuze and Guattari 1977, 1987). The two books he wrote on cinema – *Cinema 1: The
Movement-Image* and *Cinema 2: The Time-Image* (Deleuze 1986, 1989) –
are tremendously difficult to understand, but they have had a significant
impact on the field of film studies. Deleuze's approach to the study of

cinema is ruthlessly semiotic in the sense that his books on cinema are ones which classify films in terms of the kinds of *signs* they produce. In this respect he is guided by the system of semiotics pioneered by the American philosopher Charles Sanders Peirce (1839–1914) rather than by the linguistic theories of Ferdinand de Saussure which inspired Christian Metz and other structuralist film theorists.

If Peirce is one significant influence in Deleuze's *Cinema* books, then his role is secondary when compared with that of the French philosopher, Henri Bergson (1859–1941). While the *Cinema* books are books of film history and theory, they are also commentaries on the philosophy of Bergson (see Deleuze 1988a). For our purposes, there are two fundamental points Deleuze takes from Bergson. The first of these (we shall come to the second point a little later) concerns Bergson's understanding of what an 'image' is. For Bergson, an image of something is the consciousness we have of that thing. What this means is that, if I see a tree, then such a perceptual event cannot be divided into the *tree*, on the one hand, and *my consciousness of the tree* on the other. Rather, for Bergson, my consciousness of the tree *is* the tree. Furthermore, my consciousness of the tree is what Bergson calls an 'image' which means that the image of a tree is not separated from what a tree is, but rather the image of a tree *is* that tree. All of this might sound overly philosophical, but Bergson was, after all, a philosopher. The consequences of Bergson's position for a theory of cinema are, for Deleuze, immense. If there is no division between a thing and my consciousness of that thing, then there is correspondingly no division between my consciousness of a film and the film itself. Likewise, there can be no division between a film and the real world, for both have the status of 'images' produced by consciousness: one cannot be said to have priority over the other. We might infer from this that, for Deleuze, for the duration of a film, while I am watching it, while I am conscious of it, that film *is* the real world. Such, then, is the position from which Deleuze begins his *Cinema* books.

Deleuze's aim in the cinema books is to try to describe cinema in ways that are inherently cinematic. His principal question is therefore, 'How do films make meaning?' and his methods for answering that question are unapologetically aesthetic and classificatory: films make meanings by producing specific modes of presentation. That is, by utilizing features of editing, narrative arrangement, *mise-en-scène*, performance, and so on, films produce specific 'signs' by means of which meaning is created and through which the experience of cinema can be defined. There is no intrinsic or essential way in which films make meaning – Deleuze refuses to subscribe to a notion of cinema's 'ideological apparatus' or 'imaginary signifier', for example. Instead, each film and film-maker utilizes aspects of cinema's materials to produce specific systems of meaning. What this

amounts to for Deleuze is an intricate number of terms and classificatory divisions which account for the many ways in which cinema has
the capacity to produce meanings (at least up until the early 1980s when
he was writing the books). Such terms – the specifics of which need not
concern us here – are typically arranged in terms of 'images', so that in
*Cinema 1* we have terms like action-image, perception-image, affection-
image, impulse-image, relation-image, and so on, while in *Cinema 2* the
terms range from opsigns and sonsigns (or 'optical' and 'sound' images)
through to noosigns, lectosigns, and much more besides. We cannot hope
to account for this vast range of signs here. However, we can concentrate
on the major division of cinematic sign systems upon which Deleuze concentrates: the distinction between the ***movement-image*** and the ***time-
image***. In what follows we concentrate on one example of each in order
to introduce readers to Deleuze's film philosophy.

## The movement-image

(Gilles Deleuze, 'The Action-Image: The Large Form' [Deleuze 1986: 141–
59].)

First of all, the division between the movement-image and the time-image
is a historical one. The movement-image refers to a specific way in which
the cinema functioned at a certain point in history, whereas the time-
image indicates another way of understanding how the cinema functions.
For Deleuze, the crucial turning point in the history of cinema is the Second World War: films made before the Second World War are films of the
movement-image and those made after the war are those of the time-
image. But this is not a hard and fast historical division: films of the
movement-image did not suddenly end at the Second World War – indeed, forms of the movement-image continue to be common today – and
nor did the time-image simply begin at that point. Rather, Deleuze tries
to emphasize that the movement-image and the time-image constitute
*different modes of filmic expression*, and that the time-image constitutes a
different way of conceiving film that had not been dominant or typical
before the Second World War. In short, therefore, Deleuze's distinction between the movement-image and the time-image is a historical one, but in
making that distinction he is pointing to a very specific kind of 'history'.
(Deleuze is here influenced by the French philosopher of history, Michel
Foucault [see Foucault, 1970, 1984; and Deleuze 1988b].)

   What, then, is the movement-image? For Deleuze, there are complex
philosophical reasons for naming this division the 'movement-image' in
which 'time is subordinated to movement'. Some of these issues will be

discussed when we approach the time-image. However, for the moment, we can concentrate on two defining features of the movement-image. Films of the movement-image:

- are films that work towards a definitive result; and
- feature characters whose actions can bring about that result.

Two brief examples should clarify these points. D.W. Griffith's *Birth of a Nation* (1915), typically considered the birth of the American feature film, tells the story of the Ku Klux Klan's suppression of a Negro uprising. This suppression leads to a definitive ending in which order and safety are returned to the community. The definitive result is the restitution of a stable community, a result which is brought about by the heroic actions of the Ku Klux Klan members. Sergei Eisenstein's *Battleship Potemkin* (1925) serves as an equally good example: the townspeople of Odessa unite in support of the mutinous sailors aboard the Potemkin thus leading to the happy ending in which the sailors of another warship unite in sympathy with the Potemkin's crew. Again it is the actions of characters which leads to the achievement of the definitive result (a 'happy ending', in this case).

As we have already stated, there are a large number of divisions and separate classifications employed by Deleuze in his *Cinema* books. In our discussion of the movement-image, we would like to focus on one particular chapter of *Cinema 1*: Chapter 6, 'The Action-Image: The Large Form'. It is this form of the movement-image which Deleuze refers to as representing 'the universal triumph of the American cinema' (1986: 141). He first of all describes the large form of the action-image as a type of realism, and the realism he has in mind is very close to what Colin MacCabe called classic realism, which we saw in Chapter 3. More specifically, however, Deleuze identifies two main traits by means of which the 'large form of the action image' can be discerned. These are:

- the *milieu*; and
- *modes of behaviour*.

What do these terms mean? The milieu is more or less equivalent to the setting or the situation of a film. If we consider a Western, for example, we will expect it to be set in the vast West of the American landscape. But the milieu refers to a little more than just the setting. Rather, the milieu will involve aspects of the plot. If the film is a Western, therefore, what are the parameters which guide the plot? The film's actions might focus on a saloon (*Johnny Guitar* [Nicholas Ray, 1954]), or on a long and arduous cattle drive (*Red River* [Howard Hawks, 1948]). Or the characters might be on the open plains (*The Big Sky* [Howard Hawks, 1952]) or alternatively trapped within the confines of a town or building (*3:10 to Yuma* [Delmer Daves, 1957]), and so on. The milieu is therefore a way of trying to determine the 'situation' of a film, the sense of 'what is going on?' and 'what is at stake?'

What Deleuze calls 'modes of behaviour' is more or less reducible to character. But what it really refers to is the question of what kinds of behaviours are possible for specific characters. Characters in films of the 'large form of the action-image' are determined by the kinds of actions and behaviours they have the capacity to perform. Again to pursue the question of the Western, one of the defining features of that genre is the question of whether the hero will be 'up to' the challenge; will his character be strong, resolute, intelligent enough to succeed? Therefore, one of the main ways of defining the large form of the action-image is by way of *modes of behaviour*, for it is by way of a character's mode of behaviour that the action of films of this type is established.

The milieu and modes of behaviour are interrelated, for it is only by being placed in a particular milieu that a character's modes of behaviour will be put to the test. The hero of the film – for films of the large form invariably feature a hero – is forced to act because of the milieu in which he finds himself or herself. Deleuze writes that the hero 'must acquire a new mode of being (*habitus*) or raise his mode of being to the demands of the milieu and of the situation' (1986: 141–2). In other words, the hero must find a way of dealing with the situation as revealed by the milieu in order to bring about a resolution of the plot. In many ways, this form follows a quite classic trope of narrative theory, whereby a plot is arranged according to an originating situation which is subsequently de-stabilized, thus requiring an action to bring about the re-establishment of a stable situation (either the restoration of the old situation or the implementation of a new one). To put it even more simply, film narratives have a beginning, a middle and an end. In shorthand (and following a derivation originally proposed by Jean-Luc Godard which is itself modelled on Karl Marx's 'General Formula of Capital' from the first volume of *Capital*), Deleuze refers to this narrative arrangement in terms of the formula S–A–S' (see Godard 1972). This means: situation–action–modified situation; an originating situation (*the beginning*) is modified by way of action (*the middle*) in order to bring about a modified situation (*the end*).[1]

To explain how these terms function in the large form of the action-image Deleuze relies on a wide range of examples, from documentaries through social problem films, to Westerns, and a lot more besides. But more than anything else, as we have already stated, the large form signals 'the triumph of the American cinema' (1986: 141), and for our purposes we want to focus on one film, Elia Kazan's *On the Waterfront* (1954). Deleuze devotes a few pages to Kazan's films in *Cinema 1*, but his comments on *On the Waterfront* are especially revealing. He explains that one of the main tropes of Kazan's films is that of the wronged man in a wrong world, the man who is treated unjustly by an unjust world, and therefore of the man who must struggle against the odds to put the world to right. Deleuze calls this a theology that would be worthy of Cain (as in the foundational biblical story of Cain and Abel). He continues:

> *On the Waterfront* abundantly develops this theology: if I don't betray others, I betray myself and I betray justice. One has to go through many dirty permeating situations, and through many humiliating explosions, in order to catch a glimpse through them of the impression which cleanses us and the detonation which saves or pardons us ... What is curious, with Kazan, is the way in which the American dream and the action-image grow tougher together. The American dream is affirmed more and more to be a dream, nothing other than a dream; but it draws from this a sudden burst of increased power since it now encompasses actions such as betrayal and calumny . . . . And it is precisely after the war – at the very moment when the American dream is collapsing, and when the action-image is entering a definitive crisis, as we will see – that the dream finds its most fertile form, and action its most violent, most detonating schema.
>
> (1986: 157–8)

The central character in *On the Waterfront*, Terry Malloy (Marlon Brando) must struggle with his own conscience and against the power of the Mob boss, Johnny Friendly (Lee J. Cobb), who controls labour on the water-front. Terry spends much of the film, like his brother Charlie (Rod Steiger), doing the bidding of the Mob and profiting from it, until, when he falls in love with Edie (Eva Marie Saint), he decides that the Mob corruption has gone too far, he breaks from them, and dares to testify against them in court (Figure 6.1). In Deleuzian terms, Terry discovers a 'milieu' – the corrupt practices of the Mob on the waterfront – and determines upon a mode of behaviour in order to deal with that corruption. Modes of behaviour are essential to the film, for much emphasis is placed on Terry's ability to choose. He can choose the Mob (like his brother) or he can choose to 'betray others', as Deleuze puts it, by testifying against the Mob. By betraying the Mob, he no longer betrays himself or justice. This lesson presents us with the film's ethical vision and this too is Kazan's vision of the American dream.

Along with the milieu and modes of behaviour, therefore, there are two other main ingredients which constitute the large form of the action-image: the **duel** (or series of duels) and **ethics**. Typical of films of the large form is the conflict between one character or group of characters and another. Often the large form gives rise to a series of duels, that is, a se-ries of conflicts or showdowns between opposing forces which ultimately

**Figure 6.1** Johnny Friendly (Lee J. Cobb) and Terry Malloy (Marlon Brando) nearly come to blows in the courtroom in *On the Waterfront* Courtesy Kobal. *Source*: Columbia Pictures Corporation. Collection.

culminate in a final duel which is designed to 'settle things once and for all'. We can see how this form takes shape in *On the Waterfront*, as Terry engages in a series of conflicts with the Mob ending in the final scene of the film with the fist fight between Terry and Johnny Friendly on the docks. It is important to note that this series of duels is organized along *ethical* lines – the antagonists are not fighting because they feel like it or simply because they don't like one another, they are fighting because their views of the world are radically different. What is at stake, from the film's point of view, is not merely a grudge between two people or groups, but a battle between opposed world views – in short, an *ethics*. For Kazan, according to Deleuze, this ethical battle is nothing less than the battle for the American dream, a dream which becomes more and more difficult to uphold after the war, but which Kazan's films, including *On the Waterfront*, work ceaselessly to reaffirm. In more general terms, we might see this as a specific way in which American films – 'the triumph of the American cinema' – favours plots in which good is positioned against evil and which, in the final duel, features the victory of the good and the punishment of evil. It is this American dream of the triumph of good over evil that the large form of the action-image enshrines as integral to the American cinema and which is at the heart of *On the Waterfront*.

## The time-image

(Gilles Deleuze, 'The Crystals of Time' [Deleuze 1989: 68–97].)

If, in its most overt form, the movement-image works towards the triumph of good over evil, then, to echo Nietzsche's phrase, the time-image aims to go 'beyond good and evil'. We claimed above that what defined the movement-image above all else was that its films *work towards a definitive result* and that they *feature characters whose actions can bring about that result*. Such possibilities no longer remain for films of the time-image. Their results are no longer definitive and their characters are unable to act in ways that might lead to a result. With the time-image, good and evil are no longer clear-cut. Therefore, characters no longer know how to act in ways that might lead to a triumph of the good.

These definitions are perhaps too negative. If characters in films of the time-image are not defined in terms of their capacity to act, then we should not see this as a limitation, for there are many other ways in which a character might be defined. Another way to think of characters in films of the time-image is that they tend to become caught up in circumstances beyond their control. It is not so much that they cannot act, but rather that any action simply would not be appropriate for the kinds of circumstances in which these characters find themselves. Perhaps Roberto Rossellini's *Germany, Year Zero* (Roberto Rossellini, 1948) is definitive here, especially insofar as, historically, it is neorealism immediately after the war which begins to define an aesthetic of the time-image for Deleuze. In *Germany, Year Zero* the child hero, Edmund (Edmund Moeschke), can no longer discern the difference between good and evil; he can no longer determine which acts might be good and which might be evil and thus finds himself caught in a world in which he no longer knows how to act. In a world that has betrayed him, he can only choose death, and the film ends with his tragic suicide. A character who tried to act in the name of the good discovers that the good was not what he thought it was. In so doing, he loses his ability to act.

Why is the time-image called the time-image? For Deleuze, films of the time-image present us with a *direct image of time*, whereas films of the movement-image only deliver time as subordinated to movement – an *indirect image of time*. For Deleuze, these amount to somewhat complex philosophical theses derived from Bergson – indeed, this is the second main point Deleuze takes from Bergson. For our purposes, we feel the best way to point towards the philosophical distinction between the movement-image and the time-image is to declare that, first of all, in temporal terms, for the movement-image, *everything finds its place*. That is, past, present and future can be clearly discerned; we know what happened in the past and we also know how the past can be clearly differentiated from the present and from the future that is to come. For films of the movement-image, therefore, by the time we reach the end of the film, all events of the narrative can be arranged on a time-line: we know in *On the Waterfront* that in the past Terry could have been a contender, that he fought at Madison Square Gardens. One of the tasks of *On the Waterfront* is for Terry to come to the realization that 'that was then and this is now', that by taking a fall at the Gardens, he was betraying himself. Only now, when he clearly separates his past from his present and his future, can he once again be true to himself and stop betraying himself.

Might a film of the time-image therefore be one in which chronological time is 'mixed up'? Today we are quite used to seeing films which have jumbled up chronologies, with breakthrough films like *Pulp Fiction* (Quentin Tarantino, 1994), *Fight Club* (David Fincher, 1999) and *Memento* (Christopher Nolan, 2000). However, many such films still affirm a past–present–future chronology at their conclusion, so that any jumbling of time within the film is either a trick of the film-maker (*Pulp Fiction*), a playful effect of narrative time (*Memento*), or the mistaken point of view of one of the characters (*Fight Club*). Films that are genuinely of the time-image are somewhat different from a mere playing with narrative conventions and perhaps *Citizen Kane* (Orson Welles, 1941) serves as a key marker here more than any other film. When we get to the end of *Kane* we are entirely uncertain as to what a true account of Charles Foster Kane might be. Instead, what *Citizen Kane* has presented us with is a series of subjective accounts of Kane, some bits of which appear to contradict other bits and all of which, when added up, quite literally do not add up. And that is perhaps what is most important in the time-image: in contrast to the movement-image, with the time-image *not everything has its place*. That is to say, in a time-image film, not everything can be placed on a time line in which past, present and future can be clearly discerned.

There is one more aspect of the time-image to mention. Again it involves the ways in which the time-image can be distinguished from the movement-image, so that the following division can be made:

- for the movement-image, *perception is related to action*;
- for the time-image, *perception is related to memory*.

In films of the movement-image, characters see, hear and sense events and they respond to those events by acting upon them, just as Terry Malloy's response to what he sees is to act against it. Characters in films of the time-image, on the contrary, do not respond to what they see and hear by acting upon it. Instead, what they see, hear and feel serve as catalysts to memory: it forces them back into the past. Borrowing from Bergson, Deleuze asks, *when is a memory formed*? Memories are formed in the present, but they must also then immediately fall into the past. To try to account for this doubled nature of memory – something which is both in the present and of the past – Deleuze argues that there must be a *memory image* that co-exists with any *actual image* in the present. Additionally, this means that our experience of the present will always be doubled between a *perception present* and a *memory present* (see Bogue 2003: 117–18).

These are undeniably complicated and contentious philosophical points, yet they serve as the bedrock upon which Deleuze builds his conception of the **crystal-image** in Chapter 4 of *The Time-Image*. The crystal-image in the cinema initiates a split between the past and the present, between the actual present and the memory of the present that the past evokes, a split between what Deleuze calls an ***actual*** image and a ***virtual*** one, between an actual image in the present and a virtual one from the past. The most important point to grasp is, however, not that the crystal image *separates* past and present, but instead that it makes their distinction *indiscernible*. In the crystal-image past and present overlap, become confused with one another, become entangled in one another. One way to put this is to think that the crystal-image demonstrates how difficult it is to know where the present ends and where the past begins, that our experiences of the present are always entwined with our memories of the past and also that our past can always be summoned up by – and therefore implicated in – our experiences of the present. There seems little doubt that Deleuze gained these ideas not only from Bergson but also from Marcel Proust (himself influenced by Bergson and a constant reference for Deleuze): Proust's madeleine seems the perfect precursor of the crystal-image (see Proust 1998: 60; Deleuze 2000).

*And the Ship Sails On* is a film made in 1983 by one of the great auteurs of the time-image, Federico Fellini. The film is about exploring the past, and that past is explored in a definitively cinematic way. The film's opening scenes are especially evocative as they move from silent, black and white frames, through sepia tones and sound, with a final emergence into colour. This film is a film about history – it is set on the eve of the First World War – and it is also about the history of film, that is, it is about how film can capture, record or represent history. In these ways, therefore, the film is about the relationship between the actual and the virtual:

- between the actual present (1983) and the virtual past (1914);
- between the actual presents of the characters and their virtual memories of the past, for the characters are assembled aboard the

ship for the scattering of the ashes of a recently deceased opera singer, Ermea Tetua, and their conversations are full of reminiscences of her; that is, we gain access to the character of Ermea by way of multiple evocations of her memory (in a manner not dissimilar to *Citizen Kane*);

- there is a narrator, Orlando (Freddie Jones), who speaks directly to the audience in a Brechtian manner. He seems to be both from the actual present (1983) while also located in the virtual past of the film's story. This is most evident at the film's end when he discusses with us the climactic events which occur: the ship is sinking, and he tells us, from a perspective that is clearly *after* the events, even while he is still *within* those events, that 'It's almost impossible to reconstruct the exact sequence of events'.

What Orlando, the film's narrator, therefore tries to make clear is that here it is impossible to distinguish between actual and virtual, to tell which events really happened (as *actual*) and those which were imagined or have become part of historic folklore (as *virtual*). Rather, here, in this film, present and past, actual and virtual, become *indiscernible*.

*And the Ship Sails On* also foregrounds its own inability at a meta-level to discern between actual and virtual. In some of the closing scenes, the massive studio set within which the film has been constructed is revealed to us, complete with cameras, monitors, microphones and lighting equipment, not to mention the bulky mechanism which has conveyed throughout the film the movements of the ship. In this regard, the relationship of the film itself to any actuality is put into question. The film foregrounds its fabrication, but it does not do this merely to assert that 'it's all an illusion' or that 'it's all virtual'. Rather, it does so as a way of conceding that it is impossible to discern where the actual ends and where the virtual begins. *And the Ship Sails On* delivers an exemplary crystal-image.

More specifically, Deleuze locates the crystal-image of *And the Ship Sails On* in some of the spatial and social divisions on board the ship. The staff and workers of the ship are originally subordinated to the opera performers whom they serve upon the upper decks. Yet throughout the film these divisions are reversed so that the performers end up serving the staff with their performances in the kitchens and in the engine rooms inside the internal belly of the ship. Later in the film, when the ship takes on board some Serbian refugees, these refugees then reverse places with the opera singers, as the former sing and dance while the latter are reduced to being spectators. Deleuze asserts that 'here again the exchange is made between the actual and the virtual' (1989: 73) (Figure 6.2).

Not at all straightforward, Deleuze's characterizations of the movement-image and the time-image – along with the myriad other

**Figure 6.2**  Refugees on deck in *And the Ship Sails On.*
*Source*: Courtesy Kobal Collection. RAI.

sub-divisions of types of images defined in the *Cinema* books – pose intriguing and novel ways of understanding cinema and its history. It remains to be seen how enduring those categories will be.

## Stanley Cavell (b. 1926)

Cavell is the author of three books on cinema: *The World Viewed* (Cavell 1979a), *Pursuits of Happiness* (Cavell 1981), and *Contesting Tears* (Cavell 1996). He has also written numerous articles on film, most of which have been collected into a volume entitled *Cavell on Film* (Cavell 2005), and in a recent book called *Cities of Words* (Cavell 2004) Cavell re-visits many of the films discussed in *Pursuits of Happiness* and *Contesting Tears* (some might call this his fourth book on cinema). As a philosopher, he is also the author of many books of philosophy, probably the most important being *The Claim of Reason* (Cavell 1979b). Cavell's interventions into film studies represent the most sustained engagement with the medium made by any philosopher, for they span a period of 40 years, roughly the entire span of the historical period covered by the book you are now reading. In accordance with the three major contributions to film theory Cavell has made, we shall examine his theses one at a time.

## The World Viewed

First published in 1971, the subtitle of *The World Viewed* is *Reflections on the Ontology of Film*, so the overarching aim of the book is to answer the question, What is cinema? It is a long and winding book – and so too is Cavell's writing style long and winding – but we feel there are two main theories at the centre of *The World Viewed*. The first is that *films screen the world* and the second is that films are *moving images of **scepticism***.

What does Cavell mean by declaring that *films screen the world*? He means that films typically take their material from the world, that is, they offer us images and sounds which are taken from the world. These images and sounds are then projected for us on a movie screen. Cavell's notion of screening thus involves trying to work out *how* films screen the world from which their sounds and images are taken. For him, *screen* has at least two meanings. First, the screen acts as a surface upon which the sounds and images of films are projected. To put it one way, films *show us* the world by way of the screen; they make the world available to us. More emphatically, however, Cavell argues that the movie screen is also a barrier to the world. Films *screen* the world in the sense of cutting us off from it. 'The world of a moving picture is screened', he writes. 'It screens me from the world it holds – that is, makes me invisible. And it screens that world from me', he continues, 'that is, screens its existence from me' (1979a: 24).

These observations on the relation between screen and world lead Cavell to his second important argument about the nature of cinema; that films are *moving images of scepticism*. In screening the world, movies screen *us*, as viewers, from the world. As Cavell states, the screen 'makes me invisible'. We are therefore allowed to view this world even if this world cannot see us. For the world that is screened to us in a movie, we are invisible, we view that world *unseen* (1979a: 40). Cavell continues by claiming that 'In viewing films, the sense of invisibility is an expression of modern privacy or anonymity' (1979a: 40). In other words, what Cavell wants to say is that films allow us to see their worlds, but they do not allow us to partake of those worlds. We are cut off from the worlds that are shown to us on film.

Cavell does not then claim that this is a negative aspect of films and nor does he argue that films are somehow *unreal* or *false* because they are unable to show us worlds in which we can participate. Instead, he argues that, by cutting us off from the world, films demonstrate to us the nature of modern subjectivity. That subjectivity, for us, is that we are trapped inside ourselves, that we are 'subjects' whose only means of certainty is to feel *anonymous*, *invisible*, uncertain, and definitively cut off from other subjects and from the world as such. 'That is our way of establishing our connection with the world', Cavell argues: 'through viewing it, or having views of it'. He continues: 'Our condition has become one in which our natural mode of perception is to view, feeling unseen. We do not so much look at the world as look *out at* it, from behind the self' (1979a: 102).

Films, then, are a moving image of scepticism for Cavell. They demonstrate to us the difficulty of answering the question, *does the world exist?* (as well as its companion question, *do other minds exist?*). The only answer films can give is that the world only exists for us insofar as it is *screened* from and for us. From such a position, the only guarantee we have of the world is that which we, as cut off from the world, can see and hear of it from behind our own selves. That films demonstrate this notion of 'being trapped inside one's own subjectivity' is, for Cavell, the reason that 'movies seem more natural than reality' (1979a: 102), so effectively do they demonstrate the ways in which we are screened from the world.

## Pursuits of Happiness

(See Chapter 2 'Knowledge as Transgression' [Cavell 1981: 71–109].)

Cavell's 1981 book, *Pursuits of Happiness*, develops some of the themes of *The World Viewed*, specifically the question of how one goes beyond the state of being trapped inside one's own subjectivity. While he certainly provides answers for that question in *The World Viewed*, he answers it more emphatically in the later book. The way to get outside of the trap of subjectivity is to have one's view of the world affirmed by another human being and to reciprocally affirm the view that this other person has of the world. This is a task that is central for the medium of film, according to Cavell, for the medium of film shows to us views of the world that are not our own. Affirming a film's view of the world as one that we can take for a world is therefore a way of moving outside our own subjectivity and affirming the view of another (that of the view presented by a film). This achievement is, for Cavell, the great achievement of film: not only does it demonstrate to us our entrapment inside our own subjectivity, but it also demonstrates how that entrapment can be overcome. A more explicit way in which this entrapment is overcome is provided by *Pursuits of Happiness*.

*Pursuits of Happiness* presents a theory for a genre of film which Cavell calls the 'comedies of remarriage'. They are a cycle of films from the Hollywood of the 1930s and 1940s in which couples end up married – or as Cavell prefers to put it, *remarried*. The couples in these films are *remarried* because they begin these films more or less together, then become separated, so that the task of the films is to work out how the couple might get back together again. There are examples in the genre in which the couple actually does remarry (*The Awful Truth* [Leo MacCarey 1937] and *Adam's Rib* [George Cukor 1949]), but Cavell takes remarriage to be figurative more than anything, for, so his argument goes, the only way to truly be married is to court the possibility of divorce, that is, the possibility of not being married. Remarriage, therefore, might be taken as the basis for the understanding of marriage that develops in this cycle of films – at least, Cavell takes this to be one of the great discoveries of these films.

What does marriage have to do with the medium of film and the overcoming of subjectivity? Cavell's point is that in marriage the subjective view of one person can be 'married' to that of another. The point of marriage in the remarriage comedies is that the couple learns how to develop views of the world which they can share, a world which they can make together, as it were. This is how each member of the couple overcomes their own subjectivity in order that they each share a view of the world. Cavell takes this to be a primary metaphor for the medium of film *per se*; or more emphatically he argues that the films of this genre make it clear to us that the getting together of the couples is something quite specific to film, that the genre of remarriage is, for the most part, a genre that could only ever have been invented by film (though there are significant precursors).

For Capra, Frank Capra's 1934 film, *It Happened One Night*, inaugurates the cycle of 'comedies of remarriage'. His reading of the film centres on the role of the famous blanket which divides the film's yet-to-be-married couple, Peter (Clark Gable) and Ellie (Claudette Colbert) (Figure 6.3). Cavell's reasons for highlighting the blanket are manifold. The blanket acts as a screen which is analogous to the movie screen, but it also exemplifies the way in which Peter and Ellie block themselves from each other. In other words, the blanket offers a demonstration of the way that the characters remain withdrawn inside their own subjectivities. The removal of the blanket signifies the removal of the barrier that separates the couple; that in affirming the possibility of sharing one's view of the world with another one overcomes being trapped inside one's own subjectivity.

## Contesting Tears

(See Chapter 5, 'Stella's Taste' [Cavell 1996: 197–222].)

Published in 1996, *Contesting Tears* celebrates another cycle of Hollywood movies that emerges as a sequel of sorts to the remarriage comedies, a genre

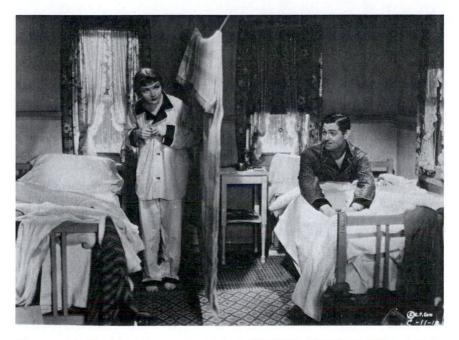

**Figure 6.3** The blanket-screen which divides Ellie (Claudette Colbert) and Peter (Clark Gable) in *It Happened One Night*.
*Source*: Courtesy British Film Institute. Columbia Pictures Corporation.

of 'women's films' of the 1940s and 1950s that Cavell calls 'melodramas of the unknown woman'. These films offer a sometimes startling variation on the theme of the 'couple getting together', for these are films in which the quest to form a couple ends in failure. If the remarriage comedies are films in which couples get together, then the melodramas of the unknown woman are ones in which the couple is an impossible one. This, however, makes neither the films nor their heroines failures. Instead, for Cavell, the triumph of these films is that the female heroines in them come to the knowledge that being in a couple – in *this* couple – is not right for them. What *is* right for them, on the other hand, is to have discovered independence as a way of knowing the world. They might remain entirely unknown and unknowable to the men in these films – hence they are 'unknown women' – but their achievement is that these women know what it is like to be unknown and, for Cavell, they can therefore choose to remain unknown.

Choosing this course of independence is a way of overcoming the isolation of subjectivity by affirming the strength of one's own subjectivity. What Cavell argues is that these women test their subjectivity in relation to others and they make their choices on the basis of that testing. If the heroines of these films end up choosing against sharing their view of the world with another, then this choice is informed, and is not a rejection of the world or a further blockage to knowing the world. Instead, it is a way of knowing the world by remaining unknown.

King Vidor's 1936 film, *Stella Dallas*, is the earliest example of the genre, and surely Cavell is correct to call it 'harrowing' (1996: 200). After marrying the debonair but dull Stephan Dallas (John Boles) as a way of moving herself up the social scale, Stella (Barbara Stanwyck) discovers that the tastes and conventions of that world are not for her. After having a child, Laurel (Anne Shirley), she soon becomes separated from Stephan and develops a strong bond with her daughter. However, after some years she realizes she cannot give her daughter the opportunities she longs for, whereas Stephan can give Laurel the entry into high society that Stella did not desire. At the end of the film, therefore, Stella 'gives away' her daughter, as it were, and Laurel goes to live with Stephan and his new wife.

Cavell concentrates on two key scenes in the film. The first occurs when, while staying at an upmarket hotel with Laurel, Stella makes a spectacle of herself by overdressing in a garish and entirely 'over the top' manner (Figure 6.4). Her dress draws the criticism of the other well-to-do patrons of the hotel, some of whom Laurel had developed friendships with. Stella is thus shamed as one who is not 'part of that world' and, as a consequence, they both immediately leave the hotel and Laurel has to give up the friendships she had made. Intuitively, any viewer of this scene is inclined to think that Stella is entirely unaware of the fact that she makes a spectacle of herself, that her overdressing is an attempt to impress the well-to-do patrons of the hotel, but that it is an attempt which backfires in a disastrous manner. Cavell argues strongly against such an interpretation and instead contends that Stella knows precisely what she is doing. What Stella is doing, for Cavell, is displaying the fact that she is not part of the well-to-do world, and nor does she want to be. Additionally, she is displaying for Laurel that she – Stella – is not part of that world with the ultimate aim of trying to make Laurel reject her. The point is this: Stella discovers that Laurel might wish to be part of the well-to-do world which Stella does not wish for, and she is determined to allow Laurel an entry into that world so that Laurel can make the decision for herself.

The second key scene occurs at the end of the film. Laurel is living 'happily ever after' with the new Stephan and Mrs Dallas. She is to be married to a well-to-do son of the right sort. As the marriage takes place, Laurel is surprised that Stella has not found out about it, for Stella has covered her tracks in such a way as to be now entirely absent from her daughter's life. Stella *does*, however, know of the marriage and manages, incognito, through a window, in the film's final scene, to see Laurel taking her vows

**Figure 6.4** The outrageous outfit worn by Stella Dallas (Barbara Stanwyck) in *Stella Dallas*.
*Source*: Courtesy Kobal Collection. United Artists.

and receiving the nuptial kiss. Having witnessed her daughter's betrothal, she then walks away, towards the camera, and smiles. Stella's achievement is to have affirmed her unknownness, to have accepted herself as unknown and to have produced herself as unknown. This achievement is an affirmation of her subjectivity, but not an affirmation that entails her still being trapped inside her subjectivity. Instead, it is a transformation or transcendence of the state of being subjectively trapped. Cavell claims that the possibility of such a transformation is one of the powers of the medium of film – and he is adamant that the window through which Stella gazes upon her daughter's marriage is a screen analogous to that of the movie screen. What the movie screen makes possible in the instances of 'melodramas of the unknown woman' is the possibility of *knowing thyself*; of moving, as Cavell claims (echoing the American nineteenth-century philosopher, Ralph Waldo Emerson) from *conformity* to *self-reliance*, of developing the power to 'think for oneself', 'to judge the world', to 'acquire . . . one's own experience of the world' (1996: 220). For Cavell, these are some of the extraordinary things which films have the capacity to do.

# Glossary

**Actual**: For Gilles Deleuze, the actual refers to actions or events which occur in the present and which are objective (i.e., they can be apprehended by more than one subject).

**Crystal-image**: A subset of the time-image for Gilles Deleuze, the crystal-image designates films in which time is split in two. When this occurs, the past and the present coexist. Therefore, for the crystal-image, the past is *in* the present as much as the present is *in* the past.

**Duel**: Gilles Deleuze argues that films of the large form of the action-image (a subset of the movement-image) feature a series a duels between opposing forces or characters. Such films will usually culminate in a final duel designed to settle things 'once and for all' and to bring about a resolution of the narrative.

**Ethics**: Used in a very specific way by Gilles Deleuze to refer to the way in which some types of the movement-image establish their narratives around a conflict between opposing points of view. Typically, such conflicts are configured in terms of a battle between 'good' and 'evil' forces, thus giving rise to a system of ethics.

**Milieu**: Term used by Gilles Deleuze in his classification of the movement-image to designate the setting or 'set-up' of a narrative. Milieu, more generally, refers to the 'situation' in which a character or group of characters find themselves in terms of a film's overall narrative.

**Modes of behaviour**: Term used by Gilles Deleuze to denote the kind of action required by a character to respond to a situation in films of the movement-image. As such, the mode of behaviour is a reaction to the 'milieu'.

**Movement-image**: Invented by Gilles Deleuze, and generally referring to modes of film-making that were dominant before the Second World War, the term movement-image designates films in which time is subordinated to movement. Therefore, for films of the movement-image, time is measurable and clearly separated into past, present and future.

**Scepticism**: Philosophical position which denies the possibility of proving that the world exists outside of the mind. Correlatively, sceptics also claim that the existence of other minds cannot be proven.

**Screen**: A central term for understanding Stanley Cavell's approach to cinema, the screen refers to a twofold process. The screen both makes the world available to us (it is the screen *through which* we apprehend the world) and simultaneously blocks the world from us (it screens us from the world).

**Time-image**: Generally referring to some kinds of film-making that emerged after the Second World War, the term time-image is a classification used by Gilles Deleuze to describe films which offer a direct image of time. By this, Deleuze means films in which the passing of time cannot be accurately measured and in which images of the past – especially in the form of memories – are not clearly distinguishable from images of the present or those of the future.

**Virtual**: For Gilles Deleuze, the virtual refers to actions or events which have occurred in the past or which might potentially occur in the future. Therefore, the virtual is associated with a subject's memories of the past or imaginings of the future.

# 7 Film as art

## Historical poetics and neoformalism

The two research traditions that form the basis of this chapter can best be understood as distinct but overlapping strands within the broader domain of poetics. In film studies, *historical poetics* has been elaborated most extensively by David Bordwell, while Kristin Thompson's *Eisenstein's Ivan the Terrible* (1981) and *Breaking the Glass Armor* (1988) represent the earliest systematizations of a *neoformalist poetics* of film. In the space of a decade Bordwell and Thompson crystallized their poetics through an outstanding succession of articles and monographs – the aforementioned works by Thompson; Bordwell's 'Lowering the Stakes' (1983), 'Historical Poetics of Cinema' (1989), *Narration in the Fiction Film* (1985), *Ozu and the Poetics of Cinema* (1988), and *Making Meaning* (1989a); and the co-authored texts *Film Art* (Bordwell and Thompson 1979) and *The Classical Hollywood Cinema* (Bordwell et al. 1985). Bordwell's most recent characterization of historical poetics is set forth in *Poetics of Cinema* (2008).

In several of these works the authors decry the state of contemporary film theory, which in the 1980s remained under the sway of a few major paradigms – psychoanalysis, semiotics, feminism, and Marxism. Detractors would eventually label these paradigms Grand Theories, indicating a tendency to subsume individual films to broad and baggy schemes, often cobbled together from other disciplines. The poetics programmes that took form in the 1980s emerged partly as reactions against **Grand Theory**, targeting in particular the dominance of interpretive criticism, which cut across and monopolized the reigning theoretical paradigms. Rooted in the premises of Russian Formalist literary criticism and theory, neoformalist and historical poetics sought a reversal of standard critical procedures. If doctrine-driven Grand Theory homogenizes films by producing 'top-down' interpretations – i.e., 'readings' that map preconceived theoretical schemas onto particular films – neoformalist and historical poetics espouse 'bottom-up' analysis, grounding propositions in the film's specific qualities.

Both Bordwell (1989a) and Thompson (1988) disdain the routinized practices of film interpretation, arguing that the unique features of disparate films are flattened out by *a priori*, 'cookie-cutter' readings. Clamping down theoretical schemata onto a film does more to reaffirm the Grand

Theory's premises than to illuminate the film's unique qualities. More-over, interpretation can be a fruitful path of inquiry, but it is not in all cases the most vital or appropriate one. Some films actively retard or dis-courage meaning-centred inquiry – they cue us to regard other textual features and effects as more important. If Grand Theorists thematize form and style in order to support particular 'readings,' a poetics of cinema con-ceives these systems as fulfilling a variety of functions, not all of which are subordinated to the transmission of themes. In all, Bordwell and Thomp-son find limitations in both the practices (schemata-mapping) and ends (a 'reading') of meaning-centred criticism. Neither critic denies, however, that interpretation can valuably contribute to a poetics of cinema. They recommend, rather, that the fruitfulness of such an approach be measured against specific cases.

Neoformalist and historical poetics tend to privilege neither evaluation nor interpretation as the default centre of inquiry. Nor do they provide Grand Theories attempting to account for broad aspects of cinematic phe-nomena. Indeed, Bordwell and Thompson specify that their poetics are not absolute theories, but conceptual frameworks (Bordwell), aesthetic approaches (Thompson), 'a set of assumptions, a heuristic perspective, and a way of asking questions' (Bordwell 2008: 20). Both poetics pro-grammes, however, can engage the critic in theorizing. For instance, the poetician could discover regulative principles within a number of films and construct a set of general propositions elucidating those principles. Furthermore, in contrast to the blanket assumptions perceived in Grand Theory, the poetician's theorizing is likely to be of a 'middle-level' sort, addressed at midrange aspects of cinematic phenomena. If Grand Theo-ries are inflexibly monolithic, the approaches proffered by Bordwell and Thompson tackle modest and focused problems, and their conclusions can be modified or contested in the light of subsequent research.

Although Bordwell and Thompson set forth polemical arguments against Grand Theory, the research paradigms they advance are not de-fined simply by this negative movement. Rather, neoformalist and his-torical poetics represent positive efforts toward an empirically reliable ap-proach to cinema, one that is at once critically incisive and sensitive to historical matters. Grand Theories tend to subsume the individual film to broad theoretical propositions, but a poetics takes the artwork itself as a point of departure. Poetics is rooted in the concrete practices and routines of craft traditions; it asks questions pertaining to the principles and purposes governing the artwork's construction; it explains the causes and functions of aesthetic features; it situates the artwork within histor-ical frames of reference; and it investigates the artwork's effects, envis-aging perceivers that are perceptually and cognitively active. In each of these emphases, neoformalism and historical poetics reveal a legacy in the work of early film theorists such as Münsterberg, classical theorists such as Arnheim, Bazin, and Eisenstein, and contemporary theorists such as Burch, as well as the Russian Formalists and Prague Structuralists – all of whom point the way for fully-elaborated poetics of cinema.

This chapter sketches the contours of the neoformalist and historical poetics approaches. Both traditions are separable into three broad areas of inquiry – *analytical poetics*, which examines the film's construction in pursuit of particular effects; *historical context*, concerned with the historically-constituted causal factors moulding the film's forms and materials; and *effects*, which centres on the film's elicited responses and its sorts of uptake by audiences. The chapter outlines each of these broad domains in turn. Bordwell (1989c: 378) describes neoformalism as a 'trend within the domain of historical poetics' – neoformalism and historical poetics are thus discrete branches within the poetics tradition. Still, the two programmes share cognate concerns, and this chapter often conflates them. Areas of distinction, however, are suggested through a discussion of two formalist concepts – the **dominant** and **defamiliarization**. These exegeses are illustrated through reference to a particular example from Hong Kong cinema, Chang Cheh's *wuxia pian* (martial chivalry, or swordplay film) *The Heroic Ones* (1970).

The latter part of the chapter provides a more extensive example, elaborating the concepts introduced below through another, more recent Hong Kong film – *Dog Bite Dog* (Soi Cheang, 2006). Partly these films have been chosen to indicate the broad compass of a poetics of cinema – the approach is not confined to typical or classical film-making, but takes as its objects of study films from different national cinemas and historical periods. A poetics is not limited to films that promote or undermine prevailing ideologies, as certain Grand Theories tend to be. Nor is it confined to a canon of chefs-d'œuvre. A poetics of cinema is as much concerned to elucidate the average, ordinary film as it is the undisputed masterworks of the medium. *The Heroic Ones* and *Dog Bite Dog* will serve also to show how enduring principles and innovation coexist within particular traditions – a key emphasis of the poetics programmes discussed here.

A brief synopsis of *The Heroic Ones* will be helpful at this point. Produced by Hong Kong's renowned Shaw Brothers studio, *The Heroic Ones* takes as its subject matter the historical conflict between the Mongol and rebel armies in China's Tang dynasty (Figure 7.1). A Mongol King and his 13 sons prepare to invade enemy territory. One son, Chun Xiao (David Chiang), offends a local warlord with his brash displays of martial skill; he also provokes the consternation of two of his own siblings, whose jealousy toward Chun bleeds into hatred when he prevents their rape of a village girl. The insurgent brothers collaborate with the warlord, murdering Chun and causing the death of Jin Su (Ti Lung), another of the Mongol King's

**Figure 7.1** The wily Chun Xiao (David Chiang) bedevils the Warlord in *The Heroic Ones*.
*Source*: Courtesy of Celestial Pictures Ltd.

favourite sons. Devastated by his sons' betrayal, the Mongol King orders their arrest. A climactic swordfight pits the surviving brothers against their disloyal kin; refusing to yield, the insurgent brothers are run through by their plaintive siblings.

## Analytical poetics

Central to the tradition of analytical poetics is the study of three levels of filmic structure – thematics, constructional form, and stylistics.

### Thematics

Thematics refers to the referential material (subject matter) and conceptual material (themes) that may be recognized within the artwork. Any film will aesthetically shape and thus transform these materials by developing them through the formal qualities of the medium. Even mundane themes can seem compelling by virtue of the formal properties that shape them. Some aestheticians assign to artworks a neat form–content split, whereby form is construed as the mere convoy of meaning, but the poetician contends that themes and subject matter are not finally separable from their formal devices of expression. Thus a film's theme does not surface autonomously of the work's stylistic and referential materials. Rather, thematic meaning is one of many formal components out of which the artwork is constructed, and it interacts dynamically with other materials to comprise the work's overall form. The poetician may be sensitive to

the ways a film-maker integrates or puts into conflict the various components to infer thematic meanings. Conceptual material in *The Heroic Ones*
rests on a cornerstone of the *wuxia* genre – the enduring value of honor
and *yi* (righteousness) among noble knights-errant – but as we'll see, this
theme becomes transparent only as a result of a dynamic tension among
the film's related formal elements.

Two further concepts are studied under the rubric of thematics: *iconography* and *motifs*. Both function as recurring elements within the work,
and thus are apt to serve as constructional principles supporting the film's
form. The poetician might examine how a film-maker employs these devices as constructive principles, e.g., how an image or motif functions to
motivate a stretch of story action, or how it is patterned for particular effect across the whole film. Often a film will motivate its use of iconography
through genre conventions. *The Heroic Ones* displays the visual iconography traditional to the *wuxia* genre: opulent palaces, ramshackle teahouses,
open battlefields, swords, and the like. It also employs motifs, most prominently the recurring shots of fire woven throughout the action. A poetician
may pause to plumb the motif for symbolic significance – e.g., to interpret the conflagrations as a visual correlative of searing conflicts within
the Mongol army – or, guided by particular research questions, she may
choose to disclose the constructional functions and effects underpinning
the motif's appearance.

### Constructional form

When an analyst examines the structural principles underpinning any
device, she investigates *constructional form* – another of the three levels of
general cinematic structure. Film form is typically governed by principles
of construction. Kristin Thompson (1999) argues that constructional form
in the classical Hollywood narrative is composed of four large-scale segments, each one linked by causal progression and identified by a shift in
the protagonist's goals (a 'turning point'). Other films, such as key works
by Sergei Eisenstein, organize their parts on the principle of conflict. Alternatively a film may construct its form out of abstract linkages and graphic
play, as do many works in the avant-garde tradition.

Episodic form characterizes the large-scale construction of *The Heroic
Ones*. Though it traces an overarching revenge plot, the film consists of a
series of small-scale narrative units. Each unit of action is signalled by the
articulation of a short-range goal (often in the form of a command issued
by the Mongol King); the achievement or deferral of this goal signals the
close of the story phase and the launch of a new stage of action. And almost every plot phase is marked by the recurring fire motif, whose appearance knits the various blocks of action together. In its broadest compass,

a poetics assumes that the form of the work results from an artist operating within certain traditions and pursuing certain effects. Bordwell (2000) has shown that Hong Kong cinematic tradition has historically favoured episodic form, not least because it permits the inclusion of piecemeal attractions such as fights, chases, and similar arousing setpieces. Most basically, *The Heroic Ones* achieves its large-scale form because director Chang Cheh configures the norms of a tradition in ways designed to achieve captivating effects.

## Stylistics

Integral to an artwork's form is its style, and the poetician analyses the principles by which stylistic parameters – e.g., music, cinematography, lighting – interact with one another, and with other components in the artwork's construction. Historical poetics terms this object of analysis *stylistics* – the third of our three levels of film structure. Along with constructional form, stylistic patterning transforms the subject matter and themes of the artwork. Often stylistic devices are subsumed to the narrative line, but occasionally style will come forward as an object of interest in its own right. When style challenges or displaces narrative as the locus of our attention, the work manifests 'parametric' form. Bordwell and Thompson have demonstrated that certain film-makers (Ozu Yasujiro, Jacques Tati, Robert Bresson, and others) create palpable surfaces by making style unusually active or subdued.

Such consistently self-conscious displays of style are untypical, however, and technique need not be laid bare in order to compel the poetician. Driven by the search for explanations, the analyst submits stylistic features to a rigorous examination of purposes and effects. What is the function of a particular cutting pattern in its given context? What kind of uptake does a chosen leitmotif provoke? *The Heroic Ones* foregrounds the fast zoom shot as a fairly overt stylistic device, and the critic can approach its usage in a variety of ways. Depending on the goals of analysis, the poetician may choose to examine the device's function as a structural element (e.g., its patterning within and across discrete story episodes), the principles motivating its selection over rival options such as axial cutting and slow dissolves, or the force of its appeals to our attention (e.g., to what degree it functions 'parametrically').

Referential and conceptual materials, constructional form, stylistic parameters – all these features are dynamically interlocking components of the artwork's construction. Distinguishing among them allows the poetician to describe and analyse precisely how each one is organized into a formal system yielding particular effects. Noticing how these elements interact can help to explain idiosyncrasies within a film too. For example, though it *prima facie* appears to manifest formal unity, *The Heroic Ones* develops its narrative lines in fairly unusual ways. Chang Cheh lets plotlines dangle, but these fugitive tropes may be revived at any moment. Stalking vengefully out of the plot's opening phase, the warlord returns to stir up conflict at the film's midway point. Other plotlines halt abruptly. A putative romance plot finds tragic resolution when the village girl is slain by bandits. At the climax, a plot surge toward the warlord's comeuppance fizzles into an unexpectedly pensive coda: no longer concerned to deliver the warlord his due, the remaining sons lament the shattered ethic of brotherhood. Few films of this genre fail to supply robust resolution of both romance and revenge tropes. How to account for *The Heroic Ones'* abruptly curtailed plotlines?

The poetician, alert to this apparent flouting of convention, seeks explanations. One promising avenue of investigation could examine the short-lived romance story as a byproduct of episodic plotting. Alternatively, the critic might look to institutional factors shaping the film's production – exigent production schedules, such as constrained Shaw Brothers' films of this period, are likely to yield a few textual imperfections. But we can approach this question more positively, in a way that lets us see how a gifted film-maker generates dynamic interplay between form and theme. Put simply, as *The Heroic Ones'* romance and revenge tropes taper off, the film's principal themes crystallize. Now the tattered ideals of brotherhood and *yi* acquire utmost saliency, while traditionally central action lines – the main antagonist plot, the secondary romance story – drop out of focus or abruptly climax.

By suppressing key plotlines Chang Cheh intensifies signature themes; or, put more technically, the film's conceptual material is inferred by a dynamic tension between narrative theme and constructional form. Moreover, *The Heroic Ones'* open plotlines no longer appear unmotivated – conceiving our three objects of study (thematic, formal, stylistic) as interlocking phenomena lets us see how one level of formal structure (plot organization) accommodates another (theme). The analyst need not attempt to account for all three components in any given work, but she stays alert to the way the different levels relate to one another across the film's duration.

## Historical context

Form is conceived as dynamic in terms of both its internal organization and its relation to historical *norms* and *backgrounds*. For the poetician, the concepts of norms and backgrounds are fundamental for placing a film in history. Backgrounds are the historically defined circumstances from which the artwork springs. These historical backgrounds are comprised by sets of standardized norms and conventions, with and against which the artist works. An original film stands out as distinctive partly by reference to a background of transtextual norms. A film's distinctiveness may arise from a *deviation* from normalized devices, but more often it involves the film-maker *recasting* existing norms in fresh ways. Even an innovative film like *Citizen Kane* (1941) does not radically break from classical Hollywood tradition, but reworks technical options already built into the classical system at its particular moment in history (Bordwell 2008: 27).

A distinctive film achieves salience by establishing ***intrinsic norms*** (principles set up by the individual work) that to a perceptible extent violate ***extrinsic norms*** – those repeated standards or 'rules' by which films within a given cinematic mode operate. The poetician constructs proximate and pertinent contexts for the work – she may, for instance, situate *Citizen Kane* against the background set of classical Hollywood cinema. By such comparative strategies the critic illuminates the principles, functions, and effects that make the work striking, as well as the debts the film owes to the tradition within which it operates.

Another type of background involves modes of production and consumption – what are the institutional forces impinging upon the film at its particular point in history? What norms of film-making practice shape the finished work? What are the standard conditions of reception for which the artwork is customized? In order to explain why a film possesses the features it does, historical poetics is apt to reconstruct the precise historical circumstances (industrial, economic, social) accompanying the film's making. Reconstructing historical norms can greatly enhance one's grasp of a film's historical uses and effects as well – by disclosing the circumstances of production and consumption, the poetician can explain, at least to some degree, the effects wrought by the film in its contemporary epoch and at subsequent historical junctures. (On this view, then, a film's effects are not fixed, but are contingent upon historical context.)

Part of the analyst's historical reconstruction often involves canvassing the range of formal options available to the film-maker at a certain point in history. Assuming that the film-maker is a rational and intentional agent, the poetician reconstructs the film-maker's choice situation – the set of historically-defined options from which the film-maker makes numerous, ends-oriented selections. Often these options are fewer than we might suppose. We ought not to assume, for instance, that a film-maker has access to every item of film technology circulating within her particular epoch. Invariably, the film-maker's choice situation is narrowed by mediating forces – budget constraints, studio policy, market trends, available technologies, and so on. Nor should we suppose that constraints necessarily hamper artistic expression. Sometimes the director himself imposes the constraints, as typified by Ozu Yasujiro. In such cases, constraints partly correlate to preferred artistic choices – Ozu sets himself artistic challenges by self-consciously streamlining his repertoire of formal options. (Of course, other constraints such as those mentioned above impinge on Ozu's choice situation as well.) Guided by particular goals, the director selects from an array of mediated options those forms that seem best suited to achieving the sought-after ends. Choices are made partly as solutions to particular problems. How to enliven a swordplay duel through formal means? Chang Cheh opts for rapid zoom shots, but a contemporary – King Hu – favours another solution, creating visual interest through an oblique presentation of characters and physical actions (Bordwell 2008: 413–30).

Assuming that forms and materials are chosen to fulfil some function, the poetician offers causal and functionalist explanations for the film-maker's choices. Creative choices are assumed to be motivated by the pursuit of certain goals; and specific goals are inferred by the preference for and patterning of particular devices. Moreover, the reconstructed choice-making situation constitutes a type of background, since it enables critics to lay out the concrete historical options (including norms and other, less orthodox devices) that are open to the film-maker in a given period. It is against this historical ground that poeticians can examine the principles underlying the film-maker's purposive choices (e.g., her conformity with, deviation from, or recasting of historical norms).

Narrative films are sometimes taken to hold a mirror to the historical and cultural epochs of their day, but historical poetics distrusts such reflectionist assumptions. Not every popular film is shot through with socio-historical commentary. Furthermore, what critics define as cultural *zeitgeists* are often amorphous and historically imprecise abstractions. Assuming that films straightforwardly reflect their historical milieu, moreover, downplays the transformative effects of the film medium. Even a film whose subject matter is culled wholesale from the *zeitgeist* is, in formalist parlance, *deformed* by various mediations – not least the manifold forms and materials out of which the film is constructed.

It might be generally true that *Five Easy Pieces* (1970), *The Parallax View* (1974), and other films of the New Hollywood echo the downbeat mood of America in the era of Vietnam and Watergate. *Cloverfield* (2008) and *The Mist* (2007) might instantiate post-9/11 sensibilities. *Chungking Express* (1994) perhaps 'reflects' collective concerns about Hong Kong's reversion to Chinese rule. None of these assumptions is very historically or conceptually precise however. Historical and cultural factors inevitably find their way into movies, but such factors – in the sense of collective 'moods' or attitudes – are not necessarily the most proximate influences impinging upon films. In place of vague abstractions such as *zeitgeists*, the poetician seeks to find shaping forces of a more concrete and historically verifiable sort. Industrial practices, norms of storytelling, and other mediating factors are likely to exert a greater practical influence on the film than do putative anxieties drifting in the ether. Thus the poetician will often treat such proximate factors as fruitful points of departure, exploring their influence upon the film's functions and effects.

Situating the film in history involves reconstructing the circumstances of reception as well. Once the poetician has established the norms and conventions specific to a given historical period, she can begin to explain why some films strike their immediate audience as innovative, bizarre, or pedestrian. Situating Jean Renoir's *The Rules of the Game* (1939) against the background of classical French storytelling, Kristin Thompson (1988) argues that the film perplexed a 1939 audience unaccustomed to the device of narrative ambiguity. Ambiguity, at odds with the canonized elements of French drama, resulted in this audience's failure of plot comprehension. Thompson goes on to trace the standardization of ambiguity as a realist device in the ensuing decades – from the neorealist exercises of the 1950s Italian directors, through the open-ended climax of *The 400 Blows* (1959), and the narrative equivocations favoured by Michelangelo Antonioni and Ingmar Bergman. Thompson notes that the device was firmly established as an art cinema norm by the 1960s. As a result, a 1960s audience could revisit *The Rules of the Game* and easily grasp its use of ambiguity as a cue for realism. (This is not to say that modern audiences could disambiguate Renoir's narrative, only that they could grasp more readily the principles governing its ambiguous cues.)

Thompson's analysis exemplifies the tendency of historical poetics and neoformalism to ground reception in concrete historical circumstances, relating the spectator's uptake to the critical concepts of historical backgrounds, norms, and conventions. Still, a poetics of cinema does not settle for historical illumination and close film analysis. Operating on the assumption that a film's form is engineered to fulfil intended goals, the analyst seeks to illuminate the achievement or otherwise of the goals themselves. The poetician, that is, combines formal and historical analysis with an explanation of the various effects produced by the work.

## Poetics of effects

The two research traditions we've here been considering advance a poetics of *effects*, a category that is both broadly empirical (exploring the viewer's uptake of the finished artwork) and conceptual (identifying the filmic cues designed to guide and constrain that uptake). 1970s film

theory popularized a conception of the spectator as ideologically positioned, psychically regressive, and passive, but the poetics programmes
advanced by Bordwell and Thompson conceive the viewer in terms of
perceptual and cognitive engagement. In mounting an explanation of a
film's effects, the critic seeks to specify and characterize the various operations that the spectator executes, along with the cinematic cues that trigger
them.

Bordwell advocates a cognitive model of the viewer's activity, one which
charts the complex range of tasks that film viewing entails – perception
of moving images, comprehension of plot events, strategies of inference,
construction of hypotheses, and so on. (We address these operations more
fully in the next chapter.) Cognitivism is one potential pathway that a poetics of effects could follow, but it does not inevitably lead off from the
neoformalist or historical poetics perspectives – the poetician may appeal
to rival explanatory frameworks in order to account for the viewer's activity. Nevertheless, adherents of a poetics approach share the assumption
that an artwork is structured to elicit certain effects, and that the perceiver is an active participant in the construction of the work's meaning
and effects.

Of central importance to the poetician are those effects that challenge
and expand viewing skills. Spectators acquire and develop such skills
through repeat encounters with the medium; in the act of viewing, our
knowledge of a tradition's formal operations combines with our competencies of everyday life to facilitate comprehension. Possessing the appropriate viewing skills is essential if a film's effects are to work upon
us. Film-makers try to achieve effects by means of salient cues built into
the work; the hypothetical viewer perceives and reacts to these cues, responding in ways that are more or less congruent with the film-maker's
intentions. But a viewer lacking the necessary viewing skills may struggle to determine which cues are important, and fail to grasp the work's
intended effects. (Recall the case of *The Rules of the Game*, whose contemporary audience had not yet developed sufficient viewing skills to absorb
the film's equivocations.) Thompson (1988: 32) notes that neoformalist
poetics 'treats audience response as a matter of education about and awareness of norms' – and as norms vary according to historical circumstance,
so too do viewing skills.

If our familiarity with norms is confined largely to the contemporary
cinema, we may find certain viewing procedures challenged by, say, *The
General* (1927), which adheres to its own set of historically constituted
norms. Occasionally we encounter a new film for which our repertoire
of norms is inadequate. Complex films of this sort hold a special appeal
for the poetician, since they may possess innovative formal schemes, or

assign old devices new functions, or otherwise rework existing norms in interesting ways – at the very least, such films offer an occasion for analysis, an opportunity to measure the original, challenging work against established norms and traditions.

One advantage of a poetics of effects is the active role it grants to the spectator. If Marxist film theory postulates a deterministic, 'hypodermic' model of reception whereby the viewer is positioned as a passive, uncritical subject, historical poetics plots effects on a continuum flanked by text and perceiver – the viewer can stick fast to the cues sprinkled through the film, or she can deviate grossly from textual cues by appropriating the film for her own purposes. An 'average' response may move between these two poles at various points in the film's progression. Bordwell (1988: 173–4) notes: 'The text cannot dictate how it will be understood. There may be "preferred readings," but spectators are always able to interpret a text in accord with their own aims and interests.'

Audiences requisition films for uses unforeseen by the film-maker. Agitated black Americans in the 1970s could construe *Fist of Fury* (1972), *Enter the Dragon* (1973), and other Bruce Lee movies as tacitly inciting uprisings among oppressed minorities. College students and midnight movie audiences appropriated *Reefer Madness* (1936) decades after its original release, ironically transforming a piece of conservative propaganda into an affirmation of liberal, anti-authoritarian attitudes. (As one critic puts it (Samuels 1983: 97), the film was embraced by audiences 'in the midst of their own reefer madness'.) A poetics studying appropriation might identify the textual cues that are primary in the perceiver's uptake, the cues that the perceiver correspondingly 'plays down' in the act of appropriation, and the social circumstances shaping both the 'ordinary' and 'aberrant' contexts of reception.

## Two formalist concepts

The objects of formal analysis, the situating of the artwork in history, the investigation into uses and effects – these concerns, so central to neoformalism and historical poetics, are strongly indebted to Russian Formalist literary criticism. Yet as their re-brandings suggest, neoformalism and historical poetics are distinct derivations from the Formalist tradition. Indeed, Bordwell (1983: 7) suggests that, partly due to the tradition's heterogeneity, 'anyone seeking to draw a coherent critical practice from [Formalism] must pick out certain concepts and downplay others'. Consequently, we find Bordwell's historical poetics 'slighting' certain Formalist concepts that in Thompson's neoformalism occupy a central role. Two of these concepts – the *dominant* and *defamiliarization* – will be discussed here. Bordwell invokes the former device in early formulations of historical poetics, as well as in his studies of Ozu (1988), Eisenstein (1993), and Dreyer (1981); he invokes the latter concept on occasion in several early writings. But he omits explicit mention of both concepts in his most recent overview of historical poetics. If these are two Formalist concepts that Bordwell 'downplays', especially in his recent work within historical poetics, they are nevertheless central to the neoformalist poetics postulated by Thompson.

## The dominant

Poetics, we have said, considers form a dynamic system consisting of more or less conflicting elements. Yet if the parts clash, how does the artwork achieve order? The Russian Formalists sought to resolve this question through the concept of the 'dominant', the central hub of an artwork around which all other components revolve. As the artwork's primary structuring principle, the dominant permeates the work's core structural levels – its theme, form, and style. Dynamism of form arises from the suppression of subordinated devices and the concomitant foregrounding of a single privileged element (the dominant). Prioritizing the dominant engenders the *deformation* of the artwork's other components; that is, the other components are *transformed* by their subordination to the dominant. An artwork is dynamized by the tension yielded by its subordinated and foregrounded components, while order is achieved by moulding conflicting elements into the service of the dominant. In Roman Jakobson's (1935: 82) words, 'it is the dominant which guarantees the integrity of the structure'. In formulating a dominant for the work, the poetician identifies and traces the influence of the foregrounded component upon any or all of the three levels of film structure.

Typically the dominant will differ from one work to another. As Boris Eikhenbaum (1927: 219) states, 'Any element of the material may become foregrounded as a formative dominant and thus as the basis of plot or construction.' Thompson (1988) suggests that ambiguous cues for subjective action become the formal dominant in Otto Preminger's *Laura* (1944), while Bordwell (1988: 76) argues that the dominant in Ozu's pictorial style is 'the urge to make every image sharp, stable and striking'. Different works will typically be seen to manifest different dominants. However, the analyst may invoke the dominant to unify several films within a tradition, or to suggest coherence among the films of an individual director. At the level of the individual film, the dominant is crucial in marking the work off from its pertinent backgrounds – a film that makes salient a highly unusual device is likely to depart from its conventional backgrounds in striking ways. The Russian Formalists placed particular value in such artworks, which, by prioritizing unusual dominant structures, subordinate familiar components to fresh, defamiliarizing ones.

## Defamiliarization

For the Russian Formalists, art succeeds by reinvigorating the habitual, ordinary perception with which we encounter the everyday world. If general perception is apt to become habitualized and automatic, art functions to renew everyday experience by restoring salience to the act of perceiving. Practical perception quashes the sensation of things, but an artwork recovers the palpability both of perception and of the things perceived – in Victor Shklovsky's (1965: 12) famous dictum, 'art exists . . . to make the stone *stony*'. The value of such artworks rests in their capacity to sharpen our perception, since they force us to perceive the familiar and commonplace as 'unfamiliar' and strange. This idea finds an echo in the 1930s writings of classical film theorist Rudolf Arnheim, who argued that the filmed object is transformed by the formal properties of film. Such properties, Arnheim (1957: 57) claims, 'sharpen [the object], impose a style upon it, point out special features, make it vivid and decorative. Art begins where mechanical reproduction leaves off, where the conditions of representation serve in some way to mold the object.'

All art forms defamiliarize the everyday world, if only by the transformative properties intrinsic to their medium. But individual artworks vary in the degree to which they make strange the everyday world and the conventions of other artworks. An artist revivifies ordinary perception by foregrounding new or scarce devices; by assigning familiar devices new functions; or by placing such devices within new contexts. The defamiliarizing device can itself become habitualized, however, as consistent deployment diminishes its estranging effects. Artists thus constantly seek fresh ways to defamiliarize habitual perception – and this, according to Thompson (1988: 11), 'explains why artworks change in relation to their historical contexts and why defamiliarisation can be achieved in an infinite number of ways'.

A device may become habitualized at the level of the individual film. Take *The Heroic Ones*, which foregrounds the fast zoom shot as a stylistic dominant. Director Chang Cheh makes the zoom device a ubiquitous element throughout the film, enlarging a character's facial gestures or punctuating the rhythms of rapid-fire action sequences. He strings several zoom shots together in woozy succession. And he recruits a single shot to execute several zoom manoeuvres, feverishly exposing and magnifying regions of dramatic space. So extensively does Chang rely on the rapid zoom that it quickly becomes a normative part of the film's structure – consequently, its value as a defamiliarizing device dwindles. Formalists argue that artworks should provide us fresh perceptual challenges, but a film that domesticates a device through compulsive repetition depletes its 'renewing' effects upon our everyday perception.

A device may become habitualized by widespread industry uptake as well. Devices lose distinctiveness when film-makers collectively adopt them as favourite storytelling options. Consider, again, the rapid zoom device. Zooms fell out of fashion in the late 1970s, but previously they had served as a popular resource among Shaw Brothers' film-makers, helping to define a house style. By the early 1970s, Chang Cheh's *wuxia pians* were awash with flashy zoom shots, and the tendency to flaunt the device in fight sequences soon spread to rival studios. Inevitably the industry's use of fast zooms reached saturation point, prompting film-makers to re-cruit the device less frequently. Noting the vogue for particular devices, such as the fast zoom, reminds us that defamiliarization depends upon historical backgrounds. In neoformalist parlance, the zoom device became *automatized* during the 1970s, its powers of perceptual renewal diminished through obsessive uptake by directors such as Chang Cheh. But at a subsequent stage a Hong Kong director could reanimate the fast zoom, and – thanks to historical distance and limited contemporary use of the device – recover its defamiliarizing force. A device whose defamiliarizing effects have become spent in one historical epoch can thus find its renewing capacity restored at a later historical juncture.

We have aligned the dominant and defamiliarization with neoformalism, but this should not suggest that the concepts have no place in a historical poetics of cinema. As noted above, Bordwell invokes both concepts in his formative writings on historical poetics and in several subsequent works. Though his latest survey of historical poetics omits explicit reference to these notions, they are nevertheless implicit in parts of his discussion. He tacitly invokes defamiliarization, albeit of a relatively mild sort, when asserting that 'form and style will transform social givens' (Bordwell 2008: 32). And we can assume that the dominant remains a relevant concept for Bordwell's historical poetics, given its central concern with constructional principles and effects. The question, rather, concerns the weight of emphasis afforded defamiliarization and the dominant within the two traditions – as Bordwell says, adapting the Formalist tradition involves the downplaying as well as the appropriation of concepts. Rather than identify these devices wholly and exclusively with neoformalism, we do better to regard them as tacit options encompassed within historical poetics, to which the analyst may have recourse in light of particular cases.

# The poetics approach and *Dog Bite Dog* (Soi Cheang, 2006)

The rest of this chapter analyses *Dog Bite Dog*, a contemporary Hong Kong crime thriller, from the perspectives of neoformalism and historical poetics. Poetics, we have suggested, investigates the contexts and traditions pertinent to the individual work. Perhaps the most proximate of these contexts is the film-maker's working situation, which mediates between the artwork itself and the broader social milieu. Significant here is the director's uptake of tried and proven production methods, those more or less tacit craft procedures that directors consciously or intuitively know. No film-maker proceeds without reference to some kind of pre-set pathway, and different national cinemas tend to offer their own variations on production routines.

Under the aegis of local veterans such as Johnnie To, Soi Cheang has inherited the Hong Kong cinema's distinctive working protocols. Cheang, like many of the region's directors, often begins production without a completed screenplay – armed with just the bare rudiments of a story, he trusts that the plot will crystallize as shooting progresses. (*Dog Bite Dog* typified this practice; during shooting, Cheang's scriptwriters would be on standby to chip in dialogue and iron out plot wrinkles.) He also eschews storyboards in favour of a more spontaneous shooting method, preferring to figure out camera set-ups by 'instinctively' reacting to the specific features of setting and location. These ways of proceeding are part of what a poetics regards as craft traditions, or *practices*, and although most Hong Kong directors adapt them to individual ends, such procedures prove remarkably durable as standardized routines guiding the film-maker's activity.

Stressing the endurance of a tradition doesn't automatically cast the film-maker as a passive recipient of bequeathed customs. Directors are often well versed in cinematic traditions, and self-consciously reach down into film history in search of effects. Of his appropriation of the rapid zoom device in *Love Battlefield* (2004), director Cheang notes:

> I was thinking about the [1960s/70s] Shaw Brothers movies and the zoom device. The zoom technique has always been there, but for some reason local film-makers haven't been using it. It's such a great technique – why don't we use it? So I decided to bring it back in.
>
> (Bettinson 2008: 222–3)

The weight of tradition does not foreclose the film-maker's agency – a director working within a tradition can exploit its norms in inventive ways.

Nor does the poetician's emphasis on backgrounds imply that cinematic practice is impervious to historical change. Bordwell (2008: 29) concedes that, from one angle, 'The historical side of poetics is conservative, often trying to remind people that things that seem brand-new almost always proceed from longer-lived conventions.' Nevertheless, the notion that film-makers recruit a tradition's norms to their own ends implies that the tradition is always steadily evolving – some elements of the tradition remain stable, while others undergo degrees of transformation. As Thompson (1981: 18) notes, 'the [individual] work is at once symptomatic of the larger backgrounds and also important in itself as a *historical development* of those backgrounds' (italics added). Situating Cheang against a ground of tradition serves not to suppress his innovations, but on the contrary, to foreground these innovations all the more sharply.

If the historical component of our poetics programmes sensitizes us to tradition and historical context, the analytical dimension orients us toward the three filmic systems of thematics, constructional form, and style. In practice, we have said, these three levels are interlocking phenomena, but by prising them apart we can examine both their respective principles of construction and the purposes and means by which they interact. Consider, first, constructional form – how best to characterize *Dog Bite Dog*'s organization of story and plot?

Cheang favours doppelgänger protagonists, and he makes this topos the mainspring of his storytelling. *Dog Bite Dog* acquires its overall form thanks to twin protagonists set in parallel formation – large-scale form radiates from the doppelgängers' diverging trajectories. A feral, individualistic assassin (Edison Chen) is fervently tracked by a mixed-up Hong Kong cop (Sam Lee). The cop is assailed by psychological demons; the killer's concerns are startlingly primal. As story events accumulate, the protagonists are pulled into analogous relation. By the final reel, the cop resembles the steely assassin of the film's opening phase – his multi-layered psychology now dwindles to the simple motive of revenge. Psychological weight is shifted to the killer, whose affections for a retarded girl threaten to blunt his instincts for survival. Tracing criss-cross paths, the cop becomes more beastlike while the killer develops greater humanity.

We can sketch a proximate background for Cheang's symmetrical formal schemes and doubled protagonists. Cheang's immediate film-making milieu – the contemporary Hong Kong cinema – has fruitfully defamiliarized narrative clichés of character doubling. Flagrant character parallels pervade *Infernal Affairs* (2002) (strongly influential upon subsequent thrillers produced in the territory), John Woo's *A Better Tomorrow* (1986) and *The Killer* (1989), and certain noir thrillers produced by local company Milkyway Image. Even an art cinema exponent like Wong Kar-wai builds character parallels out of rhyming blocks of action. Symmetrizing

**Figure 7.2** Figures arrayed diagonally in *Dog Bite Dog*.
*Source*: ©2006 Art Port Inc., ALL RIGHTS RESERVED.

plotlines can lend coherence to an episodic narrative and foster the impression of organic unity (or, at least, of basic formal cohesion). The materials and forms conventional to the urban crime genre constitute another proximate mediation.

At the analytical level of poetics, *Dog Bite Dog*'s symmetrical large-scale form is inextricable from its principal themes. Cheang mines plot schemas circulating in his milieu (symmetrical action lines and the motif of doubling) and fuses them with thematic materials. In *Dog Bite Dog*, criss-crossing plotlines cue a favourite thematic concern: the capacity for humanity in the animal, and the animalistic instincts of humankind. By pressing us to notice that large-scale form can infer themes, a poetics of cinema reminds us that style, theme, and plot – though conceptually distinct – are systematically interrelating phenomena.

Analytical poetics invites us to study aspects of style as well. Examining *Dog Bite Dog*'s visual style casts light on its shifting relation to background norms. Cheang served his film-making apprenticeship under Johnnie To, so it shouldn't surprise us that he shares To's taste for geometric compositions, lining up characters along invisible diagonals (Figure 7.2) or spreading them out horizontally (Figure 7.3). Images of this sort flaunt the art of pictorial design, and coax the viewer to an appreciation of staging and composition. *Dog Bite Dog*'s *mise-en-scène* thus asserts a fascination of its own, but Cheang ensures that even the most extroverted images serve the drama. In the police headquarters, detectives array themselves in diagonal alignment as they interrogate an offscreen suspect. Cheang constructs not

**Figure 7.3** *Dog Bite Dog*: Lateral staging flaunts the art of pictorial design.
*Source*: ©2006 Art Port Inc., ALL RIGHTS RESERVED.

simply a flamboyant visual image, but one that pointedly hierarchizes the characters within the frame. The shot begins with the cop protagonist, Wai, stationed prominently in the foreground – the better to show his boisterous tirade against the suspect (Figure 7.4). As his colleagues burst into frame to restrain him, the cop retreats into the background, and his more sober commander takes charge of questioning (Figure 7.2).

Resettling the figures in diagonal formation lets Cheang adumbrate character relationships and spotlight a shift in the action. If the initial composition (Figure 7.4) gives place to Wai's hot-headedness, the subsequent staging (Figure 7.2) indicates his outranking by the detectives that supplant him in the foreground; the recessional staging also shifts attention onto the senior detective, who now challenges the suspect with devastating evidence. Soi Cheang's staging, then, is strategic as well as decorative. He yokes flagrant pictorial strategies to the unfolding of the drama, just as he rivets dramatic themes to the device of symmetrical plotting. And he inherits Johnnie To's eye for geometric visual patterns, as well as the keynote principles of pictorial and emotional clarity that traditionally govern Hong Kong storytelling (Bordwell 2000).

The influence of To may result in visual legibility, but Cheang juxtaposes this crisp pictorial style with ferociously jarring visual devices. As *Dog Bite Dog*'s feral protagonists clash in a landfill, Cheang combines handheld, docu-style cinematography with wildly spasmodic figure movements, designating an almighty scrap. A kind of studied chaos

**Figure 7.4** Renegade cop Wai (Sam Lee) is restrained by a senior officer in *Dog Bite Dog*.
*Source*: ©2006 Art Port Inc., ALL RIGHTS RESERVED.

springs from these twin techniques – the percussive thrusts of the camera lend the action a palpable sense of disarray, while bracing figure movements belie the choreography of action, yielding an untidy, realistic tangling of bodies. This bristling style of action is far removed from the restrained cool of Johnnie To's action scenes, as well as from *Dog Bite Dog's* own displays of pictorial ornamentation. So too does Cheang's searing dogfight flout the sensuous treatment of violence in John Woo. These innovations, however, occur against a background of traditional norms. Camera and figure movement foster an impression of chaos, but Cheang keeps the action legible, ensuring that his overwrought style doesn't obscure the drama. And true to Hong Kong tradition, the writhing protagonists trade blows with an astounding appreciation of symmetry, making them kin to the chivalric figures that populate the action films of John Woo and Chang Cheh.

*Dog Bite Dog's* documentary stylistics stand out still further against another cluster of historical norms – wirework, digital effects, and sophisticated production values. *Crouching Tiger, Hidden Dragon* (2000) exemplifies the 'wire-fu' technique, blending together wirework and martial arts (a favourite Hong Kong concoction); computer-generated effects embroider the action sequences in *The Stormriders* (1998), *Shaolin Soccer* (2001), and *Kung Fu Hustle* (2004); and cosmopolitan productions such as *Gen-X Cops* (1999), *New Police Story* (2004), and *Invisible Target* (2007) supply

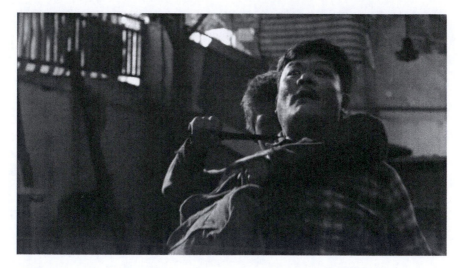

**Figure 7.5** The ferocious Cambodian assassin (Edison Chen) takes Fat Lam (Lam Suet) hostage in *Dog Bite Dog*.
*Source*: ©2006 Art Port Inc., ALL RIGHTS RESERVED.

traditional action with a sleek visual polish. As these features became familiar and normalized, directors could achieve more seemingly realistic action sequences by flouting or recasting these norms. Put differently, *Dog Bite Dog*'s documentary style carries a certain defamiliarizing force against this background of recent Hong Kong action cinema, attesting to the historically contingent nature of cinematic realism.

What of the film's dominant, that constructive lynchpin determining the relation among all the work's components? Symmetrical patterning – a principle that penetrates all three of the film's structural levels – would seem a likely candidate here. It pervades constructional form, shaping the divergent trajectories of the twin protagonists; visual style, as when echoic compositions pull the protagonists into an explicit comparison (Figures 7.5–7.7); and theme, which muddies the distinction between animality and human nature. Symmetrical patterning even underpins the film's title. Other components are symmetrically configured too. The stylistic cues to realism – 'shakycam' cinematography, apparent spontaneity of figure movement, imperfect lighting sources – are subordinated and undercut by the non-naturalistic canine growls that sometimes displace the protagonist's voices, a flourish that functions principally to establish cop and killer as analogous.

Perhaps surprisingly, treating thematics, large-scale form, and style as conceptually separable phenomena allows the poetician to describe how

**Figure 7.6** *Dog Bite Dog*: Echoing his stand-off with Fat Lam, Pang (Edison Chen) bargains with the life of another cop.
*Source*: ©2006 Art Port Inc., ALL RIGHTS RESERVED.

**Figure 7.7** Wai (Sam Lee) is pictorially aligned with the assassin at *Dog Bite Dog*'s climax.
*Source*: ©2006 Art Port Inc., ALL RIGHTS RESERVED.

closely each level is imbricated. By attending to one level of *Dog Bite Dog*'s general structure, such as style, we can examine its degree of imbrication with other levels, such as theme or form. We can explore how these general systems (theme, form, style) are organized to achieve particular effects (e.g., defamiliarization). Concretely, poetics can also cast light on Cheang's innovations by invoking such concepts as norms, conventions, and backgrounds. It is against these concepts that Cheang's recasting of received traditions stands out in relief. By stressing continuity as well as change, historical poetics and neoformalism are apt to celebrate both the ingenuity of the film-maker and the enduring appeals of particular traditions.

## Glossary

**Defamiliarization**: The 'making strange' of the habitual and everyday. Defamiliarization pertains to the artwork's capacity to renew perception by affording 'familiar' phenomena unusual prominence. If ordinary perception becomes habitualized through everyday routine, the defamiliarizing artwork refreshes and sharpens perception somehow (e.g., by wrenching familiar elements out of their customary context or inflecting familiar objects in unorthodox ways). Defamiliarization derives from the term 'ostranenie' ('to make strange'), a central concept in Russian Formalism.

**The dominant**: The dominant is a central heuristic tool employed in neoformalist criticism. Formulated by the Russian Formalist critics in the early twentieth century, the concept of the dominant describes the governing structural principle that permeates all formal levels of the individual artwork. The dominant contributes to the work's dynamic structure, jostling and sometimes conflicting with the formal components it subordinates.

**Extrinsic norms**: The principles and patterns that govern broad categories of texts. Conventions of genre, narrative organization, stylistic construction, and so on, pre-exist the individual film and constitute the extrinsic norms that connect the artwork to traditions. The extrinsic norms of the film provide a background of conventions against which more innovative elements (the film's **intrinsic norms**) stand out in relief.

**Grand Theory**: A pejorative term applied by detractors of the major theoretical paradigms that emerged in the 1960s and 1970s. Associated in particular with film theorists David Bordwell and Noël Carroll, the term invokes theories (or Theories) that attempt to account for all aspects of cinematic phenomena, subsume individual films to *a priori* readings, generate abstract and mystifying premises, and proceed doctrinally to affirm the tenets of a particular Theory. A major alternative to Grand Theory is the practice of **piecemeal theorizing**, associated chiefly with historical poetics, neoformalism, and cognitive approaches to film.

**Intrinsic norms**: The distinctive principles and patterns embodied by the individual artwork. A film may announce its intrinsic norms in more or less tacit fashion, and part of the viewer's uptake involves grasping the peculiar features that the film lays out. Intrinsic norms pertain to the unique constructional form of the artwork, and thus compel the poetician. Such norms also carry the potential to expand the viewer's repertoire of viewing skills, and thus form a central concern of the neoformalist.

**Piecemeal theorizing**: The principle of conceptualizing and theorising delimited, small-scale research questions. As a reaction to the perceived totalising enterprises of so-called Grand Theory (e.g., Marxism, semiotics, psychoanalysis), critics proceeding in piecemeal fashion pursue modest, refined, empirically-based lines of inquiry. Such midrange theories do not encompass all aspects of the cinematic experience, but attempt to account for particular aspects of filmic phenomena. The call for piecemeal theorizing has been articulated most forcefully by proponents of cognitivism and historical poetics.

# 8    The cognitive turn

## Narrative comprehension and character identification

During the 1980s, the cognitive study of film, afforded impetus by a contemporaneous 'Cognitive Revolution' sweeping through varied disciplines, emerged as a distinctive strain of theoretical inquiry within film studies. The prime movers of the cognitive approach to cinema – David Bordwell, Noël Carroll, and Edward Branigan – initially drew upon research from perceptual and cognitive psychology, cognitive philosophy, and narratology in investigating the spectator's comprehension of cinematic texts. Another flurry of cognitive inquiry followed in the 1990s, with film theorists Murray Smith, Torben Grodal, Joseph Anderson, and others illuminating the spectator's mental and emotional processes by appeals to neuroscience, evolutionary psychology, and other humanistic and scientific disciplines.

This research, and the cognitive endeavour more broadly, has served partly as a corrective to certain theoretical notions propounded by Grand Theory – chiefly those concerning identification, illusionism, and subject-positioning. But the cognitive programme has also explored terrain that Grand Theorists have left uncharted. Cognitive theorists have explored the evolutionary importance of facial expressions of emotion (Smith 2003); the ways eye movements in cinematic performance hold and direct interest (Bordwell 2003); why different media elicit different kinds of emotional response (Frome 2006); how films are tailored to an ecologically constrained perceptual system (Anderson and Anderson 2007); the role of reconstructive memory in the viewing of 'puzzle films' (Barratt 2009); and numerous other aspects of spectator cognition. The objects of enquiry are various, and the preceding sample indicates something of the diversity of the cognitive programme.

Just as poeticians reject the notion that neoformalism constitutes a *theory* of cinema, so cognitivists assert that the cognitive approach hardly provides a single theory, much less a Grand Theory, of cinematic phenomena. It is, as one theorist notes, 'by no means a monolithic enterprise' (Smith 2007: 65). Rather, cognitivism is at once a set of assumptions, a perspective, an approach, and a programme of research. Cognitivism does not currently stand as a single, unified theory of cinema partly because its proponents conceive of the phenomena they study differently, and they do not always converge upon mutually held beliefs. More properly, Noël Carroll (1996a: 321) argues, the cognitive endeavour ought to be understood in terms of a 'series of small-scale theories' organized around questions of film communication, rather than a single monolithic theory accounting for all aspects of cinematic experience. Cognitive film theory comprises a cluster of piecemeal inquiries whose contribution to film theory is registered in a variety of ways – by mid-level arguments set forth about individual phenomena; more encompassing theses (e.g. concerning medium-specific properties, or culturally shared spectatorial processes); and the falsifying or qualification of existing theories from psychoanalysis, semiotics, and other reigning theoretical paradigms within film studies.

Cognitive film theorists, then, are unified by a set of shared assumptions. What precisely are the assumptions that glue the cognitivist programme together? Apart from a collective conviction that empirical scientific method can profitably elucidate cinematic experience, several broad assumptions guide the cognitivist's inquiries:

1. *Many of the skills and procedures involved in film viewing are precisely those that we use to function in the everyday world.* Cognitivists assume, as a point of departure, that spectators rely on everyday perceptual and cognitive capacities in comprehending and responding emotionally to the fictional world of the film. Film viewing involves fairly automatic, nonconscious – or ***bottom-up*** – activities, such as perceiving figures in space and reacting to physiological stimuli; it also engages us in cognitively more complex, ***top-down*** operations such as constructing plot events, storing information in memory, and forming empathetic attachments with characters. At both levels of processing, the capacities by means of which we process and react to textual elements are identical to those that orient us within the real-world environment. In postulating this default premise, cognitivism flies in the face of psychoanalytic theories of spectatorship, which divorce film viewing from ordinary perception and cognition. Cognitivists demystify the concept of the spectator as it is conceived in psychoanalysis. The notion of the 'positioned' spectator locked into a passive, trancelike state is disdained, as are standard psychoanalytic metaphors identifying film viewing with dreams and illusions. Far from a regressive, irrational, or passive activity, film viewing in the cognitive programme is conscious, dynamic, and guided by an irreducibly 'rational' drive toward information-gathering and affective experience. As Torben Grodal (1997: 10) observes, film 'is not an illusion . . . on the contrary, *film is part of reality*' (italics in original).

A psychoanalytically inclined theorist might reply that film viewing differs from our everyday activities in quite striking ways. Theatrical film screenings foster a highly controlled environment – the lights are dimmed, the viewer is riveted to a single vantage point, her activity is regulated by cultural customs and routines of behaviour (e.g., we refrain from singing in a screening situation). Nevertheless, cognitivists don't deny that film viewing is a particular, often highly ritualized form of experience, and they mount research questions pertaining to the perception, comprehension, and affective arousal of cinematic texts (e.g. how we perceive three-dimensional objects from a two-dimensional image; how we grasp disturbances, such as flashback sequences, in a linear flow of events; why we respond emotionally to events and characters we know to be fictional). Most basically, films do not call forth some anomalous perceptual and cognitive machinery that is then 'switched off' when we step out of the theatre. Our everyday capacities are all we have to work with, and our responses to cinematic fictions are governed by the same cognitive architecture that guides us through our real-world encounters.

2. *The human mind is not a blank slate, and film spectators are psychologically predisposed to undertake certain textually-encouraged procedures.* Many cognitive film theorists hold that spectators bring to the film event not only highly developed procedures for perceiving and comprehending the environment, but also certain active *predispositions* that crucially shape uptake of narrative action. For instance, Joseph Anderson (1996) argues that spectators engage with fiction films through a kind of voluntary imaginative *play*, whereby the fictional realm is bracketed off, or *framed*, from 'the normal flow of events'; Anderson asserts, moreover, that human beings are fitted out not only with 'the capacity to play, but an active disposition to play' (1996: 116). The spectator is predisposed toward other activities too. Film-makers routinely marshal devices designed to evoke our 'identification' with characters, but Murray Smith (1995) and Torben Grodal (1999) suggest that the viewer's inclination to empathize stems from innate psychological dispositions. Ed Tan (1996) argues that the human mind is naturally predisposed toward the kind of emotionally saturated experiences that are habitually served up by popular cinema. And as 'meaning-seeking creatures' (Anderson 1996: 49), we're prepared *a priori* to undertake perceptual tasks, comprehension procedures, and other information-gathering activities demanded of us by narrative films. In the shadow of psychoanalysis, cognitivists hasten to stress that these kinds of viewer predispositions are rational, goal-oriented, and consciously acted upon.

In the view of ecological cognitivists, the predispositions that shape our viewing habits have probably been hardwired by evolution. Far from a *tabula rasa*, the spectator is pre-programmed by biology to execute certain types of activity. The phenomenon of play, the tendency to empathize, the effort to construct narrative meaning, even the act of film viewing itself – none of these practices is wholly culturally acquired, but rather has evolved biologically through a process of natural selection. Cognitive film theorists such as Anderson and Grodal posit adaptive functions for the activities that characterize film viewing – imagining, empathetic iden-tification, emotional response – all of which, they argue, have evolved in different ways to enhance our fitness in the environment. Once again, a postulate of the cognitive approach runs afoul of psychoanalysis – dif-fering sharply from the cultural relativism of subject-position theory, the evolutionary strain of cognitivism posits that the human mind has been 'formatted by evolution' (Grodal 1997: 278) and cannot wholly be ex-plained in terms of social constructivism.

3. *Audience response in the cinema is not attributable to either the specta-tor or the artwork alone, but arises from the direct interfacing of viewer and text.* Contrary to the notion that texts deterministically 'produce' spe-cific responses in viewers, cognitivism spotlights the purposeful agency of the film spectator. Perceivers form judgements, construct expectations, store information, and engage in a host of other perceptual and cogni-tive tasks – moreover, we have noted, they are biologically pre-wired to do so. Yet, cognitivists argue, spectators' responses are typically *aroused* somehow, and this arousal is provided by various kinds of stimuli situ-ated throughout the text. Neither the film's patterning of stimuli nor the spectator's activity proceeds arbitrarily. Seeking to elicit certain responses (e.g., narrative comprehension, antipathy for an antagonist, a physiolog-ical reaction) and guided by the assumption that spectators of all cultures share basic perceptual and cognitive capacities, film-makers construct the artwork in ways designed to directly tap the spectator's cognitive architec-ture. Film-makers thus adopt the mantle of intuitive psychologists, fine-tuning textual elements so as to facilitate (or in some cases, thwart) the cognitive uptake of the spectator. Spectators, on the other hand, actively seek *cues* or *prompts* within the artwork that authorize those activities to which they are naturally disposed (e.g. imaginative play, acquisition of knowledge, emotional investment, and so forth). Thus, as one theorist notes, 'although the viewer plays an active role, that role is guided by the film' (Tan 1996: 42).

Many of the theories we have examined in this book – structuralism, ap-paratus theory, *Screen* theory – presuppose deterministic structures within the text, but the piecemeal inquiries launched by cognitivists explore a continuum between text and spectator. At one end of the spectrum, re-searchers have examined the textual strategies that film-makers mobilize in order to elicit and direct spectator response – the way a music cue serves as an emotion trigger, for example, or how tactics of plotting wrong-foot the spectator's assumptions about narrative events. Theorists researching

at the other end of the continuum have investigated the spectator's biological potentialities, that is, the biological endowments that may be tapped
and exploited by film-makers for particular effect – our capacities of visual
cognition, the tendency to flinch at sudden loud noises, an ecologically
practical capacity to imagine, and so on. Much cognitive film theory os-
cillates between the twin endpoints on this continuum, indicating how
'audience response lies at the intersections of individual and general spectator characteristics, specific context, and textual cues' (Plantinga 1999:
382).

For the cognitivist, the default assumptions outlined above, and the
piecemeal theories exfoliated from them, are open to empirical confu-
tation. If many theories of film are given to speculative theorizing (e.g.,
positing abstract theories of the structure of the subject or society), cognitivists mount explanations that are empirically verifiable or falsifiable. As
assumptions, the cognitivists' tacit agreements serve as points of departure, not as irrefutable empirical facts. This apparent equivocation ought
not to be taken to signify, on the cognitivist's part, a lack of confidence
in empirical data or inductive reasoning; rather the theorist proceeds cau-
tiously, testing data against 'difficult' cases, and formulating scientifically
plausible and potentially corrigible arguments. In such ways, cognitivists
seek to avoid the perceived totalizations, miscalculations, and obscuri-
ties exemplified by many of the theories we have so far encountered in
this book.

## Narrative comprehension

What is the nature of the spectator's response to cinematic texts? If the
viewer is an active, thinking, perceiving entity, what procedures characterize the act of film viewing? We will concentrate here on narrative comprehension, though it should be emphasized that cognitive film theory
investigates a host of other viewing procedures too – cinematic perception, emotional response, spatio-temporal orientation, and so on. Cognitivists do not share a consensus for how spectators 'cognize' film narratives, but one influential characterisation is set forth by David Bordwell
(1985). Disclaiming the subject-position theory that viewers are passively
'acted upon' by a controlling text, Bordwell advances a constructivist account of spectator activity, arguing that spectators dynamically *construct*
the story by responding to *cues* woven throughout the film. Cues nudge
the spectator to execute various operations. These operations include certain high level mental processes such as *inference making* (i.e., deriving
assumptions from available data), *hypothesis framing* (constructing proba-
bilistic explanations about past events, known as *curiosity hypotheses*, and

predictions about upcoming events, known as *suspense hypotheses*), and *information processing* (e.g. storing or *encoding* salient data in working memory). All these top-down processes function to plug gaps in the film – spectators draw on memories, form inferences, and generate hypotheses to fill in story information that the text skips over or purposefully withholds.

At a broader level, such activities are governed by various types of **schemata**, structured knowledge frameworks with which the spectator comes to the film. Most films cue the viewer to apply both real-world **schemas** (e.g. cultural 'competencies,' learnt knowledge about social routines and behaviours) and schemas derived from other artworks (e.g., knowledge of canonical story structure, prototypical genre tropes, etc.). These broad schemata are activated and refined by the film's cues, and together the schemas and cues shape the spectator's inferences, expectations, and predictions. Moreover, Bordwell reminds us, film viewing is a goal-oriented activity. Not only is the spectator spurred to active participation with and by the text, but, Bordwell argues, she is 'already tuned' for such activity before the film is underway (1985: 34). Cues are *sought* phenomena; unity, coherence, and closure are looked-for attributes; information is readily grasped and finessed by applied schemata. In no sense, then, is the spectator positioned, sutured, or rendered passive. Furthermore, Bordwell's contention accords with the cognitivist premise that spectators are biologically predisposed toward the sorts of mental activity that cinematic narratives routinely exploit.

Bordwell (1985) chiefly theorizes about the cognitions entailed by *fiction* film, but the processes he itemizes govern comprehension of nonfiction films too. To illustrate this, and to demonstrate that the spectator can be mentally energetic even in passages of short screen duration, we might consider a brief moment in Eric Steel's documentary *The Bridge* (2006). Telephoto footage picks out a male figure standing by the side of the Golden Gate Bridge, overlooking the San Francisco Bay. The man empties a bottle of beer, releases the object into the bay, and looks down at the water. Interspersed with this telephoto footage are talking head interviews with friends of a man named David, who had committed suicide by jumping from the Golden Gate Bridge. The witness testimonies partly overlay the caught telephoto footage, acting as a kind of voiceover. Our cognitive processing of the sequence is shaped by contextual data – the film has earlier presented telephoto images of regular pedestrians; it has also furnished telephoto shots capturing suicidal acts at the bridge, a factor that brought some controversy upon the film. (Another source of controversy stems from the film-makers' apparent passivity, observing suicidal agents without intervening in their fatal actions.) *The Bridge* itself documents the suicides occurring at the bridge over a 12-month period.

**Figure 8.1** Ambiguous behavioural cues in *The Bridge*.
*Source*: Easy There Tiger Productions.

Bracketing and overlaying the telephoto footage, the witness testimonies constitute a foreboding cue; that is, they *inflect* the telephoto
images with negative connotations, and stimulate the spectator's activity. Tentatively, a hypothesis coalesces: the figure in the telephoto shot
is 'David', the victim alluded to in voiceover. At least two factors contribute to this hypothesis. First, documentary schemata prime us to expect
voiceovers that bear referential or denotative relation to the images they
accompany. (This assumption is activated when a voiceover invokes the
name 'David,' seeming to denote the onscreen figure poised at the side of
the bridge.) Second, our hypothesis stems from an effort to pick out salient
cues and draw inferences from them. Even tenuous cues are ripe for cognitive uptake. That the man in the telephoto shot swigs beer is of itself
insignificant (Figure 8.1), but the gesture acquires salience in light of an
earlier cue – a commentator's claim that David had been 'self-medicating
with alcohol'. (This claim is intoned seconds before the telephoto footage
appears, and thus is still active in working memory.) These twin factors –
assumption of audio-visual congruence; the effort to construct relations
among cues – trigger the hypothesis that the figure witnessed in telephoto
footage is David. Yet gaps in our knowledge remain; the cues guiding our
hypothesis are compelling, but our assumptions remain corrigible. Because the cues are not wholly equivocal, we probably hold in check an
antithetical, albeit less forceful, hypothesis: namely, that the man on the
bridge is not the person (i.e., David) being lamented by witnesses; and,
moreover, that this man may or may not be about to end his life.

Our inferential activity is set further tasks by the telephoto footage. The man casts the beer bottle over the edge, and observes its long-drawn passage into the water. Thanks to intrinsic norms set up by the film (e.g., figures poised at the edge may jump), and to the schemas and hypotheses it evokes, an otherwise innocuous gesture suddenly seems disturbingly portentous. Immediately we try to ascertain a plausible motivation for the action we have witnessed – the man drops the bottle into the bay, but *why* does he drop it? Any inference here is likely to be arranged on a continuum between a wholly innocuous motivation and one that services a more purposeful goal. Again, foregoing cues guide our expectations. If we hypothesize that the onscreen figure is David, then we are likely to search for behavioural cues that anticipate his act of suicide.

This sequence consumes very few seconds of screen duration, but it marshals our inferential mechanisms into action, pushes us to frame hypotheses, and generates cognitive uncertainty. First, we infer coherence between witness testimony and caught footage – the man on screen is the same individual being discussed by interviewees. Our hypothesis here is guided by schemas of documentary narration, as well as by an effort toward meaning and unity. (As noted, we form and suspend another, more cautious hypothesis too.) Further hypotheses proliferate with the discarded beer bottle. Perhaps the loiterer is simply dispensing of waste, but a more likely inference has him judging the distance from bridge to bay. (That he leans over the bridge to witness the object's trajectory kindles this latter inference.) Why should he want to calculate the distance of the drop? Does he plan to trace his own tragic descent into the water? Perhaps, on the other hand, he is simply a casual bystander. Moreover, if the onscreen figure *is* David, are we about to bear witness to the suicide invoked by the framing testimonies? And if he is not David, who is he? Why does the narration seem to linger on his actions?

Resolution of this cluster of hypotheses is furnished when the figure mounts a bicycle and tapers off into the street. Now our main hypotheses are short-circuited; the tactics on which we hung our assumptions shown to be false cues; and our hypotheses and predictions – is the loiterer the victim described by stricken friends? will he jump into the bay? – demystified. If the scene has aroused dysphoric (i.e., negative) emotions in the viewer, these are likely to be replaced by more positive affective states (e.g., relief that the male figure comes to no harm).

Still, cognitive effort does not wane with the thwarting of our main hypotheses. We must untangle our association of loiterer and suicide victim. Indeed we must disqualify any assumption that the witness testimonies relate referentially to the caught footage (in this instance, at least). Our most provisional assumptions are to be retroactively worked upon – the dropping of the bottle, for instance, ought not to have been construed as ominous. Furthermore, the sequence instils and reinforces a set of tacit expectations in the viewer, elaborating an intrinsic norm, namely, that the narration will salt misleading cues among more reliable ones. Expectations will be exploited, sometimes violated. Suspense hypotheses will be evoked and invalidated. *The Bridge* lays out stark subject matter, but it engages us in an almost ludic narrational stratagem, drawing us into an activity whereby we try to determine the suicidal agent from the regular passer-by. Here is one source of the film's controversy, yet in such ways the film-maker self-consciously provides us a glimpse of his own dilemma – all of a sudden everyone is apt to look sunken, tearful, putatively suicidal; equally, all are apt to appear untroubled, healthy, and robust. Faced with such ambiguous behavioural cues, how could the director and his crew have reliably intervened in the fates of the suicidal victims?

Non-fiction films call upon different kinds of schemata than those cued by fictional works, but both modes of cinema ask the spectator to make inferences, frame and test hypotheses, synthesize incoming data, and map abstract structures onto the work. These activities do not constitute a specifically 'cinematic' or 'aesthetic' mental set, but are routine practices guiding comprehension in our everyday traffic with the world. As in our real-world encounters, cognition of the scene in *The Bridge* is moulded by goals – cognitive effort goes toward unifying ambiguous textual elements into coherent, meaningful relation, dovetailing the scene within the film's wider context. We apply schemata derived from prior knowledge (e.g. we animate some concept of suicide, along with a set of expectations pertaining to documentary narration); we probabilistically rank several top-down hypotheses; and we re-examine data encoded in working memory. All these higher level processes sit on top of a non-conscious visual system that mostly, according to Bordwell (1985), Anderson (1996), Tan (1996) and others, perceives and organizes visual data 'directly', in bottom-up fashion. Notions of viewer passivity hold little water in cognitivist accounts of spectatorship. Even in concentrated bits of action, spectators summon and sharpen a multitude of perceptual and cognitive skills.

## Identification

One major facet of the spectator's activity – identification – remains to be accounted for. What, precisely, does identification in the cinema amount to? What does the spectator identify *with*? How crucial is this phenomenon to narrative comprehension? Theories of identification are a cornerstone of the discipline's major paradigms (see, for instance, Chapter 4 of this volume), but many cognitivists find the language of identification vague and ambiguous. 'Identification', as a term, has been burdened with manifold referential meanings – spectators identify with themselves, with the Other, with the camera, and with the gendered gaze. They succumb to the cinematic apparatus' illusionistic and ideological identifications. And they proceed through the work passively, constrained by the deterministic perspectives of an invisible observer. Not surprisingly, this 'hypodermic' model of identification finds no favour within the cognitivist programme. Its assertions of textual determination butt against the spectator–text *interplay* set forth in cognitive theory; its insistence on the illusory capacities of the medium presuppose an easily duped, submissive spectator; finally, certain premises lack empirical foundation, and seem out of step with actual experience – identification with the camera, for instance, would seem to entail that spectators shuttle between distinct vantage points with an agility quite beyond the bounds of normal human action.

Contemporary cognitive theorists have argued that, insofar as cinematic identification occurs at all, it does so in relation to fictional characters. Still, Noël Carroll (1990) and others suspect the term 'identification' of being baggy, elastic, and loaded with psychoanalytic implications. Theorists have thus directed their efforts toward forming finer-grained characterizations of cinematic identification. Gregory Currie (1997) argues that spectators imagine, or simulate, the mental states of characters, 'trying on' the fictive agent's beliefs and desires. Spectators run these simulated states 'off-line', 'disconnected from their normal sensory inputs and behavioural outputs' (1997: 144–5). Whereas fleeing from a frightful creature would be a normal 'behavioural output', our off-line simulation keeps us riveted when the yawning jaws of an onscreen monster thrust toward us. Currie's theory of off-line simulation accords in important ways with the concept of imaginative 'play' advanced by Anderson (1996). Similarly, Grodal (1997: 226) suggests that spectators 'bracket' identification with characters as a game-like activity. Foregrounding the primacy of *imagination* enables each theorist to register striking alternatives to hypodermic models of identification. If psychoanalytic viewers are seduced into illusory identification, cognitivist viewers purposively enter into imaginative simulation. The imaginative spectator does not mistake the fiction for reality, nor believe herself to *be* the character – the act of identifying with characters is voluntary, rational, and framed mentally as an imaginative activity 'from which we can bale out' (Grodal 1997: 102). Moreover simulation has practical value, since, as evolutionary psychologists would argue, the capacity to imagine has evolved biologically for the purposes of adaptation and survival.

Many cognitivists deplore the notion of 'identification' because it operates as a blanket term covering too diverse a range of practices, but how do cognitivists defend the concept of 'imagination' or '**simulation**' against similar charges? Chiefly by particularizing, or distinguishing between, different kinds of imagining. Elaborating distinctions proffered by Richard Wollheim (1984), Murray Smith (1999a) suggests that the viewing of fiction films involves both *central imagining* (imagining 'from the inside' the experience of a particular character, or *empathizing* with her) and *acentral imagining* (imagining an experience from 'outside' any character's perspective, akin to a *sympathetic* response). Psychoanalytic theory, without adopting this parlance, throws its weight onto central imagining – the positioned spectator grows susceptible to the text's operations by centrally imagining the protagonist's experience. Yet central imagining is only part of the picture. As Carroll (1990) notes, the spectator's thoughts and emotions frequently do not chime with those we attribute to the character. We feel concern for the oblivious swimmer about to become shark bait, but concern is not what the swimmer feels – she feels elated, unaware of the predator advancing toward her (Carroll 1990: 90). Appropriate responses to character-centred fictions involve both central and acentral forms of imagining, Smith argues. The analyst seeks to characterize the spectator's imaginative activity in particular cases, and to examine the means by which the text *cues* particular kinds of imaginative response. Discriminating varieties of imagination allows the cognitivist to posit more nuanced, finessed responses than can be suggested by catch-all terms like 'identification'.

Given the difficulty in wresting the term 'identification' from its psychoanalytic associations, Smith (1995) proposes that theorists substitute 'identification' with the term *engagement* – the better to suggest responses to a range of character types, not merely to those agents with whom we share affinities. Smith posits three levels of character engagement, collectively comprising 'the structure of sympathy'. *Recognition* pertains to the assignment of unique, individuating traits to characters, and to our *re-identification* of agents across a duration; *alignment* refers to the range and depth of access to characters, in terms of their actions (our *spatio-temporal attachment* to them) and their thoughts, beliefs, and feelings (our degree of *subjective access* to a character's internal states); finally, *allegiance* denotes the spectator's evaluation of characters, which serves as the mainspring of emotional response. The three levels of engagement interact, though by distinguishing among them Smith achieves a more precise handle on the factors shaping our engagement than does the relatively fuzzy notion of identification. Smith nuances his model of character engagement with a further set of distinctions. In the process of central imagining, spectators embody both voluntary responses such as *emotional simulation* ('imagining from the inside' the affective states of characters) and involuntary ones, such as *affective mimicry* (non-consciously mimicking character emotions, spurred on by facial and bodily expressions) and *autonomic responses* (as when loud, unexpected noises or sudden movements trigger physiological reflexes).

How does Smith's cognitive model of character engagement improve upon existing theories of cinematic identification? First, the spectator in Smith's account executes a host of imaginative operations, but Smith takes care not to substitute one type of determinism with another – that is, whom we 'identify' or engage with is not wholly prescribed by the phenomenal spectator. Rather, Smith's structure of sympathy describes psychological processes that are fostered – though not wholly determined – by various kinds of narrational structure. Engagement thus springs from two interfacing, dynamic phenomena – the spectator and the film's narration. (Anomalous here are involuntary, autonomic responses such as the startle reflex, which are prompted by sensory triggers within the text.) Second, Smith provides a more textured portrait of character engagement than is achieved by the equivocal notion of identification. Specifying distinct levels of engagement allows Smith to elucidate the text's regulation of spectator responses; it also enables a firm purchase on the wide range of viewing procedures that engagement entails. Furthermore, Smith's model flouts the notion propounded in folk psychology of a singular, unchanging identification – in Smith's account, engagement is a plural phenomenon inasmuch as our responses to a particular character are apt to change over time, and because 'we may engage simultaneously with different characters in different ways within a given sequence in the film' (1995: 93). Like other cognitive theorists of film, Smith seeks to supplant the contested notion of identification with a cluster of naturalistic, finely-specified concepts (such as motor mimicry, emotional simulation, and autonomic reactions).

What textual and psychological factors lead us to form particular evaluations of particular characters? How does allegiance operate in films that encourage identification with wrongdoers? What mechanisms cause our judgement of agents to shift? Smith, along with other cognitive theorists, has probed these questions and proffered explanations, the nature of which will emerge in the following analysis of Tim Burton's *Sweeney Todd: The Demon Barber of Fleet Street* (2007), a film that ruffles the spectator's sympathies in various ways. Our analysis of the film moves between psychological and narrational processes, for as we've noted the mental and affective uptake of films relies on commerce between both phenomena.

## Perverse allegiance and *Sweeney Todd: The Demon Barber of Fleet Street*

A soft-hearted barber, Benjamin Barker (Johnny Depp), is falsely arrested and displaced from his family and London milieu. Escaping from prison 15 years later, Barker – now under the alias of Sweeney Todd – returns to the capital and determines to wreak revenge on Judge Turpin (Alan Rickman), the sadistic magistrate responsible for his imprisonment. The landlady presiding over Todd's old barbershop, Mrs Lovett (Helena Bonham Carter), reveals that Todd's wife Lucy has died and his daughter Johanna (Jayne Wisener) is captive in the decadent Turpin's residence. Along with fellow traveller Anthony (Jamie Campbell Bower), Todd devises a plot to extricate Johanna from the magistrate's clutches; he also plots bloody retribution against Turpin and his oily henchman Beadle Bamford (Timothy Spall). When a business rival, Pirelli (Sacha Baron Cohen), threatens to blackmail Todd, the demon barber executes him, and Mrs Lovett takes in the victim's youthful apprentice, Toby (Ed Sanders).

Gradually, Todd slides deep into moral dissolution, spraying his barbershop walls with the blood of innocent clients. Mrs Lovett bakes the remains of Todd's victims into succulent meat pies, her pie shop thriving thanks to the fulsome appetites of unsuspecting patrons. Her new protégé, Toby, begins to suspect Todd of gruesome misdeeds. Finally Todd sates his craving for Turpin's comeuppance, but there follows a tragic *anagnorisis*. Todd's wife has not met the fate claimed by Mrs Lovett – a revelation that emerges only when Todd spots Lucy among the slain bodies of his own victims. Anguished by Mrs Lovett's deception, Todd sends the devious landlady hurtling into the bakehouse furnace. In a morbidly ironic final act, Toby – spurred to avenge Mrs Lovett's murder and to protect his own well-being – slashes Todd's neck with one of the barber's own razors.

As this synopsis indicates, *Sweeney Todd* generates a complex play with the spectator's allegiance. How does the film guide and constrain the spectator's sympathies? Here, as in any film, the viewer's evaluation of character is founded on the **primacy effect** – the set of first impressions erected by the film, including the judgements formed about a character when she or he is first brought to our notice. These initial judgements tacitly guide our expectations about the character as the drama unfolds, and we constantly cross-reference durable first impressions against developing plot actions. Often the primacy effect turns out to be a fairly reliable barometer of a character's attributes, while character change generally confirms our initial assumptions. About Judge Turpin we form broadly negative first impressions, and the narration simply 'deepens' our initial evaluation as the film progresses. The primacy effect can prepare us for a more ambivalent engagement with characters too. The music-led scene introducing Mrs Lovett summons various devices to elicit our allegiance – Helena Bonham Carter's star persona cues us to expect an eccentric but basically attractive character; song lyrics nakedly solicit our sympathies ('pity a woman alone'); and the bouncy melodic line bathes the character in an affirmative, giddy atmosphere (Figure 8.2). No less crucial to our initial judgement of Mrs Lovett, however, is the scene's somewhat malevolent undertone. Unsettling elements pervade the jaunty action. Song

**Figure 8.2** Sympathetic misfits: the eponymous barber (Johnny Depp) and Mrs Lovett (Helena Bonham Carter) in *Sweeney Todd: The Demon Barber of Fleet Street*.
*Source*: Courtesy British Film Institute. Dreamworks/Warner Bros.

lyrics repeatedly evoke imagery of dead animals. Skittering cockroaches get flattened by bakehouse utensils. The disquieting aspects to Mrs Lovett's character offset the narration's overt appeals to our sympathy with her. In such ways, the primacy effect hints at the ambivalent allegiance that will characterize our engagement with Mrs Lovett across the film as a whole.

The primacy effect, and the ongoing evaluation of character, are significantly shaped by the star system. Many films yoke the primacy effect to the specific attributes embodied by the star player, creating swift and schematic character delineation – once first impressions have been set up, they are reinforced, dismantled, or subverted by the film in different ways. Our schemata for particular star personas help to orient us to *Sweeney Todd*'s bizarre, antiheroic protagonists. Both Helena Bonham Carter and Johnny Depp delivered sympathetic portraits of freaks and misfits in earlier films (indeed, this is Depp's stock-in-trade – think of his protagonists in *Edward Scissorhands* (1990), *Ed Wood* (1994), *Charlie and the Chocolate Factory* (2005), and the *Pirates of the Caribbean* series (2003, 2007).) Prior knowledge of the stars' personas not only prepares us for the idiosyncratic traits we discover in Todd and Mrs Lovett; it also discourages us from regarding these traits as purposive deterrents from sympathetic engagement. Other knowledge frameworks elucidate the primacy effect too – for instance, generic schemata activate gothic or horror expectations (we may expect our protagonist to behave ominously); and familiarity with Tim Burton's previous films like *Beetlejuice* (1988), *Batman* (1989), and *Mars Attacks!* (1996) cues us to anticipate a narrative populace illuminated by outlandish freaks and outsiders.

Once the viewer has been supplied initial story information, she continues to construct character by following narrational cues, such as the primacy effect, recognition, and the narration's patterns of alignment and allegiance. Character development may serve to reinforce and 'deepen' our initial moral evaluation of a character – for instance, we evaluate Beadle negatively at the outset, and we are given no cause to revise our judgement as the plot progresses. (Indeed, our initial judgement gets forcefully reaffirmed by ensuing story action.) Alternatively, a film's narration may press-gang us into reshuffling our allegiances quite radically. Most generally, films shape our judgements of characters in more or less drastic ways. Our allegiance with Todd and Mrs Lovett wavers throughout the film, while our antipathy toward Turpin and Beadle remains relatively constant.

We might assume that our allegiance is correlated to the changing traits of the character as she or he progresses through the narrative. For instance, our affirmative moral evaluation of Terry Malloy (Marlon Brando) in *On the Waterfront* (1954) is homologous with the ex-boxer's gradual embodiment of morally admirable values across the duration of the film. Often, however, what looks like character change is actually a flexing of the narration's powers of communicativeness. Our moment-to-moment evaluation of Mrs Lovett depends not so much on the character's changing moral traits as on the way the narration controls our knowledge of character information. Apparent shifts in Mrs Lovett's moral valence suggest an arc of character change, traced across the whole film. Initially she embodies a host of affirmative traits, chiefly affection and compassion, e.g., her maternal stance toward Toby, her apparent sympathy for Todd's withered wife (articulated in the song 'Poor Thing'), and so forth. By the end of the film, personality traits of a far less desirable sort are brought to the fore.

Our moral evaluation of Mrs Lovett has changed, but crucially it has not changed in response to shifts in character psychology or morality. Rather, Mrs Lovett's personality traits remain fundamentally consistent, while our moral evaluation of her is transmogrified by the revelation of information previously withheld from us by the narration – namely, the deception spun by Mrs Lovett around the 'death' of Todd's displaced wife. Moreover, though our moral judgement has been transformed, our overall

*engagement* with Mrs Lovett is apt to remain relatively unaffected. The revelation of her deception forcefully challenges our moral assumptions, but
it is unlikely to short-circuit the fund of goodwill that we have generated
toward the character throughout the foregoing action. (We don't assume,
for instance, that her affection for Todd was ever disingenuous.) Just as a
certain equivocation defines our first impressions of Mrs Lovett, so does
an ambivalent (or 'partial') allegiance characterize our engagement with
her at the point of narrative closure.

For Smith, allegiance depends not only upon evaluating the characters
in moral terms, but also upon hierarchizing these judgements and characters according to a system of preference. Allegiance, writes Smith, 'rests
upon an evaluation of the character as representing a desirable (or at least,
preferable) set of traits, when compared with other characters within the
fiction' (1995: 62). Thus the protagonist of Fritz Lang's *M* (1931) acts in
violation of moral propriety, but comes to be regarded sympathetically
*relative to* certain other agents in the text (e.g. the lynch mob that perse-
cutes him in the final reels). A film establishes an internal system of values
whereby, Smith argues,

> [our] real-world attitudes are organised by the ongoing placement
> of characters into positions of relative desirability. On the basis of
> this process, we form preferential and hierarchized sympathies
> and antipathies towards the various characters.
>
> (1995: 194)

Morally straightforward films generate a *Manichaean* moral structure,
which pits moral agents against immoral or amoral ones. Such Manichaean structures are mobilized in films like *Star Wars* (1977), *Speed* (1994)
and *Fargo* (1996), in which the characters' values are plainly delineated,
and the viewer's moral hierarchization of the agents occurs as relatively
unqualified and automatic. Our emotional responses to such fictions and
characters are likely to be comprised of 'basic' emotional states, such as
fear, sadness, and joy. A major alternative to the Manichaean framework
is the *graduated* moral structure, characterized by Smith as manifesting
'a spectrum of moral gradations rather than a binary opposition of values' (1995: 207). Smith posits films such as Otto Preminger's *Daisy Kenyon*
(1947) and Orson Welles' *The Magnificent Ambersons* (1942) as exemplary
cases. In the graduated structure, characters do not epitomize unalloyed
moral values, but rather exhibit a finer-grained cluster of traits. The task
of hierarchizing them according to a system of preference is thus more
complex than in the Manichaean model, while the characters' amalgam
of diverse moral traits may arouse responses anchored in the 'higher' emotions (i.e. ambivalent, complex, or compound emotion states).

*Sweeney Todd* complicates the evaluation of character, but it neverthe-less arrays its agents on a graduated hierarchy of moral values. Though his actions violate moral propriety, Todd manifests a relative desirability when compared with the still more degenerate Judge Turpin. Moreover, the film's initial flashback (depicting Todd's false arrest at the hands of the magistrate) sets up a moral opposition between Todd and Turpin which prevails in working memory even after Todd switches from victim to vic-timiser – thus the power of the primacy effect. The flashback, and its precise placement near the beginning of the film, are integral to eliciting what Carl Plantinga calls 'spectator vengeance', an emotionally saturated desire to see come-uppance meted to an irredeemable wrongdoer (1999: 387). Guided by the primacy effect and the narration's maintenance of character – e.g., its refusal to supply data that might ameliorate our judge-ment of Turpin – the viewer comes to see Todd's acts of vengeance not only as a justified trope, but as a desirable one as well.

Yet the viewer also recognizes that Todd's acts of violence far outstrip his desire for revenge. An internal moral structure posits Todd's violence toward Turpin as valid, but the film disturbs our approbation of Todd's activity when he sets about slaughtering innocents without justification. Evaluating these latter actions as morally unjust entails that the spectator activates real-world schemas for revenge and justice – these schemas, along with other cognitive predispositions (e.g. moral values) and the text's ac-tivation of horror schemata, shape our ability to discriminate morally per-verse violence from 'desirable', justified retribution. Now the viewer an-ticipates a morally apt punishment to follow from Todd's unjust actions. To this extent, a film's system of value not only directs our sympathies and antipathies toward particular characters, but cues us to hypothesize upcoming story action as well. Moral structures trigger cognitive activity by pressing us to execute moral judgements, and by guiding our inclina-tions about how plot events should properly be resolved. In such ways, internal moral systems work to arouse and satisfy a desire for cognitive clo-sure, the pursuit of which motivates the spectator's moment-to-moment engagement with the drama.

The climax of *Sweeney Todd* confirms the morally skewed nature of the diegetic milieu, but it supplies, in Noël Carroll's (1990) phrase, a 'morally correct outcome' insofar as the wrongdoers (including Todd and Mrs Lovett) are punished. (The exception is the virtuous and suffering Lucy, who is afforded no mercy by story events – her death serves princi-pally to intensify the tragic flavour of the story.) Though we form a partial allegiance with Mrs Lovett, the landlady's death seems apposite in the context of the film's moral system. Moreover, the revelation of her be-trayal at the climax is likely to deepen our sympathy with Todd, who is once again unjustly wronged.

The explicit (albeit theatrical) nature of Todd's bloodletting puts our allegiance with the protagonist under further strain. Torben Grodal notes that scenes of repellent violence are apt to elicit 'a kind of schizoid numbness, an emotional dissociation from the narrative experiences'. Spectators seek to temper dysphoric emotions by distancing 'themselves from a full empathic identification with even the most positive characters' (Grodal 1999: 143) – a more or less bottom-up reflex in which spectator perception and emotion are wedged apart. Identification with the fictive agent thus becomes 'purely perceptual' (Grodal 1997: 158), divorced from emotional involvement. If an affective distance is so accomplished, the spectator's negative evaluation of Todd may be registered less forcefully than if emotional engagement occurs as 'symbiotic' and unmediated. At any rate Todd's unjustified violence, for all its visceral arousal, is not adequate to foil the spectator's allegiance, though this allegiance is notably *qualified* by Todd's perverse acts. In all, a number of pre-established factors ensure that sympathy for Todd remains intact (e.g. the primacy effect, star charisma, mapped schemata, the hierarchy of moral values, and so on).

If we are encouraged to sympathize with morally degenerate characters, isn't there a danger that the apparently innocuous activity of imagining will produce harmful, morally contaminating effects? Gregory Currie (1997: 162) cautions that beliefs and desires simulated by the spectator off-line may inadvertently be brought online, due to a glitch in the viewer's 'inhibiting mechanism' – that is, the default brain activity that brackets off imaginative 'play' from 'normal' activities and responses. Currie states:

> [B]y imagining ourselves in the situation of a character with destructive, immoral desires, and thereby coming to have, in imagination, the desires of the character...we may be in danger of really acquiring those desires through failure of the inhibitory mechanism.
>
> (1997: 163)

Similarly, Stephen Prince (1998: 114) floats the prospect that justified violence in movies stirs up genuinely aggressive propensities within the spectator. Thus, in *Sweeney Todd*, our simulated 'trying on' of Todd's retaliatory cognitions may bleed into *actual* beliefs and desires, and potentially degrade our moral valence in the everyday world. If we do adopt Todd's immoral desires, and moreover if we remain sympathetically disposed to him, then our engagement in this instance may be characterized as *perverse allegiance* – Murray Smith's term for sympathetic responses to characters on the basis of their immoral traits and actions (Smith 1999b). For Currie, this kind of dubious engagement carries with it a risk of 'moral damage', since our simulation of immoral mental states may transmogrify the moral schemata we apply to real-world situations.

Smith (1999b) argues that perverse allegiance is in fact a strikingly rare species of spectator engagement. A genuinely perverse allegiance entails that spectators sympathize with morally undesirable traits and actions. But often what looks like perverse allegiance in popular cinema is only *apparently* so – sympathy for the character obtains *in spite of* that agent's perversity, not because of it. Engaging with Sweeney Todd's vengeful desires amounts to an 'imaginative slumming' by the spectator: we simulate malignant desires (e.g. meting out revenge to Judge Turpin) while reassuring ourselves that the agent we 'identify' with is – at heart – morally worthy.

Moreover, moral degradation may be foreclosed by the mechanism of 'schizoid numbness'. If Todd's heinous acts prompt the viewer to disengage from empathetic identification with the protagonist (i.e., to effect schizoid numbness), then the spectator does not simulate Todd's illicit desires – and since the spectator does not simulate immoral desires, there can be no danger that she *acquires* those desires through simulation. Schizoid numbness thus renders unlikely both moral damage by simulation, and allegiance of a genuinely perverse sort.

The viewer of *Sweeney Todd* also applies a schema for 'justified revenge' that helps her execute the appropriate moral judgments (a schema, moreover, that the film-makers trust will be activated). In concert with textual cues such as the primacy effect, this schema cues the spectator to regard Judge Turpin's come-uppance as a sanctionable, even desirable trope. Crucially, moreover, the schema calls attention to any actions that *transgress* the parameters of justified vengeance, such as Todd's wanton slaughter of unfortunate clients. Once again, a genuinely perverse allegiance is discouraged. Todd's moral perversity, exceeding the spectator's schema for justified vengeance, does not draw our moral approbation, hence does not elicit our allegiance. Our disapprobation of Todd's perversity, cued by schemata and the film's moral structure, leads us to regard Todd's grisly demise as the morally correct outcome – even though our overall engagement with the protagonist remains a sympathetic one. (The spectator's schema for narrative closure – particularly prototypes of 'poetic' resolution and dramatic symmetry – is also likely a factor here.)

For all the suspicion of moral degradation, some cognitivists have stressed the positive moral development that empathetic identification may engender. Simulating the cognitive and emotion states of characters provides, they suggest, a form of 'moral' and 'emotional learning' (Gaut 1999: 213; Smith 1999b: 228; Neill 1996: 180), an expansion and ripening of the spectator's moral schemata. As Noël Carroll proposes, narrative artworks *exercise* 'our pre-existing moral powers [...and thus] the texts may become opportunities for enhancing our already existing moral understanding' (Carroll 1996b: 237n4). In other words, the activity of character engagement may be endowed with educative value, sharpening and expanding the spectator's moral and emotional repertoire, priming her for use of these capacities in real-world situations.

This is not to deny that debasement of moral values through empathetic engagement might occur. Nor is it to repudiate the notion of a genuinely perverse allegiance. (Smith argues that truly perverse allegiances do occur in film viewing, if infrequently.) It is only to suggest that, typically, spectators are guided – by a combination of strategic cues and activated schemata – toward morally sound identifications. Still, sympathetic reflexes may be triggered in unforeseen ways. Bordwell (2007) suggests that an unsympathetic character shown emoting – displaying, for instance, facial symptoms of sadness or fear – is apt to invoke *emotional contagion* in the spectator, an involuntary affective response whereby viewers 'catch' the emotion state etched on the character's face. As a byproduct of legible, emotive facial expression, 'a wisp of empathy' may be felt for the unsympathetic agent, despite a more global condemnation of the figure. Such bottom-up responses of sympathy may be unanticipated and perhaps unsought by the film-maker, while the spectator's brain continues to function in more or less autonomic or deliberative ways in response to stimuli. This interactivity between text and viewer – so central to the cognitive study of how films work upon us – gives 'filmmakers enormous power, along with enormous responsibilities' (Bordwell, 2007).

# Glossary

**Bottom-up processing**: The term given to data-driven perception. Bottom-up processing occurs as a fast, mandatory response to stimuli. Such automatic processing, operating in tandem with **top-down processes**, is vulnerable to errors of perception, but possesses positive evolutionary value (e.g., an instantaneous appraisal of an unexpected noise or moving object can trigger motor responses that, in turn, rescue us from an oncoming threat).

**Primacy effect**: An aspect of narrative structure and comprehension pertaining to the forceful first impressions established by a film. The primacy effect is crucial in providing viewers with an initial orientation to the text, cuing expectations about upcoming action. Films exploit the primacy effect in various ways, undercutting, modifying, or extending the viewer's initial cluster of assumptions. The concept occupies poeticians and cognitivists in particular, since it guides and constrains the spectator's activity and mobilizes basic cognitive procedures.

**Schema**; **schemas/schemata** (pl.): A knowledge cluster, comprising of a bounded set of beliefs, assumptions, expectations, and other *a priori* associations that the viewer brings to an artwork. Central to cognitivist accounts of spectator activity, a schema orients the viewer to the moment-by-moment unfolding of the film. Viewers make sense of a text by applying real-world schemas (knowledge sets pertaining to everyday experience) and intertextual schemas (knowledge of other artworks, including generic conventions, narrative topoi, stylistic norms, and so on).

**Simulation**: A term employed within cognitivism to describe the spectator's capacity to imagine the experience of a fictional character. Cognitivists have employed the term in slightly different senses, but the broad assumption holds that spectators imagine, or simulate, the mental states of the narrative agent, nevertheless remaining cognizant of the fictional status of the film event. Set against the notion of psychoanalytic 'identification', simulation is conceived by cognitivists as a voluntary, active, and conscious activity that is, moreover, a basic part of our biological inheritance.

**Top-down processing**: The term given to cognitively mediated, deliberative responses. If **bottom-up processing** operates in quick, involuntary fashion, top-down processes are organized by the perceiver's prior knowledge and **schemas**. Such higher-level cognitions include hypothesis-forming and inference-making, activating the expectations and memory functions of the perceiver.

# 9   Recent developments

## Phenomenology, attractions and audiences

Despite reports of its death, film theory is alive and well today, even if it does not carry with it the bravado and solemnity of 'Theory' (with a capital 'T') that so energized the field during the 1970s and 1980s. Theories of film are flourishing and many new titles influenced by continental philosophy (for recent contributions see Beller 2006; Frampton 2006; Harbord 2007; McGowan 2007; Rodowick 2007; Stadler 2008), as well as cognitivism and analytic philosophy (for example, see Branigan 2006; Grodal 2009; Plantinga 2009), are continuing to appear. We cannot hope to chart each of these new contributions to the field here, but, alongside developments in cognitive theory and historical poetics, we do feel there are three theoretical areas of investigation that have flourished since the late 1980s. Each of these new areas of film theory has proven its longevity so that the future of these areas does not seem to us to be in doubt. The fields are *phenomenology and film*, the *cinema of attractions*, and *audience research*.

## Phenomenology and film

(Vivian Sobchack, *The Address of the Eye* [Sobchack 1992].)

Two works appeared in the early 1990s which aimed to turn film theory back to the 'things themselves' in accordance with Edmund Husserl's claim that phenomenology was a science which advocated a 'return to things themselves'. The books were Vivian Sobchack's *The Address of the Eye* (Sobchack 1992), which has had an enduring impact on film studies in the years following its publication, and Allan Casebier's *Phenomenology and Film* (Casebier 1991), which sadly has had very little impact at all. Casebier's book grounds its approach firmly in Husserlian phenomenology and supports a realist argument in which film has the capacity to show to us 'things themselves'. The guiding trope of the book is that cinema has the ability to reveal the real world to us. One of Casebier's closing claims is that 'the cinematic medium may be recognized as having a most valuable capacity to guide spectator perception to the things themselves' (1991: 157–8). It is perhaps understandable that, when the world of cinema was just about to embark on the journey towards its digital future – the break-through films of *Terminator 2* (1992) and *Jurassic Park* (1993) – Casebier's reiteration of a realist theory of film fell on deaf ears. With digital cinema, many argue, there simply are no longer any 'things themselves'. Rather, there are merely combinations of digital data, so any claim for a return to 'things themselves' might already have appeared outdated shortly after it appeared.

A more forceful intervention was made by Sobchack. Instead of Husserl, her phenomenologist of choice was the French post-war philosopher, Maurice Merleau-Ponty, author of works such as the *Phenomenology of Perception* (Merleau-Ponty 1962). There are two guiding threads in Sobchack's *Address of the Eye*. First, there are arguments against structuralism, semiotics and psychoanalysis. Each of these domains of thought, Sobchack argues, grounds experience in symbolic significations, so that, for film scholars who use such methods, all experience is reducible to codes, symbols and systems of signification (see our discussions of *Young Mr. Lincoln* and *The Birds* from Chapter 1). Sobchack claims that such analyses miss an important dimension of experience: that which *precedes* acculturation and signification. Much of *Address of the Eye* is therefore devoted to charting elements of the cinematic experience which are not entirely determined by symbolic, cultural, signifying processes.

Second – though it is a point derived from the first – in *Address of the Eye*, Sobchack emphasizes the importance of the spectator's experience of his or her own body during the screening of a film. Film theory, she argues, has reduced film spectatorship to being a process undertaken by disembodied eyes (and, to a lesser extent, ears). Against such claims, Sobchack is determined to give spectators their bodies back. It is not too difficult to see how this second point relates closely to the first: the bodily zones of spectator engagement are ones which are freed from the restrictions of symbolic determination; or, at the very least, Sobchack wishes to focus on what she considers the *primary* experiences of embodied engagement as opposed to the *secondary* experiences of coded and signified things. As she puts it at one point, 'The "thought" of Self is a secondary and reflexive reflection of [an] original subjectivity' (1992: 117). A thought self is an encoded and symbolic one, while an embodied self is freed from the layers of acculturation that language and other symbolic structures impose upon subjectivity. What Sobchack's phenomenology of film tries to recover are the experiences of that primary self which are normally covered over and hidden by the symbolic encrustations of existence.

These arguments quite radically reconfigure some of the arguments of contemporary film theory as we have seen them elucidated throughout this book. Where film theory has most of the time dedicated its analyses to pointing to the symbolic layers which pertain to the cinema apparatus and to individual films, Sobchack finds something worthwhile in following a completely opposite strategy. In other words, she tries to figure out what happens to the spectator and to the film *beneath the coded layers* which film theorists have always been keen to point to. Sobchack does not at all deny that the codified layers of meaning are there and that they are important for the cinematic experience. But her book aims (and some subsequent writings; see Sobchack 2004) to chart a something else – a phenomenological realm – that underlies the symbolic structures of filmgoing. Film theory had to that date overlooked these aspects of the cinema experience.

Sobchack's more controversial claim is that, in conjunction with the body of the spectator, films themselves might be said to have bodies. At first sight this seems an outrageous claim, but what Sobchack wishes to point out is that cinemagoing is an *intersubjective* experience. Going to the cinema is a process in which a spectator engages in modes of communicative exchange with a film. From such a perspective, Sobchack considers that films themselves have thoughts and feelings. This does not necessarily mean that films are sentient beings. Rather, it is a claim that *we* have to posit thoughts and feelings *in* films in order for them to be meaningful and for their experiences to be ones with which we engage. Sobchack writes:

> The direct engagement, then, between spectator and film in the film experience cannot be considered a monologic one between a viewing subject and a viewed object. Rather, it is a dialectical engagement of *two* viewing subjects who also exist as visible objects . . . Both film and spectator are capable of viewing and of being viewed, both are embodied in the world as the subject of vision and object for vision.
>
> (1992: 23)

This might sound a little bit crazy: the film *sees me* when I watch it! But Sobchack's logic is rigorous: in order, as spectators, that we posit the film's world, narrative, characters and so on as existing in meaningful ways, we must acknowledge that the film *addresses* us as viewers who are looking at the world it displays for us. Another way of conceiving of this is to discern that any film *includes us* in its world as that film unfolds. To this extent we can say the film 'sees' us. As Sobchack claims, in a manner befitting a phenomenologist: 'Watching a film is both a direct and mediated experience of direct experience as mediation' (1992: 10). What can this mean?

Sobchack argues that the film experience is a combination of direct and mediated sensations. If what we see and hear in a film is a process of direct sensations conveyed to our senses, then these direct sensations are also given shape only within the overall meaning-structure of the film as a whole. In other words, the sense-perceptions we receive from a film – say, two characters kissing each other – might cause physical sensations in our bodily perceptions, but that kiss can only be fully experienced if put in the context of the film's mediating processes. The *direct* phenomenological experience is vitally important, but part of that experience involves the mediations of a film's narrative forms and situational motivations – for example, that these characters are kissing after having been separated for a number of weeks by unforeseen circumstances. The processes of direct experience and mediated experience combine in order to provide a fuller account of the filmic experience.

Furthermore, for Sobchack, the *film itself* will also have direct and mediated experiences. What is inscribed on celluloid is the material matter of images – those things that are portrayed on film are, for all intents and purposes, *the film's own direct experiences*. If the film presents a tree on screen, then we can say that *that* image shows us the film's direct experience of a tree. The tree will, of course, be situated within a filmic 'world' which the film itself constructs – for example, this tree might be the tree where two lovers have arranged to meet. Therefore, much as the spectator's relation to a film is composed of both direct and mediated experiences, so too is the film itself a composite of both direct and mediated instances.

This complex phenomenology of the film experience enables Sobchack to tackle *Screen* and apparatus theories head-on. She argues that the dominant modes of contemporary film theory are all deeply suspicious of the cinema and that many theories of the cinema tend to focus on its deceptive qualities. Those of you who have read the earlier chapters of this book might judge the degree to which Sobchack's argument is correct. We believe it to be partly correct, for both *Screen* theory and apparatus theory claim that some forms of film-making foster illusions (mainstream and Hollywood films are the typical culprits), while other forms (usually avant-garde or politically committed cinemas) break those illusions. (As for the position of Metz, we believe his position to be somewhat more complicated.) However, the main point which shines through in Sobchack's arguments is that her book is not intended as a guide for judging which films are good or bad, and in doing so she effectively argues against some of the main trends of 1970s and 1980s film theory. Her project in *Address of the Eye* is to chart the ways in which the dialectic between screen and spectator sets into play a communicative exchange. In charting many of those ways, her book makes an invaluable contribution to film theory.

# The cinema of attractions

(Tom Gunning, 'The Cinema of Attractions: Early Film, its Spectator, and the Avant-Garde' [Gunning 1990].)

If *Screen* theory had sought to theorize forms of cinema which opposed the norms of mainstream Hollywood film, then the theorization of the 'cinema of attractions' has similarly attempted to discover alternative ways of conceiving of cinema. Strictly speaking, unlike the avant-garde cinemas advocated by *Screen* theory, the 'cinema of attractions' was not an *oppositional* cinema. Rather than discovering alternatives to Hollywood in the avant-garde or overtly politicized modes of film-making, theorists of the cinema of attractions have found alternative practices in examples from the earliest years of cinematic production, that is, roughly the period beginning in 1894–95 with the birth of cinema, and lasting up until about 1906–07. Theorists have discovered many films of this period in which there is a conception of cinema almost entirely antithetical to the feature length narrative films which came to dominate most conceptions of cinema after the 1910s. As we saw in Chapter 2 on Metz, what became generally understood by the term 'cinema' was a feature-length narrative film in which spectators were encouraged to become swept up in a story universe. Early cinema, however, was based on entirely different desires and expectations. Instead of producing story films where the need to follow a story was paramount, and rather than portraying characters with whom audiences would sympathize and become emotionally involved, the films of the cinema of attractions were typically not centred on stories or on deep, well-constructed or 'rounded' characters. Instead, this was a cinema of tricks, games, gags and chases. The early years of cinema were comprised of films which provided shocks, thrills and spectacles for their audiences rather than complex plots and emotionally-driven characters.

In a number of articles published throughout the 1980s and 1990s, Tom Gunning – along with some other authors (the precursor was Burch [1973, 1990]; but there have been invaluable contributions from André Gaudreault [1990] and Charles Musser [1990, 1991]) – tried to account for what early cinema *was* rather than simply specifying what it *wasn't*. In other words, if early cinema was *not* driven by storytelling or characters, then what *was* it shaped by? For Gunning, the key term was *attractions*. He made a link between the notion of 'attractions', which had been theorized by the Soviet film-maker, Sergei Eisenstein, during the 1920s (Eisenstein 1988a, 1988b), and some of the formal qualities of early films. Eisenstein defined attractions as any element of a film (or theatre, for Eisenstein originally came up with the term 'attractions' when working in the theatre) which impacted upon the spectator, either sensually (as with Eisenstein's celebrated 'kino-fist') or psychologically (see Gunning 1990: 59). A type of cinema which aggressively shocks or jolts the spectator is, according to the terms of these arguments, a form of film-making imbued with aims entirely different from those of voyeurism, absorption or narrative involvement which are central to the mainstream feature film.

First published in 1986, Gunning's article on 'The cinema of attractions' (Gunning 1990) set in place many of the arguments that would be fleshed out by him in future years. The main tenets of the cinema of attractions are clearly described there:

- it is a cinema of showing and exhibition;
- it is a cinema that eschews the drive for narrative; and
- it is a type of cinematic exhibition where the spectator is conceived in a markedly different way from the kinds of spectators expected of feature films.

In clarifying these points, Gunning makes an example of the commonly conceived distinction between the films of the Lumière brothers and those of Georges Méliès. Where the former are often thought of as precursors of the realist, narrative tradition and the latter associated with fantastical, magical films, Gunning sees much more of a similarity than a difference. He writes that 'one can unite [the Lumières and Méliès] in a conception of cinema that sees cinema less as a way of telling stories than as a way of presenting a series of views to an audience, fascinating because of their illusory power' (1990: 57). The point to make here is that the films of the Lumières and Méliès should not be judged by virtue of the kinds of narrative films that eventually came to dominate cinema. Instead, the entire conception of their mode of film-making was of an entirely different nature to the kinds of cinema we are used to today. Perhaps more than anything else, the kind of relationship between screen and spectator was radically different.

One particular characteristic of early cinema highlighted by Gunning is the fact that, in many early films, actors look directly at the camera. In doing so, they acknowledge they are being watched by an audience. Therefore, such actors are not withdrawing into a world of make-believe but are instead openly recognizing that they are part of a cinematic display, as though they are declaring to us, as we watch them, 'Hey, you there! Look at me!' Gunning asserts:

> It is the direct address of the audience, in which an attraction is offered to the spectator by a cinema showman, that defines this approach to film making. Theatrical display dominates over narrative absorption, emphasizing the direct stimulation of shock

or surprise at the expense of unfolding a story or creating a diegetic universe.

(1990: 59)

At this point in history too, right at the end of the nineteenth century, cinema itself was a novelty. Nowadays, we are probably jaded by the media that have saturated our existences since birth, but for those living at the end of the nineteenth century, no such thing as a cinematic moving image had existed before. It is somewhat impossible today to imagine just how astonishing it must have been to have seen early cinematic projections – a stunning shock to perception. Cinema itself was therefore an attraction, argues Gunning: people wanted to see what the cinema's tricks were; they wanted to see what cinema could do. He argues that one of the primary aims of early films was to display and exploit the tricks of the cinema. Many films, therefore, were specifically geared towards exploring the possibilities of the medium. 'Many trick films', he suggests, 'are, in effect, plotless, a series of transformations strung together with little connection and certainly no characterization' (1990: 58). As a specific example of this kind of 'plotless' cinema, Gunning mentions Meliès's *Voyage to the Moon* (1902): 'The story simply provides a frame upon which to string a demonstration of the magical possibilities of cinema' (1990: 58). The demonstration of the magical possibilities of cinema was central to the cinema of attractions.

The cinema of attractions lasted barely a decade. Gunning argues – most convincingly in a study of D.W. Griffith's short films (see Gunning 1991) – that narrative forms of cinema began to dominate after about 1907. By around 1916 (as is argued by Bordwell, Staiger and Thompson in their magisterial study of the classical Hollywood cinema [Bordwell, Staiger and Thompson 1985]), most of the techniques and methods that would come to dominate what we now call 'cinema' were in place. The period between these two dates is generally regarded as a period of 'transition' (see Keil and Stamp 2004). What this concentration on dates and different modes of cinema highlights is the way that research into the cinema of attractions was motivated as much by an appreciation of the *historical* aspects of cinematic experience as it was by anything *theoretical*. Gunning certainly foregrounded the theoretical aspects of the notion of the cinema of attractions, but less theoretically-inclined historians have found a great deal to be gained from historical research into the earliest periods of cinema (Abel 1999, 2006; and Grieveson 2004).

The notion of the cinema of attractions therefore calls attention to an important *turn to history* in film studies which has replaced many of the regions of the discipline formerly occupied by film *theory*. Gunning points to the importance of a historical approach to theories of cinema in his 'cinema of attractions' article when he claims that 'Every change in film history implies a change in its address to the spectator, and each period constructs its spectator in a new way' (1990: 61). This claim seems to be a direct evocation of a theorist who has inspired much of the historical turn in film theory, Walter Benjamin. Benjamin was one of the great soothsayers of film theory in the first half of the twentieth century and is responsible for making the somewhat contentious claim that 'Just as the entire mode of existence of human collectives changes over long historical periods, so too does their mode of perception' (Benjamin 2003: 255). Claims like this underpin many of the arguments central to the cinema of attractions. Those arguments are based on the notion that both *cultural* and *perceptual* expectations can be radically different in one historical period when compared with another. Quite simply, in early cinema, people *saw films differently* from the ways in which people typically see films nowadays.

In one of Gunning's other breakthrough articles, 'An Aesthetic of Astonishment' (Gunning 1989), observations on early cinema are guided by a discussion of the audience responses to the very first cinema screenings. Gunning argues that a kind of folklore grew up in relation to those first screenings, a folklore which posited early cinema spectators as naive and childlike. The fabled responses to the Lumière's *Arrival of a Train at the Station* (1896) were especially hyperbolic. It was believed that viewers fled screaming in terror as the train approached the station, apparently fearful that the train was going to burst through the cinema screen and crush them all to death (Figure 9.1). And yet, Gunning was unable to discover any contemporary accounts of those screenings which could support such suppositions. Why, he therefore asks, have many historians considered that the cinema's first spectators did react in such a way? And if they did not respond in that fashion, how did they react?

Gunning argues that many historians have imposed upon early cinema audiences a set of beliefs which simply did not pertain to early cinema. Rather, these historians have taken the suppositions of classical narrative filmgoing and imposed those conditions on the spectators of early cinema. If at the cinema today – and the theories of Christian Metz are a good guide here – audiences are supposed to willingly suspend disbelief (or 'double up their belief', as Metz argues) in order to partake of the cinematic illusion, then historians have merely projected the same beliefs onto the cinema's earliest spectators. If *we* today suspend disbelief while watching films, then *they* must also have suspended their disbelief back then. To therefore *believe* in the cinematic mechanism was to also believe both in its reality and the reality of the objects it filmed, like the train that might be hurtling towards one during a screening. Gunning's argument is vehemently opposed to such accounts – he is convinced that spectators

**Figure 9.1**  From the Lumière Brothers' *L' Arrivée d'un train à La Ciotat.*
Lumière.
*Source*: Courtesy British Film Institute.

at the earliest screenings did not engage in a willing suspension of disbelief, for the cinema was not yet an 'imaginary signifier' in the sense Metz
gives to that term. Gunning's theorization of the cinema of attractions is
therefore a full-blown critique of Apparatus theory:

> The terrorized spectator of the Grand Cafe [location of one of
> the first cinema screenings] still stalks the imagination of film
> theorists who envision audiences submitting passively to an all-
> dominating apparatus, hypnotized and transfixed by its illusionist
> power.
>
> (Gunning 1989: 32)

In place of Metz's fetishistic spectator – 'I know very well (*it's not
real*)...but all the same (*I shall believe that it is real*)' – Gunning places
his own equation: 'I know, but yet I see' (Gunning 1989: 33). Gunning's
equation is the inverse of fetishism, for where fetishism is a matter of dis-
avowing what one sees (*I see that it's not real, but I'll nevertheless believe that
it is real*), Gunning posits that the initial approach to the cinema is one of
disbelief: *I know it's not real, and yet...I am astonished that it appears here
before me!* For cinema's earliest audiences, going to the cinema was not

about a disavowal of illusion or a suspension of disbelief. It was a matter of an acceptance and relishing of the astonishing powers of illusion possessed by the cinema.

Finally, therefore, early cinema was focused on staging illusions, presenting and exhibiting illusions, and *not* on discovering ways of making illusions believable. In this way, it owed a great deal to the fairground and its attractions as well as to the tradition of the magic show. Indeed, one of the cinema's first geniuses, Georges Méliès, had been a magician before he began making moving pictures.

> The craft of the nineteenth century stage illusions consisted of making visible something which could not exist, of managing the play of appearances in order to confound the expectations of logic and experience. The audience this theatre addressed was not primarily gullible country bumpkins, but sophisticated urban pleasure seekers, well aware that they were seeing the most modern techniques in stage craft.
>
> (Gunning 1989: 33)

The interjections of Gunning and others onto the terrain of film theory completely changed the landscape of film studies. The discovery of radical historical variability in film reception was something that had rarely been considered by film theorists and the fact that an entirely different mode of audience engagement was discovered among early cinema audiences necessitated a substantial re-think of the presuppositions of film theory, especially Apparatus theory.

## Audience research

(Martin Barker, 'The Pleasures of Watching an "Off-Beat" film: The Case of *Being John Malkovich*,' [Barker 2008].)

Audience research represents one of the first ways in which the 'effects' of the cinema were investigated. Emilie Altenloh's 1914 study (Altenloh 2001) of cinema-going in two German cities provides extraordinary insights into the habits and expectations of some of cinema's earliest audiences, while a range of other studies from the 1920s to the 1950s ensures that audience research in one form or another has an impressive history (see, for example, Blumer 1933; Mayer 1948). At the same time, many such instances of audience research were driven by various 'public decency' initiatives with aims of highlighting the potential harmful effects of moviegoing, most notably the Payne Fund studies undertaken in the USA in the late 1920s and 1930s (see Forman 1933). Audience research became virtually non-existent during the 1960s and 1970s, however, as academic courses in Film Studies tended to focus on issues of aesthetic taste or, as we have seen in the early chapters of this book, took on board trends in structuralism and semiotics.

Audience research re-emerged at the end of the 1970s. Much of this was a result of efforts made by academics at the Birmingham Centre for Contemporary Cultural Studies whose immediate efforts related to television more than cinema. The breakthrough works were David Morley's *The 'Nationwide' Audience* (on the British current affairs programme, *Nationwide*) and Ien Ang's *Watching Dallas* (on the popular soap opera of the 1980s, *Dallas*) (Morley 1980; Ang 1985). Even if the focus of these works was on television, their theoretical approaches were at odds with the then dominant *Screen* and apparatus theories that dominated Anglo-American discussions in both film and media theory during the 1970s. There are important reasons for this. First of all, these authors argued that the text-centred approaches associated with structuralism, *Screen* and apparatus theories ignored the wider factors of film (and television) reception. By focusing too narrowly on the ways in which the formal properties of 'texts' generate meanings, scholars had overlooked the ways in which *contextual*, *historical* and other factors surrounding a film screening or television broadcast might influence the ways in which those texts are understood and interpreted. Perhaps an easy way to think of this point is in terms of the question of why any one person might go to see any one particular film. Most of the time it is because one has heard something about the film beforehand, so one knows what kind of film its is (e.g., a gangster film or a musical), knows who is acting in it and has heard about some aspects of the plot from reviews or trailers or, finally, one might know or be interested in who directed the film. These kinds of expectations serve to guide what kinds of responses a viewer might intend to have to a film and, as such, it is not only the specifics of a film's *textual qualities* – its narrative or editing strategies and so on – that influence the ways in which a film is interpreted and experienced by viewers. Rather, there is a vast range of factors *beyond the text* that determine how one might respond to a film.

Another reason audience researchers criticized *Screen* theory was the latter's lack of verification. *Screen* theorists, like Colin MacCabe or Laura Mulvey, relied on their own hypotheses and speculations and hoped those speculations might be convincing if backed up by Freudian or other theories. Their arguments related to purely hypothetical audiences, not actual audiences. Audience researchers are therefore keen to make their conclusions empirically verifiable – their conclusions are based on the actual testimonies of 'real' audience members.

Audience research is just that: research into the behaviour and responses of audiences. Because of the influence of the Birmingham School,

research of this type in the United Kingdom has tended to utilize questionnaires handed out to or interviews conducted with actual audience
members. In the United States, by contrast, this approach has been less
common. Researchers in the USA have tended to pursue methodologies
pertaining to what has become known as *reception studies*. This strategy of
research relies less on interviews with or the personal testimonies of actual cinemagoers than on historical, promotional and exhibition factors
which surround and influence the ways in which films might have been
received. Such work is often focused on historical factors – contemporary
reviews or censorship practices, for example, or the relationship between
specific historical events and a particular film's production and release.
There is little question that some of the best work in film studies in recent
years has been in reception studies, especially the pioneering research undertaken by Janet Staiger (Staiger 1992, 2000, 2005) along with scholars
focusing on early and silent cinema (Petro 1989; Hansen 1991; Klinger
1994; Smoodin 2004). These works definitely bridge the divide between
*history* and *theory* and thus function as something of a challenge to theory *per se*. Reception studies can rightly be counted as a key area of film
studies' 'turn to history'.

In the United Kingdom, as we saw in Chapter 4, Jackie Stacey's *Star
Gazing* (Stacey 1994) is a key work that crosses a number of boundaries. It
is first of all a work of feminist film theory, but second, it offers one of the
most effective uses of audience research yet published. Third, even though
its conclusions rely heavily on the interviews and questionnaires central
to audience research methodology, *Star Gazing* remains a thoroughly theoretical work which draws upon a range of theoretical inspirations in order to refine its arguments. With the publication of *Star Gazing*, audience
research was put well and truly on the film studies map.

Martin Barker is probably the one scholar who has been most forceful
and passionate in defending the audience research paradigm, especially
insofar as it is practised in the United Kingdom. Across a range of works –
on *Judge Dredd* (Barker and Brooks 1998), on David Cronenberg's *Crash*
(Barker et al. 2001), in *From Antz to Titanic* (Barker 2000) and, more recently, a global project on the *Lord of the Rings* (Barker and Mathjis 2007) –
Barker has honed his methodologies, both expanded and qualified his
conclusions, all the while taking aim at many of the major trends in film
theory, from *Screen* theory to cognitivism and beyond. While most of his
research pertains to popular film and popular cinemagoing, in a recent
article – the article upon which we shall concentrate here – he investigates the significance of a film that is not entirely mainstream: *Being John
Malkovich* (directed by Spike Jonze, 1999). He describes this as a film that is
not necessarily an 'art-house' film, but nor was it an entirely mainstream
production. Rather, Barker describes it as an 'off-beat' or 'off-mainstream'

film. In investigating this film, Barker was interested to discover what motivated people to go to see a film such as this, while he also carefully considered the specific responses audience members had to the film so as to ascertain what they 'got' from the film and of what their experiences of the film consisted.

It was a small sample group: only 17 recorded interviews. Barker's article focuses closely on four responses which he compares and contrasts. His key questions are quite straightforward: 'What kinds of pleasures are involved . . . [and] what senses of identity and community are summoned up in the process of watching and then discussing *BJM*?' Against claims that responses to a film must be textually determined – or determined by the kinds of 'cues' which someone like David Bordwell emphasizes (see Chapter 8 above) – Barker finds another way of thinking about how audiences engage with this film. He argues that many of those who found the film interesting and engaging seemed to be motivated by a '*wish to be part of* certain kinds of community' and that such wishing was central to their responses. In other words, the process of going to see *Being John Malkovich* entailed a process of imagining a community of the 'kinds of people' who go to see such films – off-beat, quirky, and at the margins of the mainstream. For many viewers, identifying themselves as part of such a community seemed an important part of the experience of *Being John Malkovich*.

For one respondent, Katherine, seeing the film was part of an attempt to identify herself with an 'alternative' community, a community different from the mainstream and the 'norm'. Before seeing the film, *Being John Malkovich* was, in her imagination, an aesthetic example which, if she enjoyed and understood it, would ensure her an entry into a certain type of off-beat community. The film was therefore important for her gauging her own sense of self-worth. In a sense, she wanted to be *good enough* for the film. To be able to appreciate and understand the film – and it is not a straightforwardly easy film to understand! – would be a mark of her own prowess, even her 'superiority', she claims at one point. If nothing else, Katherine's response is important for highlighting the kinds of investments and hopes spectators have the ability to inject into a film, for she invests an extraordinary amount of personal expectation in *Being John Malkovich*. And certainly, as a cognitivist might argue, the film contains 'cues' which both encourage and thwart understanding, but the importance of that understanding was not simply one of *comprehending* the film. Rather, for Katherine, understanding the film formed part of a complex structure of self-identity in which her own self-worth was at stake. We do not think it is overstating the case to believe that many filmgoers – especially those interested in difficult or off-beat films – are motivated by similar concerns. It is also worth pointing out that such

**Figure 9.2**  Maxine Lund (Catherine Keener) and Craig Schwartz (John Cusack) in *Being John Malkovich*.
*Source*: Courtesy British Film Institute. Gramercy Pictures.

points have very rarely been made in the fields of film studies or film theory.

Two of the respondents had very negative responses to particular characters. Emma, who admitted to being quite attracted to John Cusack (the actor who plays Craig Schwartz) found his character repugnant, and she also found certain elements of the plot to be a little disturbing – the 'wrong sort of weird' as she so aptly puts it. For her, watching and appreciating the film are a matter of how the film conforms to her prior expectations. And the film did, in fact, disappoint her because it failed to live up to those expectations. Therefore, again, the response to the film is not based entirely on specific aspects of the 'text', but rather, the formal and narrative properties are filtered through a series of spectator expectations. Richard was another respondent who plainly did not like one of the characters – Maxine (played by Catherine Keener) (Figure 9.2). He too was disturbed by certain aspects of the plot and his conclusions were somewhat similar to those of Emma: the film had disappointed his expectations; he failed to 'get into' the film.

A fourth respondent, Graham, was delighted by *Being John Malkovich*'s intellectual tricks. Unlike the other respondents who were keen to be swept up by the film and 'lost' in it, Graham preferred to keep his distance, something he does for most films he sees. In a Brechtian fashion, he contentedly appreciates actors who 'play at being characters' while he watches films, and he therefore found this film particular delightful, especially as it involves questions of identity, of identity-mixing and simulation. Again, therefore, it was Graham's predilections and expectations which acted as significant markers of his response to the film.

In his conclusions, Barker is impressed quite simply by the wide and varying range of responses it is possible to have to a single film (see Barker 2005, for more on this point). But responses to *Being John Malkovich* also highlighted some generalizable traits. Audience members typically knew beforehand that this was going to be a challenging film, one they would have to think about, and they relished this challenge and wanted it to be part of their experience of the film. Barker thus claims that the film acted as a catalyst or environment in which there was a 'wish for a certain kind of experience'. Furthermore, the wish for this kind of experience also mapped onto the ways in which respondents conceived of themselves as subjects: they wanted to think of themselves and be perceived by others as smart, off-beat and alternative. As Barker puts it, 'In enjoying the film, my audiences seem also to invest in the notion that they are the kind of people who do this.'

Barker makes a final point derived from 'reader response' research in literary studies. He tries to work out what aspects of the film experience might trigger memories of one's own life experiences. In this sense he is treading near the same territory we charted via Barbara Klinger's response to a scene in *The Piano* (see Chapter 4 above). Yet, where Klinger's observations were highly speculative and personal, Barker here seeks ways of making such observations part of more general patterns of cinemagoing. In truth, his own conclusions are still highly speculative and tentative, a point he readily admits. But he couches his claim in terms of the correlation between the expectations audiences have when they go to the cinema and the expectations they have of their own lives. His conclusion is that 'some imaginative forms might *remind us of the kind of people we want to be* and the *kinds of world we could imagine inhabiting*'. We think that, with such claims, film theory is certainly alive and well.

# Glossary

**Attractions**: A term first used by Sergei Eisenstein when writing about the theatre, attractions refer to the specific effects elicited by physical actions, shocks and tricks. The term is derived from fairground 'attractions', such as the rollercoaster or merry-go-round. In the cinema, it is generally taken to mean moments of activity (such as slapstick comedy or explosions) or emphatic editing designed to induce a physical response in the viewer.

**Phenomenology**: Phenomenology is a philosophical method developed by Edmund Husserl in the early twentieth century. It is predicated on reducing things to their essences by means of strict observation and by suspending all extraneous influences or presumptions. It therefore involves the systematic reflection and critical analysis of the objects which make themselves available to consciousness. Maurice Merleau-Ponty expanded Husserl's investigation to include not just objects of consciousness, but bodily, corporeal experiences as well.

# Notes

## Introduction

1. The phrase was coined by Stanley Kauffmann. See Kauffmann (1966: 415–28).

## 5 Cinemas of the other

1. Significantly, Van Sant's, *Milk* (2007) is a biopic of the first openly gay elected official in the USA, Harvey Milk.

## 6 Philosophers and film

1. The following chapter in *Cinema 1* is on the 'small form' of the action-image, the formula for which is A–S–A'.

# References

Abel, R. (1999) *The Red Rooster Scare: Making Cinema American, 1900–1910*. Berkeley, CA: University of California Press.

Abel, R. (2006) *Americanizing the Movies and 'Movie-Mad' Audiences, 1910–1914*. Berkeley, CA: University of California Press.

Altenloh, E. (2001) A sociology of the cinema: the audience, trans. K. Cross, *Screen*, 42(3): 249–93.

Althusser, L. (1971) Ideology and Ideological State Apparatuses (notes toward an investigation), in *Lenin and Philosophy and Other Essays*. New York: Monthly Review Press, pp. 85–126.

Althusser, L. and Balibar, E. (1970) *Reading Capital*, trans. B. Brewster. London: New Left Books.

Anderson, J.D. (1996) *The Reality of Illusion: An Ecological Approach to Cognitive Film Theory*. Carbondale, IL: University of Southern Illinois Press.

Anderson, J.D. and Anderson, B. F. (eds) (2007) *Moving Image Theory: Ecological Considerations*. Carbondale: Southern Illinois University Press.

Ang, I. (1985) *Watching 'Dallas': Soap Opera and the Melodramatic Imagination*. London: Methuen.

Arnheim, R. (1957) *Film as Art*. Berkeley: University of California Press.

Baker, H.A. (1993) Spike Lee and the culture of commerce, in M. Diawara, *Black American Cinema*. New York: Routledge, pp. 154–76.

Barker, M. (2000) *From Antz to Titanic: Reinventing Film Analysis*. London: Pluto Press.

Barker, M. (2005) The Lord of the Rings and 'identification', *European Journal of Communication*, 20(3): 353–78.

Barker, M. (2008) The pleasures of watching an 'off-beat' film: the case of *Being John Malkovich, Scope: an Online Journal of Film Studies* 12, October 2008. http://www.scope.nottingham.ac.uk/issue.php?issue=11.

Barker, M., Arthurs, J. and Harindranath, R. (2001) *The Crash Controversy: Censorship Campaigns and Film Reception*. London: Wallflower.

Barker, M. and Brooks, K. (1998) *Knowing Audiences: Judge Dredd, Its Friends, Fans and Foes*. Luton: University of Luton Press.

Barker, M. and Mathijs, E. (eds) (2007) *Watching The Lord of the Rings: Tolkein's World Audiences*. New York: Peter Lang.

Barratt, D. (2009) 'Twist blindness': the role of primacy, priming, schemas, and reconstructive memory in a first-time viewing of *The Sixth Sense*, in W. Buckland (ed.) *Puzzle Films: Complex Storytelling in Contemporary Cinema*. Oxford: Blackwell, pp. 62–86.

Barthes, R. (1972) *Mythologies*, trans. A. Lavers. London: Jonathan Cape.

Barthes, R. (1975) *S/Z*, trans. R. Miller. London: Jonathan Cape.

Barthes, R. (1977a) Diderot, Brecht, Eisenstein, in S. Heath (ed.) *Image-Music-Text*. New York: Farrar, Strauss and Giroux, pp. 69–78.

Barthes, R. (1977b) *Image-Music-Text*, ed. S. Heath. New York: Farrar, Strauss and Giroux.

Barthes, R. (1981) *Camera Lucida: Reflections on Photography*, trans. R. Howard. New York: Hill and Wang.

Barthes, R. (1983) *The Fashion System*, trans. M. Ward and R. Howard. New York: Hill and Wang.

Baudry, J-L. (1976) The apparatus, *Camera Obscura*, 1: 104–26.

Baudry, J-L. (1985) Ideological effects of the basic cinematographic apparatus, trans. A. Williams in B. Nichols (ed.) *Movies and Methods*, Volume II. Berkeley, CA: University of California Press, pp. 531–42.

Bazin, A. (1967) *What is Cinema?* trans. H. Gray. Berkeley, CA: University of California Press.

Bazin, A. (1971) *What is Cinema?* Volume II, trans. H. Gray. Berkeley, CA: University of California Press.

Bazin, A. (1997) *Germany Year Zero*, in B. Cardullo, *Bazin at Work: Major Essays and Reviews from the Forties and Fifties*. London: Routledge, pp. 121–24.

Beller, J. (2006) *The Cinematic Mode of Production: Attention Economy and the Society of the Spectacle*. Hanover, NH: University Press of New Hampshire.

Bellour, R. (1985) Analysis in flames, *Diacritics*, Spring, 54–6.

Bellour, R. (2000a) System of a fragment (on *The Birds*), in *The Analysis of Film*. Bloomington, IN: Indiana University Press, pp. 28–68.

Bellour, R. (2000b) The unattainable text, in *The Analysis of Film*. Bloomington, IN: Indiana University Press, pp. 21–7.

Benjamin, J. (1990) *The Bonds of Love: Psychoanalysis, Feminism and the Problem of Domination*. London: Routledge.

Benjamin, W. (2003) The work of art in the age of its technological reproducibility (third version), in H. Eiland and M.W. Jennings, *Walter Benjamin, Selected Writings*, Volume 4, *1938–1940*. Cambridge, MA: Harvard University Press, pp. 251–83.

Bettinson, G. (2008) New blood: an interview with Soi Cheang, *Journal of Chinese Cinemas*, 2(3): 211–24.

Bhabha, H. (1994) *The Location of Culture*. London: Routledge.

Blumer, H. (1933) *Movies and Conduct*. New York: Macmillan.

Bogue, R. (2003) *Deleuze on Cinema*. London: Routledge.

Bordwell, D. (1981) *The Films of Carl-Theodor Dreyer*. Berkeley, CA: University of California Press.

Bordwell, D. (1983) Lowering the stakes: prospects for a historical poetics of cinema, *Iris*, 1(1): 5–18.

Bordwell, D. (1985) *Narration in the Fiction Film*. London: Methuen.

Bordwell, D. (1988) *Ozu and the Poetics of Cinema*. Princeton, NJ: Princeton University Press.

Bordwell, D. (1989a) *Making Meaning: Inference and Rhetoric in the Interpretation of Cinema*. Cambridge, MA: Harvard University Press.

Bordwell, D. (1989b) A case for cognitivism, *Iris*, 9 (Spring): 11–40.

Bordwell, D. (1989c) Historical poetics of cinema, in R. Barton Palmer (ed.) *The Cinematic Text: Methods and Approaches*. New York: AMS Press, pp. 369–98.

Bordwell, D. (1993) *The Cinema of Eisenstein*. Cambridge, MA: Harvard University Press.

Bordwell, D. (2000) *Planet Hong Kong: Popular Cinema and the Art of Entertainment*. Cambridge, MA: Harvard University Press.

Bordwell, D. (2003) Who blinked first? How film style streamlines nonverbal interaction, in L. Højbjerg and P. Schepelern (eds) *Film Style and Story: A Tribute to Torben Grodal*. Copenhagen: Museum Tusculanum Press, pp. 45–58.

Bordwell, D. (2007) This is your brain on movies, maybe (March 7). Online at: http://www.davidbordwell.net/blog/?p=300

Bordwell, D. (2008) *Poetics of Cinema*. New York: Routledge.

Bordwell, D. and Carroll, N. (eds) (1995) *Post-Theory: Reconstructing Film Studies*. Madison, WI: University of Wisconsin Press.

Bordwell, D., Staiger, J. and Thompson, K. (1985) *The Classical Hollywood Cinema: Film Style and Mode of Production to 1960*. London: Routledge and Kegan Paul.

Bordwell, D. and Thompson, K. (1979) *Film Art: An Introduction*. Reading, MA: Addison-Wesley.

Branigan, E. (2006) *Projecting a Camera: Language-Games in Film Theory*. London: Routledge.

Brecht, B. (1964) *Brecht on Theatre*, trans. J. Willet. London: Methuen.

Burch, N. (1973) *Theory of Film Practice*. London: Secker and Warburg.

Burch, N. (1990) *Life to Those Shadows*. London: BFI.

Butler, J. (1990) *Gender Trouble: Feminism and the Subversion of Identity*. New York: Routledge.

Butler, J. (1993) *Bodies that Matter: On the Discursive Limits of 'Sex'*. New York: Routledge.

Carroll, N. (1982) Address to the Heathen, *October*, 23 (Winter): 89–163.

Carroll, N. (1990) *The Philosophy of Horror, or Paradoxes of the Heart*. New York: Routledge.

Carroll, N. (1996a) *Theorizing the Moving Image*. Cambridge: Cambridge University Press.

Carroll, N. (1996b) 'Moderate Moralism', *British Journal of Aesthetics*, 36(3): 223–38.

Casebier, A. (1991) *Phenomenology and Film: Toward a Realist Theory of Cinematic Representation*. Cambridge: Cambridge University Press.

Cavell, S. (1979a) *The World Viewed: Reflections on the Ontology of Film*, enlarged edn. Cambridge, MA: Harvard University Press.

Cavell, S. (1979b) *The Claim of Reason: Wittgenstein, Skepticism, Morality, and Tragedy*. New York: Oxford University Press.

Cavell, S. (1981) *Pursuits of Happiness: The Hollywood Comedy of Remarriage*. Cambridge, MA: Harvard University Press.

Cavell, S. (1996) *Contesting Tears: The Hollywood Melodrama of the Unknown Woman*. Chicago: University of Chicago Press.

Cavell, S. (2004) *Cities of Words: Pedagogical Letters on a Register of the Moral Life*. Cambridge, MA: Harvard University Press.

Cavell, S. (2005) *Cavell on Film*, ed. W. Rothman. New York: SUNY Press.

Clover, C.J. (1992) *Men, Women and Chain Saws: Gender in the Modern Horror Film*. Princeton, NJ: Princeton University Press.

Comolli, J-L., and Narboni, J. (1990) Cinema/ideology/criticism, in N. Browne, (ed.) *Cahiers du cinéma*, Volume III: *The Politics of Representation*. London: BFI, pp. 58–67.

Cowie, E. (1997) Fantasia, in *Representing the Woman: Cinema and Psychoanalysis*. London: Macmillan, pp. 123–65.

Creed, B. (1993) *The Monstrous-Feminine: Film, Feminism, Psychoanalysis*. London: Routledge.

Currie, G. (1997) *Image and Mind: Film, Philosophy and Cognitive Science*. Cambridge: Cambridge University Press.

De Lauretis, T. and Heath, S. (1980) *The Cinematic Apparatus*. New York: St. Martin's Press.

De Saussure, F. (1966) *Course in General Lingustics*. New York: McGraw-Hill.

Deleuze, G. (1986) *Cinema 1: The Movement-Image*, trans. H. Tomlinson and B. Habberjam. London: Athlone.

Deleuze, G. (1988a) *Bergsonism*, trans. H. Tomlinson and B. Habberjam. New York: Zone Books.

Deleuze, G. (1988b) *Foucault*, trans. S. Hand. London: Athlone.

Deleuze, G. (1989) *Cinema 2: The Time-Image*, trans. H. Tomlinson and R. Galeta. London: Athlone.

Deleuze, G. (2000) *Proust and Signs: The Complete Text*, trans. R. Howard. Minneapolis: University of Minnesota Press.

Deleuze, G. and Guattari, F. (1977) *Anti-Oedipus: Capitalism and Schizophrenia*, trans. R. Hurley, M. Seem and H. Lane. New York: Viking.

Deleuze, G. and Guattari, F. (1987) *A Thousand Plateaus: Capitalism and Schizophrenia*, trans. B. Massumi. Minneapolis: University of Minnesota Press.

Doane, M.A. (1988) *The Desire to Desire: The Woman's Film of the 1940s.* London: Macmillan.

Doane, M.A. (1991) *Femmes Fatales: Feminism, Film Theory, Psychoanalysis.* New York: Routledge.

Doty, A. (2000) *Flaming Classics: Queering the Film Canon.* New York: Routledge.

Dyer, R. (1990) *Now You See It: Studies on Gay and Lesbian Film.* London: Routledge.

Edgerton, S.Y. (1975) *The Renaissance Rediscovery of Linear Perspective.* New York: Basic Books.

Editors of *Cahiers du cinéma.* (1976) John Ford's *Young Mr. Lincoln,* in B. Nichols, *Movies and Methods,* Volume I, Los Angeles: University of California Press, pp. 493–529.

Eikhenbaum, B. (1927) Leskov and contemporary prose, in *Literatura. Teoriya. Kritika. Polemika.* Leningrad, pp. 210–25.

Eisenstein, S.M. (1988a) The montage of attractions, in *Selected Writings* Volume 1 *1922–1924.* London: BFI, pp. 33–8.

Eisenstein, S.M. (1988b) The montage of film attractions, in *Selected Writings* Volume 1, *1922–1924,* London: BFI, pp. 39–58.

Feuer, J. (1986) The self-reflexive musical and the myth of entertainment, in B.K. Grant (ed.) *Film Genre Reader.* Austin, TX: University of Texas Press, pp. 329–43.

Flaxman, G. (ed.) (2000) *The Brain is the Screen: Gilles Deleuze and the Philosophy of Cinema.* Minneapolis: University of Minnesota Press.

Forman, H.J. (1933) *Our Movie Made Children.* New York: Macmillan.

Foucault, M. (1970) *The Order of Things: An Archaeology of the Human Sciences.* London: Tavistock.

Foucault, M. (1984) Nietzsche, genealogy, history, in P. Rabinow (ed.) *The Foucault Reader.* London: Penguin, pp. 76–100.

Frampton, D. (2006) *Filmosophy.* London: Wallflower Press.

Freud, S. (1955) 'A child is being beaten': a contribution to the study of the origin of sexual perversions, in J. Strachey (ed.) *The Standard Edition of the Complete Psychological Works of Sigmund Freud,* Vol. XVII. London: Hogarth Press, pp. 179–204.

Freud, S. (1977a) *Three Essays on Sexuality,* in *On Sexuality: Three Essays on the Theory of Sexuality and Other Works.* Harmondsworth: Penguin, pp. 31–169.

Freud, S. (1977b) Fetishism, in *On Sexuality: Three Essays on the Theory of Sexuality and Other Works.* Harmondsworth: Penguin, pp. 345–57.

Freud, S. (1977c) The dissolution of the Oedipus complex, in *On Sexuality: Three Essays on the Theory of Sexuality and Other Works*. Harmondsworth: Penguin, pp. 313–22.

Freud, S. (1977d) Some psychical consequences of the anatomical distinction between the sexes, in *On Sexuality: Three Essays on the Theory of Sexuality and Other Works*. Harmondsworth: Penguin, pp. 323–43.

Freud, S. (1984) On narcissism: an introduction, in *On Metapsychology: The Theory of Psychoanalysis*. Harmondsworth: Penguin, pp. 59–98.

Freud, S. (1985) Creative writers and day-dreaming, in *Art and Literature: Jensen's Gradiva, Leonardo Da Vinci and Other Works*. Harmondsworth: Penguin, pp. 129–41.

Frome, J. (2006) Representation, reality, and emotions across media, *Film Studies: An International Review*, 8 (Summer): 12–25.

Gaudreault, A. (1990) Film, narrative, narration: the cinema of the Lumière brothers, in T. Elsaesser (ed.) *Early Cinema: Space, Frame, Narrative*. London: BFI.

Gaut, B. (1999) Identification and emotion in narrative film, in C. Plantinga and G.M. Smith (eds) *Passionate Views: Film, Cognition, and Emotion*. Baltimore, MD: The Johns Hopkins University Press, pp. 200–16.

Godard, J-L. (1972) *Godard on Godard*, trans. Tom Milne. New York: Secker and Warburg.

Grieveson, L. (2004) *Policing Cinema: Movies and Censorship in Early Twentieth-Century America*. Berkeley, CA: University of California Press.

Grodal, T. (1997) *Moving Pictures: A New Theory of Film Genres, Feelings, and Cognition*. Oxford: Oxford University Press.

Grodal, T. (1999) Emotions, cognitions, and narrative patterns in film, in C. Plantinga and G.M. Smith (eds) *Passionate Views: Film, Cognition, and Emotion*. Baltimore, MD: The Johns Hopkins University Press, pp. 127–45.

Grodal, T. (2009) *Embodied Visions: Evolution, Emotion, Culture, and Film*, New York: Oxford University Press.

Guerrero, E. (2001) *Do the Right Thing*. London: BFI.

Gunning, T. (1989) An aesthetic of astonishment: early film and the (in)credulous spectator, *Art & Text*, 34, (Spring): 31–45.

Gunning, T. (1990) The cinema of attractions: early film, its spectator, and the avant-garde, in T. Elsaesser and A. Barker (eds) *Early Cinema: Space, Frame, Narrative*. London: BFI, pp. 56–62.

Gunning, T. (1991) *D.W. Griffith and the Origins of American Narrative Film: The Early Years at Biograph*. Urbana, IL: University of Illinois Press.

Hall, S. (2000) Cultural identity and cinematic representation, in R. Stam and T. Miller, *Film and Theory: An Anthology*. Oxford: Blackwell, pp. 704–14.

Hansen, M. (1991) *Babel and Babylon: Spectatorship in American Silent Film*. Cambridge, MA: Harvard University Press.

Harbord, J. (2007) *The Evolution of Film: Rethinking Film Studies*. London: Polity.

Heath, S. (1981) *Questions of Cinema*. London: Macmillan, pp. 113–30.

Heath, S. (1992) Lessons from Brecht, in F. Mulhern (ed.) *Contemporary Marxist Literary Criticism*. London: Longmans, pp. 230–57.

Henderson, B. (1973) Critique of Cine-Structuralism (Part 1), *Film Quarterly*, 27(1): 25–34.

Henderson, B. (1973–74) Critique of Cine-Structuralism (Part 2), *Film Quarterly*, 27(2): 37–46.

Henderson, B. (1985) *The Searchers*: an American dilemma, in B. Nichols (ed.) *Movies and Methods*, Volume II. Berkeley: University of California Press, pp. 429–49.

Jakobson, R. (1935) The dominant, in L. Matejka and K. Pomorska (eds) *Readings in Russian Poetics: Formalist and Structuralist Views*. Cambridge. MA: MIT Press, pp. 82–7.

Kauffmann, S. (1966) The film generation: celebration and concern, in *A World on Film: Criticism and Comment*. New York: Delta, pp. 415–28.

Keil, C. and Stamp, S. (eds) (2004) *American Cinema's Transitional Era: Audiences, Institutions, Practices*. Berkeley, CA: University of California Press.

Kellner, D. (1997) Aesthetics, ethics, and politics in the films of Spike Lee, in M.A. Reid (ed.) *Spike Lee's* Do the Right Thing. Cambridge: Cambridge University Press, pp. 73–106.

Klinger, B. (1994) *Melodrama and Meaning: History, Culture, and the Films of Douglas Sirk*. Bloomington, IN: Indiana University Press.

Klinger, B. (2006) The art film, affect and the female viewer: *The Piano* revisited, *Screen*, 47(1): 19–41.

Kristeva, J. (1998) The subject in process, in P. French and R-F. Lack (eds) *The Tel Quel Reader*. New York: Routledge, pp. 133–78.

Kuhn, A. (2004) The state of media and film feminism, *Signs: Journal of Women in Culture and Society*, 30(1): 1221–9.

Lacan, J. (2006a) The function and field of speech and language in psychoanalysis., in *Écrits: The First Complete Edition in English*, trans. B. Fink. New York: Norton, pp. 197–268.

Lacan, J. (2006b) The signification of the phallus, in *Écrits: The First Complete Edition in English*, trans. B. Fink. New York: Norton, pp. 575–84.

Lacan, J. (2006c) The mirror stage as formative of the *I* function as revealed in psychoanalytic experience, in *Écrits: The First Complete Edition in English*, trans. B. Fink. New York: Norton, pp. 75–81.

Laplanche, J. and Pontalis, J-B. (1986) Fantasy and the origins of sexuality, in V. Burgin, J. Donald and C. Kaplan (eds) *Formations of Fantasy*. London: Methuen, pp. 5–34.

Lévi-Strauss, C. (1977) *Structural Anthropology*, trans. C. Jacobson. Harmondsworth: Penguin.

MacCabe, C. (1975) The politics of separation, *Screen*, 16(4): 46–57.

MacCabe, C. (1985a) Realism in the cinema: notes on some Brechtian theses, in *Theoretical Essays: Film, Linguistics, Literature*. Manchester: Manchester University Press, pp. 33–57.

MacCabe, C. (1985b) Class of '68: elements of an intellectual biography 1967–81, in *Theoretical Essays: Film, Linguistics, Literature*. Manchester: Manchester University Press, pp. 1–32.

MacCabe, C. (2003) *Godard: A Portrait of the Artist at 70*. London: Bloomsbury.

Mannoni, O. (1969) Je sais bien, mais quand même…, in *Clefs pour l'imaginaire de l'autre scène*. Paris: Seuil.

Mayer, J.P. (1948) *British Cinema and Their Audiences*. London: Dennis Dobson.

McGowan, T. (2007) *The Real Gaze: Film Theory After Lacan*. New York: SUNY Press.

Mehler, C.E. (2007) *Brokeback Mountain* at the Oscars, in J. Stacy (ed.) *Reading* Brokeback Mountain: *Essays on the Story and the Film*. Jefferson, NC: McFarland and Co., pp. 135–51.

Merck, M. (2007) Mulvey's manifesto, *Camera Obscura*, 22(3): 1–23.

Merleau-Ponty, M. (1962) *Phenomenology of Perception*, trans. C. Smith. London: Routledge.

Metz, C. (1974) The cinema: language or language-system, trans. M. Taylor. *Film Language: A Semiotics of the Cinema*. New York: Oxford University Press, pp. 31–91.

Metz, C. (1979) The cinematic apparatus as a social institution: an interview with Christian Metz, *Discourse: Journal for Theoretical Studies in Media and Culture*, 3: 7–38.

Metz, C. (1982) The imaginary signifier, in *Psychoanalysis and Cinema: The Imaginary Signifier*, trans. C. Britton, A. Williams, B. Brewster, et al. London: Macmillan, pp. 1–87.

Miller, D.A. (2007) On the universality of *Brokeback*, *Film Quarterly*, 60(3): 50–60.

Morley, D. (1980) *The 'Nationwide' Audience*. London: BFI.

Mulhall, S. (2008) *On Film*, 2nd edn. London: Routledge.

Mulvey, L. (1989a) Visual pleasure and narrative cinema, in *Visual and Other Pleasures*, London: Macmillan, pp. 14–26.

Mulvey, L. (1989b) Film, feminism and the avant-garde, in *Visual and Other Pleasures*. London: Macmillan, pp. 111–26.

Mulvey, L. (1989c) Afterthoughts on 'Visual Pleasure and Narrative Cinema' inspired by King Vidor's *Duel in the Sun* (1946), in *Visual and Other Pleasures*. London: Macmillan, pp. 29–38.

Münsterberg, H. (1970) *The Film: A Psychological Study*. Mineola, New York: Dover Publications.

Musser, C. (1990) *The Emergence of Cinema: The American Screen to 1907*. New York: Scribner's.

Musser, C. (1991) *Before the Nickelodeon: Edwin S. Porter and the Edison Manufacturing Company*. Berkeley, CA: University of California Press.

Myrdal, G. ([1944] 1962) *An American Dilemma: The Negro Problem and Modern Democracy*. New York: Harper and Row.

Neill, A. (1996) Empathy and (film) fiction, in D. Bordwell and N. Carroll (eds) *Post Theory: Reconstructing Film Studies*. Madison, WI: University of Wisconsin Press, pp. 175–94.

Penley, C. (1989) *The Future of an Illusion: Film, Feminism, and Psychoanalysis*. Minneapolis: University of Minnesota Press.

Perez, H. (2007) Gay cowboys close to home: Ennis Del Mar on the Q. T., in J. Stacy (ed.) *Reading* Brokeback Mountain*: Essays on the Story and the Film*. Jefferson, NC: McFarland and Co, pp. 71–87.

Petro, P. (1989) *Joyless Streets: Women and Melodramatic Representation in Weimar Germany*. Princeton, NJ: Princeton University Press.

Pisters, P. (2003) *The Matrix of Visual Culture: Working with Deleuze in Film Theory*. Stanford, CA: Stanford University Press.

Plantinga, C. (1999) Notes on spectator emotion and ideological film criticism, in R. Allen and M. Smith (eds) *Film Theory and Philosophy*. Oxford: Oxford University Press, pp. 372–93.

Plantinga, C. (2009) *Moving Viewers: American Film and the Spectator's Experience*, Los Angeles: University of California Press.

Prince, S. (1998) *Savage Cinema: Sam Peckinpah and the Rise of Ultraviolent Movies*. London: Athlone Press.

Proust, M. (1998) *Swann's Way (In Search of Lost Time*, Vol. 1), New York: Modern Library.

Rich, B.R. (2004) New Queer Cinema, in M. Aaron (ed.) *New Queer Cinema: A Critical Reader*. Edinburgh: Edinburgh University Press, pp. 15–22.

Rich, B.R. (2007) Brokering *Brokeback:* Jokes, backlashes, and other anxieties. *Film Quarterly*, 60(3): 44–8.

Rodowick, D.N. (1997) *Gilles Deleuze's Time Machine*. Durham, NC: Duke University Press.

Rodowick, D.N. (2007) *The Virtual Life of Film*. Cambridge, MA: Harvard University Press.

Rosenbaum, J. (1997) Say the right thing (*Do the Right Thing*), in *Movies as Politics*, Chicago: University of Chicago Press, pp. 13–21.

Rothman, W. and Keane, M. (2000) *Reading Cavell's 'The World Viewed': A Philosophical Perspective on Film*. Detroit: Wayne State University Press.

Said, E. (1978) *Orientalism*. London: Routledge.

Said, E. (1993) *Culture and Imperialism*. New York: Knopf.

Samuels, S. (1983) *Midnight Movies*. New York: Macmillan.

Sarris, A. (1996) Toward a theory of film history, in *The American Cinema: Directors and Directions 1929–1968*. New York: DaCapo Press, pp. 19–37.

Shklovsky, V. (1965) Art as technique, in L.T. Lemon and M.J. Reis (eds) *Russian Formalist Criticism: Four Essays*. Lincoln, NE: University of Nebraska, pp. 3–24.

Smith, G.M. (2007) *Film Structure and the Emotion System*. Cambridge: Cambridge University Press.

Smith, M. (1995) *Engaging Characters: Fiction, Emotion, and the Cinema*. Clarendon: Oxford University Press.

Smith, M. (1999a) Imagining from the inside, in R. Allen and M. Smith (eds) *Film Theory and Philosophy*. Oxford: Oxford University Press, pp. 412–30.

Smith, M. (1999b) Gangsters, cannibals, aesthetes, or apparently perverse allegiances, in C. Plantinga and G.M. Smith (eds) *Passionate Views: Film, Cognition, and Emotion*. Baltimore, MD: The Johns Hopkins University Press, pp. 217–38.

Smith, M. (2003) Darwin and the directors: film, emotion and the face in the age of evolution. *Times Literary Supplement* (7 February), 13–15.

Smoodin, E. (2004) *Regarding Frank Capra: Audience, Celebrity and American Film Studies, 1930–1960*. Durham, NC: Duke University Press.

Sobchack, V. (1992) *The Address of the Eye: A Phenomenology of Film Experience*. Princeton, NJ: Princeton University Press.

Sobchack, V. (2004) *Carnal Thoughts: Embodiment and the Moving Image*. Berkeley, CA: University of California Press.

Stacey, J. (1994) *Star Gazing: Hollywood Cinema and Female Spectatorship*. London: Routledge.

Stadler, J. (2008) *Pulling Focus: Intersubjective Experience, Narrative Film, and Ethics*. New York: Continuum.

Staiger, J. (1992) *Interpreting Films: Studies in the Historical Reception of American Films*. Princeton, NJ: Princeton University Press.

Staiger, J. (2000) *Perverse Spectators: The Practices of Film Reception*. New York: New York University Press.

Staiger, J. (2005) *Media Reception Studies*. New York: New York University Press.

Stam, R. and Spence, L. (1985) Colonialism, racism, and representation, in B. Nichols (ed.) *Movies and Methods* Volume II. Berkeley, CA: University of California Press, pp. 632–49.

Studlar, G. (1988) *In the Realm of Pleasure: Von Sternberg, Dietrich, and the Masochistic Aesthetic*. Urbana, IL: University of Illinois Press.

Tan, E.S. (1996) *Emotion and the Structure of Narrative Film: Film as an Emotion Machine*. Teaneck, Princeton, NJ: Erlbaum.

Thompson, K. (1981) *Eisenstein's Ivan the Terrible: A Neoformalist Analysis*. Princeton, N-Princeton University Press.

Thompson, K. (1988) *Breaking the Glass Armor: Neoformalist Film Analysis*. Princeton, NJ: Princeton University Press.

Thompson, K. (1999) *Storytelling in the New Hollywood: Understanding Classical Film Technique*. Cambridge, MA: Harvard University Press.

White, J. (1972) *The Birth and Rebirth of Pictorial Space*. London: Faber.

Williams, L. (1989) *Hard Core: Power, Pleasure, and the 'Frenzy of the Visible'*. Berkeley, CA: University of California Press.

Wollen, P. (1998) *Signs and Meaning in the Cinema*. London: BFI.

Wollheim, R. (1984) *The Thread of Life*. Cambridge, MA: Harvard University Press.

Wood, R. (2007) On and around *Brokeback Mountain, Film Quarterly*, 60(3): 28–31.

# Index

# CINEMA ENTERTAINMENT

Essays on audiences, films and film makers

Alan Lovell and Gianluca Sergi

Entertainment is a defining feature of contemporary culture, yet it is often accused of being superficial and even harmful. In this thought-provoking book, the authors challenge this negative view and argue for a reconsideration of the value of entertainment and the effect it has on the world in which we live.

Taking Hollywood cinema as its central focus, this exciting book explores the range of debates that the phenomenon of cinema entertainment has aroused. It is packed with examples from modern, popular films throughout, including a whole chapter on the hugely successful film *The Dark Knight*.

The book features interviews with Randy Thom and Walter Murch, filmmakers involved in creating some of the most successful films of recent years. There is an interesting discussion of the work and reputation of renowned filmmakers, Steven Spielberg and Alfred Hitchcock, names which have become synonymous with cinema entertainment.

The authors consider what makes a film successful by looking at box office figures as well as detailed description and critique of current debates surrounding what it means to entertain and be entertained.

*Cinema Entertainment* is important reading for film and media students as well as anyone interested in contemporary mass culture.

**Contents:** *Introduction: cinema as entertainment / What audiences go for: elite and mass taste / Sensual pleasure, audiences and The Dark Knight / Alfred Hitchcock: the entertainer becomes an artist / Steven Spielberg, Indiana Jones and the Holocaust / Filmmakers as entertainers? Interviews with Randy Thom and Walter Murch / The entertainment discourse Bibliographical notes / Appendix 1: Methodology for statistical analysis / Appendix 2a: Walter Murch's filmography / Appendix 2b: Randy Thom's filmography / Appendix 3: Art / Appendix 4: Credits for The Dark Knight*

2009   140pp

978-0-335-22251-3 (Paperback)      978-0-335-22252-0 (Hardback)

# THE BOLLYWOOD READER

Rajinder Dudrah and Jigna Desai (eds)

*"From its historical roots through to the contemporary moment, the collection of essays, written by eminent scholars in the field, demonstrate so clearly how Indian cinema is more than the sum of its parts. An essential text for anyone wishing to understand properly the full complexities of Hindi cinema."*
Professor Susan Hayward, University of Exeter, UK

*"We are finally at a point when the study of Bollywood is a fully fledged field in Film Studies."*
Professor Dina Iordanova, University of St. Andrews, Scotland

*"The Bollywood Reader extends the discursive boundaries of Indian popular cinema in interesting and complex ways. In putting together this volume, the editors have performed magnificently."*
Professor Wimal Dissanayake, University of Hawaii, USA

- What is Bollywood cinema?
- How does it operate as an industry?
- Who are the audiences of Bollywood cinema?

These are just some of the questions addressed in this lively and fascinating guide to the cultural, social and political significance of popular Hindi cinema, which outlines the history and structure of the Bombay film industry, and its impact on global popular culture.

Including a wide-ranging selection of essays from key voices in the field, the Reader charts the development of the scholarship on popular Hindi cinema, with an emphasis on understanding the relationship between cinema and colonialism, nationalism, and globalization.

The authors address the issues of capitalism, nationalism, Orientalism and modernity through understandings of race, class, gender and sexuality, religion, politics and diaspora as depicted in Indian popular films.

*The Bollywood Reader* is captivating reading for film, media and cultural studies students and scholars with an interest in Bollywood cinema.

**Contents:** *List of contributors - Acknowledgements - Publisher's acknowledgements - Part 1 Theoretical frameworks - Part 2 Recent trajectories - Part 3 Bollywood abroad and beyond - Select keywords - Select timeline - Further reading - Index.*

2008   384pp

978-0-335-22212-4 (Paperback)      978-0-335-22213-1 (Hardback)

# THE CULT FILM READER

Ernest Mathijs and Xavier Mendik (eds)

*"A really impressive and comprehensive collection of the key writings in the field. The editors have done a terrific job in drawing together the various traditions and providing a clear sense of this rich and rewarding scholarly terrain. This collection is as wild and diverse as the films that it covers. Fascinating."*
Mark Jancovich, Professor of Film and Television Studies, University of East Anglia, UK

*"It's about time the lunatic fans and loyal theorists of cult movies were treated to a book they can call their own. The effort and knowledge contained in The Cult Film Reader will satisfy even the most ravenous zombie's desire for detail and insight. This book will gnaw, scratch and infect you just like the cult films themselves."*
Brett Sullivan, Director of Ginger Snaps Unleashed and The Chair

*"The Cult Film Reader is a great film text book and a fun read."*
John Landis, Director of The Blues Brothers, An American Werewolf in London and Michael Jackson's Thriller

Whether defined by horror, kung-fu, sci-fi, sexploitation, kitsch musical or 'weird world cinema', cult movies and their global followings are emerging as a distinct subject of film and media theory, dedicated to dissecting the world's unruliest images.

This book is the world's first reader on cult film. It brings together key works in the field on the structure, form, status, and reception of cult cinema traditions. Including work from key established scholars in the field such as Umberto Eco, Janet Staiger, Jeffrey Sconce, Henry Jenkins, and Barry Keith Grant, as well as new perspectives on the gradually developing canon of cult cinema, the book not only presents an overview of ways in which cult cinema can be approached, it also re-assesses the methods used to study the cult text and its audiences.

With editors' introductions to the volume and to each section, the book is divided into four clear thematic areas of study – The Conceptions of Cult; Cult Case Studies; National and International Cults; and Cult Consumption – to provide an accessible overview of the topic. It also contains an extensive bibliography for further related readings.

Written in a lively and accessible style, *The Cult Film Reader* dissects some of biggest trends, icons, auteurs and periods of global cult film production. Films discussed include *Casablanca*, *The Rocky Horror Picture Show*, *Eraserhead*, *The Texas Chainsaw Massacre*, *Showgirls* and *Ginger Snaps*.

**Contents:** *Section One: The Concepts of Cult - Section Two: Cult Case Studies - Section Three: National and International Cults - Bibliography of Cult Film Resources - Index.*

2007    576pp

978-0-335-21923-0 (Paperback)    978-0-335-21924-7 (Hardback)